International Perspectives in Geography

AJG Library

Volume 19

Aim and Scope

The AJG Library is published by Springer under the auspices of the Association of Japanese Geographers. This is a scholarly series of international standing. Given the multidisciplinary nature of geography, the objective of the series is to provide an invaluable source of information not only for geographers, but also for students, researchers, teachers, administrators, and professionals outside the discipline. Strong emphasis is placed on the theoretical and empirical understanding of the changing relationships between nature and human activities. The overall aim of the series is to provide readers throughout the world with stimulating and up-to-date scientific outcomes mainly by Japanese and other Asian geographers. Thus, an "Asian" flavor different from the Western way of thinking may be reflected in this series. The AJG Library will be available both in print and online via SpringerLink.

About the AJG

The Association of Japanese Geographers (AJG), founded in 1925, is one of the largest and leading organizations on geographical research in Asia and the Pacific Rim today, with around 3000 members. AJG is devoted to promoting research on various aspects of human and physical geography and contributing to academic development through exchanges of information and knowledge with relevant internal and external academic communities. Members are tackling contemporary issues such as global warming, air/water pollution, natural disasters, rapid urbanization, irregular land-use changes, and regional disparities through comprehensive investigation into the earth and its people. In addition, to make the next generation aware of these academic achievements, the members are engaged in teaching and outreach activities of spreading geographical awareness. With the recent developments and much improved international linkages, AJG launches the publication of the AJG Library series in 2012.

Atsushi Taira · Rolf D. Schlunze
Editors

Management Geography

Asian Perspectives Focusing on Japan and Surrounding Regions

Springer

Editors
Atsushi Taira
Kagawa University
Takamatsu, Kagawa, Japan

Rolf D. Schlunze
Ritsumeikan University
Ibaraki, Osaka, Japan

ISSN 2197-7798 ISSN 2197-7801 (electronic)
International Perspectives in Geography
ISBN 978-981-19-4402-4 ISBN 978-981-19-4403-1 (eBook)
https://doi.org/10.1007/978-981-19-4403-1

This Springer imprint is published by the registered company Springer Nature Singapore Pte Ltd.
The registered company address is: 152 Beach Road, #21-01/04 Gateway East, Singapore 189721, Singapore

Preface

Management geography explores the spatial characteristics of management-related issues, especially of firms. The research group, *Kokusai Keizai Keiei Chirigaku Kenkyū Gurūpu* (the Research Group of the Spaces of International Economy and Management), was founded at the Spring Meeting of the Association of Japanese Geographers (AJG) in 2007. Ever since, we have been exploring diverse theoretical and methodological approaches for empirical management research to grasp new developments in economic and management issues in Asia, especially in multinational enterprises (MNEs) headquartered in Japan. Before the Corona crises the research group members usually met twice a year at the AJG Conference. The Japanese members collaborate with the independent research group of the Spaces of International Economy and Management (SIEM) which is now renamed into Management Geography Research Group (ManGeo). Both research groups, led by Dr. Rolf D. Schlunze (Ritsumeikan University) and Dr. Atsushi Taira (Kagawa University), aim to promote theoretical and empirical research in the field of management geography domestically and internationally.

Both research groups have been intending to investigate the issues and the topics related to management geography described below in a broad sense:

a. Theorizing management practices in a geographic space using approaches related to leadership, international human resource management, innovative practices, and interactions of managers with boundary-spanning functions.
b. Proposing new methodologies for investigating managerial practices, preferences, networking, and decision-making in private and governmental organizations transforming international economy and management spaces.
c. Providing empirical evidence on the range of management issues, including knowledge transfer and management, as well as localizing and globalizing practices. In particular, studies focusing on managerial embeddedness, corporate social responsibility (CSR), community of practices (CoPs), global production networks (GPNs), and strategic coupling of transnational firms are relevant.
d. Developing concepts for building international social capital in corporate entities and global city locations.

An important achievement of our co-leadership on behalf of the above two research groups has been their collaboration to discuss relevant topics and to introduce young scholars from different schools of thought and disciplines to the field of management geography. A common challenge of our work has been to systematically locate the topic of managers in real, relational, and topical spaces between the fields of economic geography and international business (IB). Despite our great efforts and availability of excellent work published in recent years by scholars working independently, alone or in groups both within and outside of the research group, only a few overarching publication initiatives have been realized to date. This book attempts to highlight the agenda of management geography, spurring theoretical and methodological research, and framing opportunities. We expect this book to raise the profile and promote collaboration among researchers. We wish to provide a new platform for further dissemination of the concept of management geography among economic geographers and scholars of IB and adjacent disciplines.

Based on the outcomes of the regular meetings of the Research Group of the Spaces of International Economy and Management at the annual conferences of the AJG and the special session, "Management Geography- An Asian perspective," organized by the SIEM and represented by Schlunze and Taira, at the 5th Global Conference in Economic Geography (GCEG) in Cologne, Germany, in July 2018, this book was published in English to disseminate agendas on management geography using the AJG's grant program. Our book aims to promote theoretical advancements in the field of management geography and provide empirical evidence on the changing features of international businesses. The contributors to the book examine the spatial and managerial features of Asian MNEs, especially Japanese ones, and other related agents from the broader perspective of management geography. We expect that this book will contribute to the theoretical, methodological, and empirical advancement of management geography.[1]

Takamatsu, Japan Atsushi Taira
Ibaraki, Japan Rolf D. Schlunze

[1] For further details about ManGeo and SIEM, please refer to www.mangeo.org.

Contents

List of Contributors

Abe Yasuhisa Graduate School of Social and Cultural Studies, Kyushu University, Fukuoka, Japan

Chen Lin School of Geograhy & Center for Asian Geographical Studies, South China Normal University, Guangzhou, China

Kamakura Natsuki Graduate School of Arts and Sciences, The University of Tokyo, Tokyo, Japan

Kawakubo Atsushi Faculty of Law, Toyo University, Tokyo, Japan

Niwa Takahito Faculty of Economics, Teikyo University, Tochigi, Japan

Schlunze Rolf D. College of Business Administration, Ritsumeikan University, Osaka, Japan

Su Guandong ZENRIN Co., Ltd, Fukuoka, Japan

Taira Atsushi Faculty of Education, Kagawa University, Kagawa, Japan

Yamamoto Kenta Faculty of Economics, Kokugakuin University, Tokyo, Japan

Introduction: Management Geography—Asian Perspectives Focusing on Japan and Surrounding Regions

Atsushi Taira and Rolf D. Schlunze

Abstract This introductory chapter argues for the potential of management geography in relation to two distinct disciplines of social sciences—management studies, which is rather new and mainly consists of organizational and strategic analyses, and economic geography, which involves the study of the spatial characteristics of a variety of economic-related actors ranging from local to global scales. With the globalization of firm activities, an increasing number of economic geographers have begun paying attention to the management of economic entities, particularly multinational enterprises (MNEs). In addition, as firms have recognized the importance of creating knowledge for innovation, academics have started investigating the knowledge economy, that is, the meaning of knowledge and relationships between knowledge creation and innovation. Economic geographers have been tackling management issues in the context of the spatial features of firm activities. This book is an attempt to launch management geography through the perspectives of Asian countries, especially Japan, which is significant in the global economy and has not been much investigated in geography in the literature in English.

Keywords Management geography · Economic geography · Management studies · Knowledge economy · Japan

A. Taira (✉)
Kagawa University, Kagawa 760-0016, Japan
e-mail: taira.atsushi@kagawa-u.ac.jp

R. D. Schlunze
Ritsumeikan University, Osaka 567-8570, Japan
e-mail: rolf@mangeo.org

A. Taira and R. D. Schlunze (eds.), *Management Geography*, International Perspectives in Geography 19, https://doi.org/10.1007/978-981-19-4403-1_1

1 Introduction: Management Studies and Economic Geography

In international business (IB) and economic geography, management geography is attracting increasing attention from researchers studying economic activities ranging from micro to macro levels and from social to cultural features (Hayter and Watts 1983; Laulajainen 1995, 1998; Laulajainen and Stafford 1995; Abo 2004; Schlunze et al. 2012; Jones 2018). Management geography is a new branch of economic geography that focuses on the nexus of practices and decision-making of firms and related agencies in a globalizing world from a geographical perspective. The research objectives are manifold, including the analysis of the socio-economic and cognitive spatial behavior of managerial actors.

In social science, management studies are a rather new discipline. Crainer (2000) claims that while the nineteenth century was the industrial century, the twentieth century was the management century. Broadly speaking, management studies consist of organizational and strategic analyses (Ohmae 1982). Representative researchers have reported their work on different topics of management studies, for example, Taylor (1911) on scientific management; Ford (1923) on mass production system; Schumpeter (1934) on innovation; Barnard (1938) on organization theory; Drucker (1954, 1985) on practice, innovation, and management; Chandler (1962, 1977) on organization structure and strategies ("Organization depends on strategy"); and Porter (1980, 1985) on competitive strategy and competitive advantage. However, leading cross-cultural management scientists testify that Asian management follows a different approach not emphasizing an *inner direction* as a firm's corporate strategy but an *outer direction* that emphasizes "scanning the business environment" and "customer orientation" (Trompenaars and Harpden-Turner 2006: 145). With the shifting of the global economy to Asia, the twenty-first century was believed to have become an Asian century, which necessitated the observation of managerial developments foremost in Asia.

Management studies in Japan progressed after the Second World War, especially after the 1980s. The decades of the 1980s and the 1990s saw active publication of Japanese works in English. Itami (1987) explored the mobilization of invisible assets, which led to the argument of the meaning of knowledge creation of firms and to the theory of the Japanese word *ba* as the place of creation of innovation (Itami 1991, 1999). In Japan, knowledge-acquiring concepts with a spatial component have been developed over decades (Nonaka and Takeuchi 1997). According to these concepts, knowledge is embedded in the space of *ba*. Mental, virtual, or physical spaces, such as places of experience, internet, and offices, play an important role in acquiring and spreading knowledge. *Ba* offers the opportunity to transform experimental knowledge into tacit knowledge through internalization. Synergetic knowledge, which is created through exchange and socialization in workplaces, is converted into models and implicitly used by means of *ba* to enable effective collaboration in workplaces. As localized knowledge, *ba* is tacit and can only be made explicit through the exchange of feelings, thoughts, and experiences in spaces (Bennett 2001). Many Japanese researchers see knowledge as primarily tacit, as something that is not easily visible or expressible (Nonaka and Konno 1998: 42). The perception of *ba*, in the sense of a protected and empowering space, becomes important in order to bring multifaceted knowledge carriers and networks together (Brinkhoff et al. 2015: 27). Nonaka and Konno (1998: 43) not only see self-transcendence but also walk around within the company as a process of acquiring knowledge. These activities, which are not only an important indicator for assessing the spatial mobility of managers, but also for their cognitive behavior and participation at different locations, serve to create company-relevant knowledge. Accordingly, Nonaka and Takeuchi (1995) pointed out the importance of knowledge-creating firms in the competitive market and their potential to lead the relevant market. Clearly, this potential derives from a different management approach that builds internal capabilities by observing shifts and changes in the external business or market environment.

Witnessing the progress of globalization, Ohmae (1990) pointed out that the world is getting smaller and borderless. In economics, some researchers have been attracted to the spatial aspects of economic activities and have launched the studies of geographical economics. Fujita et al. (1999) studied international trade focused on cities and regions using secondary data and created a mathematical model to explain spatial economy in an economic fashion. In contrast, management studies have been based more on primary data. Abo (1994) conducted a series of studies on Japanese-affiliated firms transplanted to the United States, highlighting the model of hybrid plant management based on empirical data obtained through interviews at companies. Here, we can observe an early divide of economics and management studies, both of which try to incorporate the spatial aspects of a globalizing economy. Kawabata (2000) argued the internationalization of Japanese retailers focusing on locations and strategies. Globalization of the manufacturing and service industry has led to the management geography studies of the application and adaptation of managerial practices and community of practices (CoPs).

1.1 International Business (IB) Studies

Jones (2018) claimed that an increasing body of work in economic geography straddles the disciplinary boundaries of management and IB studies. With the advancement of globalization of the economic activities of firms, IB studies progressed, focusing strongly on management across national borders. For example, as a pioneer in this field, Håkanson (1979) examined the spatial expansion processes of firms, including the internationalization of operations. In the 1990s, economic geographers began to adopt a firm-level approach to examine the core dimensions of management; Schoenberger (1997) explored the corporate culture; Gertler (2004) discussed the management of innovation, and Taylor and Oinas (2006) argued the roles of senior managers. The corporate service sector has been a major arena of relevant studies in management geography. Jones (2003, 2007) discussed the characteristics of management consultancy and banking and investigated the complex role of face-to-face interaction in globalizing law firms. A range of "practices" is key for understanding the business performance of firms.

Until now, the IB literature has been mostly based on experiences and theoretical building observed in MNEs from the United States and other Western countries, wherein advanced information and communication practices in industries, such as the media, Information technology (IT), and finance sector, have received attention among economic geographers. Consequently, a new geography of financialization has emerged. Clark et al. (2015) proposed the concept of global financial networks to situate offshore finance in the nexus of global value chains and took the lead in the formation of this dynamic research group of economic geographers promoting financial management studies. Academic activities on Facebook and GEOFIN (Western Banks in Eastern Europe: New Geographies of Financialization) have brought the attention of economic geographers to global finance and management. Their output from GEOFIN research includes up-to-date journal articles, such as the TESG article of Martin Sokol and Leonardo Pataccini (2020), highlighting the role of debt-based financial chains in shaping economic geographies during major global crises.

1.2 Impact of International Business (IB) Theories and Concepts

Iammarino and McCann (2013: 33) indicated the lack of a unifying or comprehensive approach to multinational behavior and tried to assess the state of art of theoretical thinking on the spatial dimension of MNEs. They critiqued the ownership-location-internationalization (OLI) paradigm of Dunning (1979), who stated that OLI is a three-legged stool, by asking whether this stool was evenly balanced. They concluded that the location was the Achilles' heel of the OLI in the quest for the needed theoretical explanations of multi-nationality. In order to understand the locational aspects of the multi-nationality of MNEs, they advocated a novel way of integrating the insights of IB with economic geography.

McCann and Mudambi (2004) viewed economic geography as *international geography*. Their theory of MNE developed along the lines of a sharp distinction between firms as organizations that centralize control and build capacities and full arm-length transactions with diverse independent actors in the market environment (Iammarino and McCann 2013: 60). A new wave of economic geography observes the growing multi-nationality and discusses how through experiences and capability accumulation, internal and external means can be exploited by MNEs. According to Iammarino and McCann (2013: 63), the lenses of economic geography perceive firm- and region-specific advantages.

Previously, Japanese scholars have contributed to the intersection of geography and management. Beika (1970) emphasized that managers always need to adjust actively or passively to internal and external changes in conditions. Totsuka (1990) suggested that the locational adjustment plays an important role in the process of globalization. The Japanese MNE study group (JMNESG; Abo 2012, 2015) has investigated more than 400 Japanese overseas factories around the world since the 1980s to analyze the transferability of Japanese management models. Initially called the dilemma approach, the "hybrid model" (Abo 1994, 2002) is based on the relationship between application and adaptation and focuses on the evaluation of the application degree of Japanese managerial practices. The fundamental idea of the "hybrid model" is the dynamism with which the Japanese management system transferred to overseas factories creates a mix of local and Japanese managerial practices. According to Kawamura (2005), the outcomes of the hybridization process vary not only by industrial sectors but also by country and region. Abo (2002) proposed a preliminary concept of management geography, emphasizing that cross-cultural differences need to be incorporated into management geography.

1.3 Japanese Managerial Practices Becoming Global Practices (Globalization and CoPs)

A review of the recent business literature, including the MNE theory (Dunning 1979; Buckley and Ghauri 1999) and culture-based approaches towards the analysis of Japanese MNEs (Koike 1988; Abo 1994), show that there has been no acceptance of the best-practice orientation of management gurus preaching global standards. However, Wenger et al. (2002) discussed the CoPs that nurture the idea of the existence of best practices. In the automotive industry, Japanese manufacturing practices are often described as the best practices that can now be found, for example, at the level of German transplants like that of Mercedes Benz in East London and South Africa (Kumon and Itohisa 2019). Initially, Japanese management studies were a domain of ethnic studies that emphasized the unique "Japanese-ness" or the so-called *nihonjinron*. However, these studies appear to be related to the mainstream studies on competitive management practices within IBs. The strong global expansion of Japanese firms that started in the 1980s and that led to Japanese foreign direct investment (FDI) in the USA and Europe also brought attention to the "best practices" from Japan (Schlunze 1997, 2001, 2002). The influence of the triad—the USA, Japan, and Europe—in international trade and manufacturing remained dominant for a long time, but the best practices have spread globally and have become detached from the particular country of origin.

1.4 *Industrial Clusters, Global Buzz, and Global Production Network (GPN)*

Local industrial clusters are facing global challenges and new competition nowadays. Industrial agglomeration has been a focus of study in economic geography (Perroux 1955; Polanyi 1967). In particular, the 1980s and onwards saw an increasing interest of researchers in industrial agglomeration, with themes of studies ranging from flexible specialization (Piore and Sabel 1984) to new industrial spaces (Scott 1988; Tomozawa, 1995), relational assets (Storper 1997), knowledge embedded in localities (Granovetter 1985; Konno 1998), and learning regions as centers of innovation (Florida 1995; Tomozawa 2000). Porter (1990, 1998) argued that the most sustainable competitive advantage in the global economy is pursued through local factors because many leading firms are located in certain cities or regions with desirable geographic advantages. Krugman (1991) pointed out the cumulative locational behaviors of firms. Recently, the concepts of related variety and spinoffs (Boschma and Wenting 2007; Klepper 2007; Content and Frenken 2016) have been advocated by an increasing number of researchers in the argument that the existence of a related variety of industries and spinoffs from the host industry has the potential to keep the industrial cluster lively [about industrial agglomeration, refer to Yamamoto (2005) and Matsubara (2013)].

In addition, recent decades saw increasing interest in the concepts of global value chain (GVC) and global production network (GPN). The Manchester School started a summer school on GVCs a decade ago and since then has been leading in the discussion of GVCs within economic geography. In 2004, Coe et al. (2004a, 2004b) launched a GPN perspective and along with Coe and Yeung (2015, 2019) expanded their perspectives, pointing out how critical it is to use the concept of GPN to understand the current world economy. Yeung (2016) emphasizes the importance of the strategic coupling of relevant industries to lead to an increasingly competitive business environment.

A review of the geographical literature on innovation management and clusters emphasizes various proximity dimensions. According to Boschma (2005), while the effects on institutional and social proximity innovation are enhanced by territorial dynamics, cognitive and organizational proximity spurs innovation in non-territorial spaces. In contrast, Nunes and Lopes (2015) argued that territorial and non-territorial approaches should be seen as complementary because companies need to belong to both global networks and locally incorporated spatial networks to maximize their economic values. Therefore, Boschma's five-fold classification of proximity dimensions, consisting of geographical, institutional, organizational, social and cognitive proximity, needs to be extended to grasp the dynamics of innovation and knowledge networks in the context of *glocal* or intercultural settings. A theory of proximity and knowledge networks that also applies to the context of innovation in intercultural contexts is still missing (Balland et al. 2015: 908). This book aims to provide empirical evidence nurturing a theory that explains the formation of cross-cultural innovation communities from a management geography perspective (Schlunze 2004; Jones 2016).

1.5 Evolutionary and Relational Economic Geography

Along with the debate on industrial agglomeration, the evolutionary aspects of regional growth and innovation have attracted the growing interest of economic geographers (Sotohebo 2012; Nojiri 2013; Mizuno 2019). According to Sotohebo (2012), evolutionary economics has argued around the key concept of "routines." Stimulated by the discussions of evolutionary economics, some economic geographers have begun to adapt to the concept of the evolution of economic systems at a variety of scales. There are two main approaches: the pass-dependency and generalized Darwinism. The concept of "related variety" is related to the latter approach. In the management context, the roles and evolution of actors inside and outside firms will be the issues to be investigated. Nojiri (2013) claimed that the concept of "routine" is equivalent to a "genome" in firms. Mizuno (2019) pointed out the importance of examining the formation and development of inter-firm networks as an evolutionary process and that firms that are tightly connected in local knowledge networks have advantages in obtaining more knowledge than firms that are isolated on the network. Furthermore, Mizuno (2019) argued that evolutionary economic geography crossovers with relational economic geography. However, observing economic changes in Asia, there is still space to theorize from evolutionary research following the call of Nelson (1995).

Another important keyword is "relational" (Yeung 2005; Bathelt and Glückler 2011), which refers to the interactions of various actors amid business transactions across space. Space itself could be relational in the context that human interactions affect business performance. The concepts of "pipelines" and "buzz" have been increasingly utilized by researchers (Bathelt et al. 2004). Taira (2020) defines "pipeline" as the trust-based information and knowledge flows among firms as well as between firms and related actors beyond the cluster and "buzz" as the coincidental effect of being close to others in the same or similar businesses (see also Storper and Venables 2004). We can regard expanding IB networks as the dispersal of cluster activities based on relational proximity. Interpersonal connections outside the cluster are crucial in order to obtain new knowledge for further innovation and to avoid negative lock-in of the cluster (Maskell et al. 2006). Thus, the term *glocal* has become a key focus for the success of firms.

Instead of treating space as a container, geographers have recently provided a conceptualization of space as a perspective (Glückler 1999; Bathelt and Glückler 2011), referring to this concept as the geographical lens, in which economic exchange, rather than space, becomes the main focus of analysis. The focus of the geographical lens is precisely the spatial overlap of different social and economic processes. Analysis in relational economic geography is based on a deeper understanding of economic actors. The critique of Thrift (2000a: 698) on the lack of explanation in traditional economic geography spurred development in relational economic geography. He argued that the division of the "wheres" for geographers and the "whys" for economists is no longer useful. We see economic action embedded in the structure of social (and economic) action. Relational economic geography pays attention to economic action as a social process.

2 Perspectives in Management Geography

Management geography deals with the spatial manifestations of management-related matters, especially of firms. In the field of geography, it is fair to say that management geography has stemmed from economic geography. Jones (2018) claimed that studies on management geography date back to the 1980s and that Peter Dicken's *Global shift* (1986, 1998) shared common concerns with management theorists about how firms internationalize their operations, how international production systems are organized, and what kind of relationships parent firms have with their subsidiaries. The decades of the 1990s and the 2000s saw an increasing interest of economic geographers in management-related affairs (Taira 1999, 2002; Jones 2003, 2007; Schlunze 2003, 2004; Beaverstock 2004). However, the term "management" is still spontaneous in major economic geography textbooks. While Coe et al. (2007) referred to management processes in the discussion of commodity chains, Dicken (1986, 1998), Aoyama et al. (2011), and MacKinnon and Cumbers (2019) have not apparently dealt with the concept. However, it is important to note that all of them have emphasized the spatial activities of firms, especially those of MNEs, as key players in the global economy.

Previously, management geography was proposed by management scientists such as Beika (1970) and Abo (2002). Various labels can be assigned to research that deals with managerial behavior from a geographical perspective; prominent labels included managerial geography (Laulajainen 1998), management geography (Schlunze and Plattner 2007; Schlunze et al. 2012; Suwala and Oinas 2012), and economic geographies of management (Jones 2018). Within geography, we followed the call of the late Risto I. Laulajainen, who raised the question about managerial geography in the *Geojournal* (Laulajainen 1998). Instead of founding a new academic field, it was widely ignored by traditional economic geographers. However, geographical studies require the notion of management behavior (Thrift 2000b). This behavioral approach is distinguished from the previous approaches that focus on environmental determinants affecting international managers' decision-making (Krumme 1969; Nishioka and Krumme 1993). Instead, nowadays, managers are seen as "change agents," coordinating and modifying interests in overlapping spheres of work and life. Owing to the increasing competition among firms, managers need to become change agents, who are the fastest and best managers, by adjusting to and creating new practices and skills (Czinkota et al. 1999). Jones (2002) critiqued that a global city was misperceived and claimed that a deeper understanding of managerial practices within multiple spaces of a globalizing economy is needed. Schlunze et al. (2012) published a conference book that was reviewed later in the *Journal of Regional Studies*, which is now perceived as an important step towards the foundation of management geography (Jones 2016). From the perspective of management geography, a global city itself is perceived as a heterogeneous assemblage of practices, materials, and actors drawn from within and without the city limits.

Management geography was introduced as a new avenue integrating IB studies and economic geography. Our initial concept that centered on real and relational spaces, such as a global city and other regional studies, was introduced at the annual conference of the Association of Japanese Geographers (AJG) by the leading members of the SIEM Research Group in 2007. Organizing a symposium at Ritsumeikan University at the Biwako Kusatsu Campus in 2010 and special sessions at leading international geography conferences, including the Annual Conference of American Geographers in New York in 2012, the Regional Conference of the International Geographical Union in Cologne in 2012, and the Global Conference in Economic Geography (GCEG) in Cologne in 2018, we made efforts to refine the definition of what constitutes management geography. Management geography is a new subfield of economic geography that focuses on the nexus of managerial decision-making and practices in a globalizing corporate world targeting managerial subjects as research objectives by applying a geographical lens. Following a call to progress our understanding in the socio-economic world (Sayer 2000), our research objective is to analyze the management of economic, social, and cognitive spatial realms in multi-scalar configurations that influence corporate performance through concentration, interaction, and/or perception. New methodologies have been developed to analyze the socio-economic and cognitive spatial behavior of managerial subjects influencing organizational performance through perceptions and preferences (see also chapter "Performance Analysis of Boundary Spanners in Multinational Enterprises Through the Lens of Management Geography"). The application and adaptation of managerial practices, the preference for localization and/or globalization strategies, and the resulting interactions and networking behavior are at the core of the analyses in management geography.

The question is how this contributes to theory building in geography. Locational theories of von Thünen (1842), Weber (1909), Lösch (1939 [1954]), Christaller (1933 [1966]), Isard (1956, 1960), and Greenhut (1956) have built a foundation of theory in economics and geography. However, Dicken (1971) expressed dissatisfaction with the normative theory claiming that it omitted personal factors in location decisions. Dicken's plea was that economic geographers need to have a wider knowledge of behavioral sciences in order to improve their understanding of the spatial behavior of business organizations. He did not advocate a particular inductive model, but he found that it was useful to conceive a business organization as an open system operating within an external environment (Dicken 1971: 427). Interestingly, he found that it was not a profit-making model, but survival is the only fundamental business goal common to all businesses, regardless of their organizational structures (Dicken 1971: 428). The information feedback from the environment is vitally important to the survival that helps to maintain the energy flow of an organization. Dicken designed a model seeking to explain that the behavioral environment can be perceived as a component of the total objective environment. His model that seeks to analyze the perceptions and behavior of actors in the context of a given business environment is discussed in detail in chapter "Performance Analysis of Boundary Spanners in Multinational Enterprises Through the Lens of Management Geography" on the boundary-spanning function of global managers, contributed by Rolf Schlunze. Essentially, Dicken observed that a geographical impact exists at all stages of the perception process and influences how the information is processed for decision-making in business organizations by individual and collective actors. Group affiliation results from physical and temporal co-location or relational place-making. Socio-economic status was reflected by the presidential office on an upper floor, but recently this and many other concepts have been challenged under the pressure of pandemic and global crises. Personality and personal attributes were used to encourage mutual understanding and friendship among humans, which resulted in co-location (Nicholson et al. 2001). The question is to what extent can Western concepts of behavioral geography and economic geography be applied to explain the behavior of managerial subjects in a rapidly globalizing Asian world.

3 Asia: A Hot Spot for Management Geography

Next, it is important to clarify the Asian perspective. Asia is a broad geographical space consisting of a range of sub-regions: East Asia, Southeast Asia, South Asia, and the Middle East. However, in this book, we focus on East Asia, which is divided into distinctive sub-regions mainly based on the nation-states: China (and Taiwan), Mongolia, Korea, and Japan. However, in management practices, similar emphasis is laid on human networks tied together by kinship and community relations. Yeung (1998) highlighted the role of Chinese business networks based on personal relationships as a key means of transnational operations in Asian firms. Through qualitative case studies using a business network perspective, he explained how Hong Kong firms organize their operations in Southeast Asia through overseas Chinese business and personal *guanxi* networks. Zhu (2012) examined the emerging role of human resource management in industrial firms of China. Lee (1997) explored the relationships between the state, society, and big businesses in Korean firms, especially those called *chaebol* (conglomerates). Furthermore, Richter (2014) highlighted the dynamics of Japanese organizations and Laage-Hellman (1997) explained the characteristics of business networks in Japan.

Recent decades saw an increasing number of books and articles on the global economy, including management aspects. Dicken and Miyamachi (1998) examined the changing geography and strategies of Japanese *sogo shosha* in Europe. Olds et al. (1999) investigated the contested meanings of globalization in the Asia–Pacific region after the economic crisis in the late 1990s. Peck and Yeung (2003) examined the changing features of global capitalism and processes of globalization—flows, knowledge, and governance—discussing modishly hostile takeovers related to perpetual fears of global contest for corporate control by Japanese MNEs (Kester 1991). Moreover, Yeung (2016) explored East Asian industrial transformation in the new global economy by introducing the concept of 'strategic coupling.' However, although Japan is still the third largest economy in the world and has a range of global companies in the variety of industries represented by Toyota in automobiles and Studio Ghibli in animation, it has not been investigated in detail. Japan has been famous for life-long employment and successive promotions based on ages in both private and public sectors. However, after the bubble economy burst in the beginning of 1990s, along with the neoliberal policies of the administration, the traditional system has faded away. Life-long employment has become a dream and approximately 40% of the workforce is found in part-time sectors. Is that because of the deteriorating roles of the Japanese economy and firms or because of the lack of interests/efforts by researchers? Because Japan is a country that still matters and will matter in the future in the globalizing economy, we need to expand the studies of Japan and Japanese firms in economic and management geography.

3.1 How to Open Up the Black Box of Corporate Life?

The research of Abo's MNE Study Group brought about enlightening insights to the subject but was naturally limited by the group's narrow focus on the application and adaptation of managerial practices at the level of Japanese overseas management. Inspired by Abo's teamwork, in 2007, Schlunze and Taira initiated two international and multidisciplinary research groups: Kokusai Keizai-Keiei Chirigaku Gurupu (the Research Group of Spaces of International Economy and Management as an AJG Research Group) and the SIEM Research Group. These groups consist of interdisciplinary teams of researchers who aim to investigate management issues from various socio-economic perspectives. As many economic geographers trained in the 1980s and 1990s in Japan, the co-leaders of the research group experienced the bubble economy and saw Japanese MNEs' vibrant outward investment. The founding group members (Schlunze 1992, 1997; Taira 1999, 2002) started with the FDI studies and locational decision-making of Japanese MNEs, but the focus of the research group shifted to other management-related affairs that addressed relational and topical spaces as well. Since then, several young researchers joining our group have conducted more actor-centered research, providing new insights into the spatial activities of Japanese firms and their management as key players in the global economy. Attention was brought to actors not only in MNEs but also in small- and medium-sized enterprises (SMEs) for global expansion.

So far, our important achievements have been to bring together key thinkers to discuss relevant topics and introduce young scholars from different schools of thought and disciplines to the field of management geography. A common challenge of this work has been to systematically locate the topic of 'managers in space' between the fields of economic geography and IB. Contributors to this book have tried to tackle management issues of Asian firms, especially Japanese-affiliated firms, and related entities in the globalized era from a geographical perspective. Schlunze et al. (2015) examined the roles of Chinese managers' *guanxi* networking for their managerial success. Taira (2020) argued the significance of *glocal* strategies of the glove-related industry in Eastern Kagawa drawing on the pipeline and buzz concepts. Abe and Fan (2010) examined changes in the spatial environment of the Japanese machinery and instrumental industry in China through a case study of the Dalian economic and technological development area. Kamakura (2018) illustrated the spatial divisions of labor in R&D by analyzing the organizational and locational restructuring of Japanese chemical firms. Niwa (2019) explored the characteristics of manufacturing firms in Tochigi Prefecture, located north of Tokyo, through network analysis. Yamamoto (2014) highlighted the geographical features of the animation industry in East Asia. Chen (2016) investigated enterprise development and employment transformation in the inland rural areas of Fujian province, China. Finally, Kawakubo (2011) argued for upgrading the scale of Wagyu cattle breeding in the context of the development potential for large-scale farming in Miyazaki Prefecture in Kyushu. The survival of our research groups with a variety of theoretical, conceptual, methodological, and empirical approaches, bears manifold opportunities for the development of a subfield called management geography. We believe that our shared interest in managerial issues might still unite diverse researchers joining our research groups' activities under the label or umbrella of management geography. Global challenges such as COVID-19, global warming and financial crisis forcing the changes that lead to new paradigms explaining our global economy. Therefore, theorizing from empirical case studies has become more important not only on macro and meso but also on micro-economic level grasping the changes within a firm. At the same time, there is a need for qualitative research to understand how and why management alters in spaces of international trade, international investment, and investment R&D. Thus, we promote the case study approach with concept building. New theories and methods have been developed to learn about managerial practices within firms that many economic geographers still perceive as a black box. We believe that managers' and entrepreneurs' boundary-spanning practices need to be mapped out in real, relational, and cognitive spaces developing unique theoretical and methodological approaches able to grasp new developments in the sphere of Asian business. Therefore, it is important to address adequate research questions that create a potential for the promising field of management geography.

4 Research Perspectives

From an Asian perspective, we wish to show that the nexus of managerial practices is created in interconnected locations within GPNs (Yeung 2016). Asian firms are taking the lead in many industries in the world economy, thus making Asian management a research focus among economic geographers. The study of Yeung (2016) on 'Strategic Coupling,' explaining East Asian industrial transformation, provided a better understanding of the new global economy. However, little light has been shed on, especially in English literature, how Japanese firms, mainly Japanese MNEs, have succeeded in dominating and controlling global and local value chains, sustaining their corporate power in Asia.

In recent decades, we have witnessed the growth of protectionism and neoliberalism, which affects global businesses, in the United States and the United Kingdom. The divide between the global north and south is widening. Some MNEs are criticized for their operations in developing countries in terms of inhuman local working conditions, including child labor. At the same time, however, there are regions and cities in the world, such as California and some cities in the United States, which advocate international cooperation and efforts to find solutions for sustainable development goals (SDGs). Increasing complexity needs to be analyzed at the managerial level, drawing on implications for the GVC and the GPN of Japanese and other Asian MNEs. It will be essential for MNEs with stakeholders to explore solutions to global challenges.

Thus, we would like to address a set of the critical questions to our readers: What kind of challenges face multinational corporations in Japan and other Asian countries?; How are managerial actors in MNEs enfolding boundary-spanning activities in global context?; How do firms and related entities cultivate pipelines and buzz within and beyond local regions?; How do actors of Japanese MNEs, SMEs, and related institutions embed various managerial processes at overseas locations?

This book consists of two parts: Part I argues Japanese and international managerial practices in the world, and Part II examines changing business communities in the industrial and rural spaces of East Asia, focusing primarily on Japan and China. Part I consists of four chapters. Chapter "Performance Analysis of Boundary Spanners in Multinational Enterprises Through the Lens of Management Geography" analyzes the performance of boundary spanners in MNEs from a management geography perspective. Chapter "Changes in the Locational Conditions of the Japanese Machinery and Instrument Industry in China: A Case Study of Dalian Economic and Technological Development Zone" discusses changes in the locational condition of the Japanese machinery and instrument industry in China through a case study of the Dalian Economic and Technological Development Zone. In chapter "Management Issues in Global R&D of Japanese Chemical Companies," management issues in the global R&D of Japanese chemical companies are explored. Chapter "Small- and Medium-Sized 'Global-Niche' Firms in Japan: A Key for the Rejuvenation of Japan's Local Economy?" discusses the characteristics and strategies of small- and medium-sized "global-niche" firms in Japan. Part II includes seven chapters. Chapter "Industrial Agglomeration and Regional Development Planning Analyzing by GIS in the City of Utsunomiya, Tochigi, Japan" explores industrial agglomeration and regional development planning in the city of Utsunomiya by GIS. In chapter "Unique Functions of a Co-Working Space in a Metropolis. A Case Study in Tokyo, Japan," the unique functions of a co-working space in a metropolis are examined through a case study in Tokyo. Chapter "How Customer Service Centers in Foreign Cities Serving Japan Changed Their Business?: A Case Study of the City of Dalian, China" discusses how Japanese customer service centers in foreign cities have evolved through a case study of the city of Dalian, China. Chapter "Factors Influencing Enterprise Development in the Inland Regions of Fujian Province in China" explores the factors for enterprise development in the inland regions of Fujian province in China. Finally, in chapter "Transformation of Agricultural Management in Japan Under Globalization Pressure: A Focus on Product Differentiation Strategy," the transformation of agricultural management in Japan under globalization pressure is discussed with a focus on product differentiation strategies.

References

Abe Y, Fan J (2010) Changes in locational environment of Japanese machinery and instrumental industry in China: a case study of Dalian economic and development area. Geogr Sci 65: 266–283. (J)

Abo T (ed) (1994) Hybrid factory: the Japanese production system in the United States. Oxford University Press, New York

Abo T (2002) An approach for management geography: in the case of Japanese hybrid factories in the three major regions. Annual Meeting, San Juan, June 28–July 1. Academy of International Business

Abo T (2004) An integrated theory of management geography: Japanese hybrid factories in three major regions. In: Gupta V (ed) Transformative organizations: a global perspective. Response Books, New Delhi, pp 231–246

Abo T (2012) Global operations of Japanese MNE's hybrid factories: management geography framework. In: Schlunze RD, Agola NO, Baber WW (eds) Spaces of international economy and management. Palgrave Macmillan, London, pp 176–199

Abo T (2015) Researching international transfer of the Japanese-style management and production system: hybrid factories in six continents. Asian Bus Manag 14:5–35

Aoyama Y, Murphy JT, Hanson S (2011) Key concepts in economic geography. Sage, Los Angeles

Balland P-A, Boschma R, Frenken K (2015) Proximity and innovation: from statics to dynamics. Reg Stud 49(6):907–920. https://doi.org/10.1080/00343404.2014.883598

Barnard CI (1938) The functions of the executive. Harvard University Press, Cambridge, MA

Bathelt H, Glückler J (2011) The relational economy: geographies of knowing and learning. Oxford University Press, Oxford

Bathelt H, Malmberg A, Maskell P (2004) Clusters and knowledge: local buzz, global pipelines and the process of knowledge creation. Prog Hum Geogr 28:31–56

Beaverstock JV (2004) Managing across borders: knowledge management and expatriation in professional service legal firms. J Econ Geogr 4:157–179

Beika M (1970) Keiei kankyoron (Business environment theory). Maruzen, Tokyo. (J)

Bennett R (2001) 'Ba' as a determinant of salesforce effectiveness: an empirical assessment of the applicability of the Nonaka-Takeuchi model to the management of the selling function. Mark Intell Plan 19:188–199

Boschma, R. A. (2005) Does geographical proximity favour innovation? Économie et institutions 6–7. http://journals.openedition.org/ei/926, doi: https://doi.org/10.4000/ei.926. Accessed 3 May 2019

Boschma RA, Wenting R (2007) The spatial evolution of the British automobile industry: does location matter? Ind Corp Chang 16:213–238

Brinkhoff S, Suwala L, Kulke E (2015) Managing innovation in 'localities of learning' in Berlina and Seville. In: Micek G (ed) Understanding innovation in emerging economic spaces: global and local actors, networks and embeddedness. Ashgate, Farmham, pp 185–201. https://doi.org/10.4324/9781315549163-9

Buckley PJ, Ghauri PN (1999) The internationalization of the firm. International Thomson Business Press, London

Chandler AD (1962) Strategy and structure. MIT Press, Cambridge, MA

Chandler AD (1977) The visible hand: the managerial revolution. The Belknap Press of Harvard University Press, Cambridge, MA

Chen L (2016) Enterprise development and employment transformation in inland rural areas of Fujian Province, China. Chiri Kagaku (Geogr Sci) 71:39–59

Clark GL, Lai KPY, Wójcik D (2015) Editorial introduction to the special section: deconstructing offshore finance. Econ Geogr 91:237–249

Coe NM, Dicken P, Hess M (2004a) Global production networks: realizing the potential. J Econ Geogr 8:271–295

Coe NM, Hess M, Yeung HW, Dicken P, Henderson J (2004b) 'Globalizing' regional development: a global production networks perspective. Trans Inst Br Geogr 29:468–484
Coe NM, Kelly PF, Yeung HWC (2007) Economic geography: a contemporary introduction. Blackwell, Malden, MA
Coe N, Yeung H (2015) Global production networks: theorizing economic development in and international world. Oxford University Press, Oxford
Coe NM, Yeung HW (2019) Global production networks: mapping recent conceptual developments. J Econ Geogr 19:775–801
Content J, Frenken K (2016) Related variety and economic development: a literature review. Eur Plan Stud 24:2097–2112
Crainer S (2000) The management century. Jossey-Bass, Hoboken, NJ
Christaller W (1933 [1966]) Central places in Southern Germany. Prentice-Hall, Englewood Cliffs, NJ
Czinkota MR, Ronkainen IA, Moffett MH (1999) International business. Harcourt Brace, Orlando
Dicken P (1971) Some aspects of the decision making behavior of business organizations. Econ Geogr 47:426–437
Dicken P (1986) Global shift. Harper & Row, London
Dicken P (1998) Global shift: transforming the world economy, 3rd edn. Guilford Press, New York
Dicken P, Miyamachi Y (1998) 'From noodles to satellites': the changing geography of the Japanese sogo shosha. Trans Inst Br Geogr 23:55–78
Drucker P (1954) The practice of management. Harper & Brothers, New York
Drucker P (1985) Innovation and entrepreneurship. Heinemann, Portsmouth, NH
Dunning JH (1979) Explaining changing patterns of international production: in defense of the eclectic theory. Oxford Bull Econ Stat 41:269-295. https://doi.org/10.1111/j.1468-0084.1979.mp41004003.x
Florida R (1995) Towards the learning region. Futures 27:527–536
Ford H (1923) My life and work. Heinemann, London
Fujita M, Krugman P, Venables AJ (1999) The spatial economy: cities, regions, and international trade. MIT Press, Cambridge, MA
Gertler MS (2004) Manufacturing culture: the institutional geography of industrial practice. Oxford University Press, Oxford
Glückler J (1999) Neue Wege geographischen Denkens? Eine Kritik gegenwärtiger Raumkonzepte und ihrer Programme in der Geographie. Verlag Neue Wissenschaft, Frankfurt A.M.
Granovetter M (1985) Economic action and social structure: the problem of embeddedness. Am J Sociol 91:481–510
Greenhut ML (1956) Plant location in theory and practice. University of North Carolina Press, Chapel Hill, NC
Håkanson L (1979) Towards a theory of location and corporate growth. In: Hamilton FEI, Linge GJR (eds) Spatial analysis, industry and the industrial environment. Progress in research and applications, 1. Industrial systems. John Wiley & Sons, Chichester, pp 115–139
Hayter R, Watts HD (1983) The geography of enterprise: a reappraisal. Prog Hum Geogr 7:157–181
Iammarino S, McCann P (2013) Pentitled multinationals and the economic geography: location. Technology & Innovation. Edward Elgar, Cheltenham, UK, pp 33–66
Isard W (1956) Location and space economy. MIT Press, Cambridge, MA
Isard W (1960) Methods of regional analysis. MIT Press, Cambridge, MA
Itami (1987) Mobilizing invisible assets. Harvard University Press, Cambridge, MA
Itami (1991) Ba no manejimento josetsu (Introduction to management of Ba). Soshiki Kagaku (Organizational Science) 24. (J)
Itami (1999) Ba no manejimento (Management of Ba). NTT Shuppan, Tokyo. (J)
Jones A (2002) The "global city" misconceived: the myth of "global management" in translation service firms. Geoforum 33:335–350
Jones A (2003) Management consultancy and banking in an era of globalization. Palgrave Macmillan, Basingstoke

Jones A (2007) More than "managing across borders?": the complex role of face-to-face interaction in globalizing law firms. J Econ Geogr 7:223–246
Jones A (2016) Geographies of production II: political economic geographies: a pluralist direction? Prog Hum Geogr 40(5):697–706. https://doi.org/10.1177/0309132515595553
Jones A (2018) Geographies of production III: economic geographies of management and international business. Prog Hum Geogr 42(2):275–285. https://doi.org/10.1177/0309132516680756
Kamakura N (2018) Kenkyu kaihatsukino no kukanteki bungyo: Nikkei kagaku kogyo no soshiki ricchi saihen to gurobaruka (Spatial divisions of labor in R&D: organizational and locational restructuring with the globalization of Japanese chemical firms). University of Tokyo Press, Tokyo. (J)
Kawabata M (2000) Kourigyo no kaigaishinshutsu to senryaku (The internationalization of Japanese retailers: locations and strategies). Shinhyoron, Kyoto. (J)
Kawakubo A (2011) Upgrading the scale of Wagyu cattle breeding and the future issues in further development of the large-scale farming in Nango district, Nichinan city, Miyazaki Prefecture. Chiikichirigaku Kenkyu (Journal of Systematic Regional Geography) 17:1–18. (J)
Kawamura T (ed) (2005) Gurobaru keizaika no amerika nikkei kojo (Japanese factories in America in global economy). Toyokeizai Shimposha, Tokyo. (J)
Kester WC (1991) Japanese takeovers: the global contest for corporate control. Boston, Harvard Business School Press
Klepper S (2007) Disagreements, spinoffs and the evolution of Detroit as the capital of the U.S. automobile industry. Manage Sci 53:616–631
Koike K (1988) Understanding industrial relations in modern Japan. Macmillan, Basingstoke
Konno N (1998) Chishiki shisan no keiei (Management of knowledge assets). Nihon Keizai Shinbunsha, Tokyo. (J)
Krugman P (1991) Geography and trade. Leuven University Press, Leuven
Krumme G (1969) Toward a geography of enterprise. Econ Geogr 45:30–40
Kumon H, Itohisa M (2019) Ahurica no nihon kigyo – Nihonteki keiei seisan shisutemu no iten kanosei (Japanese firms in Africa: the possibility of a transfer of Japanese management production system). Jichosha, Tokyo. (J)
Laage-Hellman J (1997) Business networks in Japan: supplier-customer interaction in product development. Routledge, New York
Lee YH (1997) The state, society and big business in South Korea. Routledge, New York
Laulajainen R (1995) Corporate geography relaunched. Geogr Rev Japan 68:185–197
Laulajainen R (1998) What about managerial geography? Geol J 44:1–7
Laulajainen R, Stafford HA (1995) Corporate geography: business location principles and cases. Kluwer, Dordrecht
Lösch A (1939 [1954]) The economics of location. Yale University Press, New Haven, CT
MacKinnon D, Cumbers A (2019) An introduction to economic geography: globalization, uneven development and place, 3rd edn. Routledge, London
Maskell P, Bathelt H, Malmberg A (2006) Building global knowledge pipelines: the role of temporal clusters. Eur Plan Stud 14:997–1013
Matsubara H (ed) (2013) Nihon no kurasuta seisaku to chiiki inobeshon (Cluster policies of Japan and regional innovation). University of Tokyo Press, Tokyo. (J)
McCann P, Mudambi R (2004) The location of the multinational enterprise: some analytical issues. Growth Chang 35(4):491–524
Mizuno M (2019) Evolutionary approaches to regional clusters and networks: a review of empirical studies by "the Utrecht School" of evolutionary economic geography. Ann Jpn Assoc Econ Geogr 65:239–259. (J)
Nelson RR (1995) Recent evolutionary theorizing about economic change. J Econ Lit 33:48–90
Nicholson Y, Larry D, Rajesh S (2001) The role of interpersonal liking in building trust in long-term channel relationships. Acad Mark Sci J 29:3–15

Nishioka HG, Krumme G (1993) Location conditions, factors and decisions: an evaluation of selected location surveys. Land Econ 14:195–205
Niwa T (2019) Network analysis of manufacturing companies in Tochigi Prefecture. Ann Jpn Assoc Econ Geogr 65:213–216. (J)
Nojiri W (2013) What is evolutionary economic geography? Jimbun Chiri (Japanese Journal of Human Geography) 65:397–417. (J)
Nonaka I, Takeuchi H (1997) Die Organisation des Wissens - Wie japanische Unternehmen eine brachliegende Ressource nutzbar machen. Campus-Verlag, Frankfurt am Main
Nonaka I, Konno N (1998) The concept of "ba": building a foundation for knowledge creation. Calif Manage Rev 40:40–54
Nonaka I, Takeuchi H (1995) The knowledge creating company: how Japanese companies create the dynamics of innovation. Oxford University Press, New York
Nunes S, Lopes R (2015) Firm performance, innovation modes and territorial embeddedness. Eur Plan Stud 23(9):1–31. https://doi.org/10.1080/09654313.2015.1021666
Ohmae K (1982) The mind of the strategists. McGraw-Hill, New York
Ohmae K (1990) Borderless world. HarperPerennial, New York
Olds K, Dicken P, Kelly PF, Kong L, Yeung HW-C (1999) Globalization and the Asia-Pacific. Routledge, London
Peck J, Yeung HW-C (eds) (2003) Remaking the global economy. Sage, London
Perroux F (1955) Note on the concept of growth poles. In: Mckee DL, Dean RD, Leahy WH (eds) (1970) Regional economics. Free Press, New York: 93–103. (translated by Gates L, Mcdermott AM)
Piore M, Sabel CF (1984) The second industrial divide: possibilities for prosperity. Basic Books, New York
Polanyi M (1967) The tacit dimension. University of Chicago Press, Chicago
Porter ME (1980) Competitive strategy. Free Press, New York
Porter ME (1985) Competitive advantage. Free Press, New York
Porter ME (1990) The competitive advantage of nations. Free Press, New York
Porter ME (1998) On competition. Harvard Business School Publishing, Boston
Richter F-J (2014) The dynamics of Japanese organizations. Routledge, New York
Sayer A (2000) Realism and social science. Sage, London
Schlunze RD (1992) Spatial diffusion of Japanese firms in West Germany and West Berlin from 1955 to 1989. Geogr Rev Jpn 65B:32–52
Schlunze RD (1997) Japanese investment in Germany: a spatial perspective. Lit-Verlag, Münster
Schlunze RD (2001) The spatial structure of Japanese business activities in Europe. TESG 92(2):217–230
Schlunze RD (2002) Locational adjustment of Japanese management in Europe. Asian Bus Manage 1:267–283
Schlunze RD (2003) Locational adjustments of the European manufacturing management in Japan. Ann Jpn Assoc Econ Geogr 49:271–288
Schlunze RD (2004) Managerial embeddedness of European manufacturing firms in Japan. Jpn J Hum Geogr 56:512–530
Schlunze RD, Ji W, Mori M, Li M (2015) Does Chinese managers' guanxi networking matter to their managerial success? A multiple-case study from Japan. Ritsumeikan Bus J 9:1–17
Schlunze RD, Agola NO, Baber WW (eds) (2012) Spaces of international economy and management: launching new perspectives on management and geography. Palgrave Macmillan, London
Schlunze RD, Plattner M (2007) Evaluating international managers' practices and locational preferences in the global city: an analytical framework. Ritsumeikan Bus Rev 16(1):63–89
Schoenberger E (1997) Cultural crisis of the firm. Blackwell, Oxford
Schumpeter JA (1934) The theory of economic development. Harvard University Press, Cambridge, MA
Scott AJ (1988) New industrial spaces. Pion, London

Sokol M, Pataccini L (2020) Winners and losers in coronavirus times: financialisation, financial chains and emerging economic geographies of the COVID-19 pandemic. Tijdschr Econ Soc Geogr 111:401–415
Sotohebo D (2012) Evolutionary economic geography: development path and perspectives. Geogr Rev Jpn 85:40–57. (J)
Storper M (1997) The regional world: territorial development in a global economy. Guilford Press, New York
Storper M, Venables AJ (2004) Buzz: face-to-face contact and the urban economy. J Econ Geogr 4:351–370
Suwala L, Oinas P (2012) Management geography: a conceptual framework. Paper presented at the International Geographical Congress (IGC), Cologne, August. Available at: http://www.siemrg.org/images/PDF/4-Oinas-Suwala.pdf. Accessed 10 September 2019
Taira A (1999) Localization processes of Japanese-affiliated companies in the Chicago Metropolitan Area. Geogr Rev Jpn 72:508–535. (J)
Taira A (2002) Spatial characteristics and strategies of Japanese-affiliated companies in the Midwest of the United States: localization or specialization? Geogr Rev Jpn 75:730–749
Taira A (2020) Beyond the cluster: a case study of pipelines and buzz in the glocal relational space of the glove-related industry of Shikoku, Japan. Geogr J 186:45–58
Taylor FW (1911) The principles of scientific management. Harper & Brothers, New York
Taylor M, Oinas P (2006) Understanding the firm: spatial and organizational dimensions. Oxford University Press, Oxford
Thrift N (2000a) Pandora's box? Cultural geography of economies. In: Clark G, Feldman M, Gertler M (eds) The Oxford handbook of economic geography. Oxford University Press, Oxford, pp 689–704
Thrift N (2000b) Performing cultures in the new economy. Ann Am Assoc Geogr 90:670–692
Tomozawa K (1995) Kogyo chirigaku ni okeru "flexibility" kenkyu no tenkai (A review essay on "flexibility" debates in industrial geography). Geog Sci 50:289–307. (J)
Tomozawa K (2000) Seisan shisutemu kara gakushu shisutemu e: 1990 nendai obei ni okeru kogyo chirigaku no doko (From production systems to learning systems: research trend of industrial geography in Europe and America in the 1990s). Ann Jpn Assoc Econ Geogr 46:323–336. (J)
Totsuka H (1990) Kokusai bungyo no shintenkai to Nihonkigyo (A new turn of international division of labor and Japanese firms). Shakai Seisaku Gakkai Nenpo (Ann Soc Study Soc Policy) 34:3–22. (J)
Trompenaars F, Hampden-Turner C (2006) Waves of culture—understanding cultural diversity in business. Nicholas Brealey, London
von Thünen JH (1842) Der Isolierte Staat. In: Hall P (ed) von Thünen's isolated state. Pergamon, London
Weber A (1909) Theory of the location of industries. University of Chicago Press, Chicago
Wenger E, McDermott R, Snyder WM (2002) Cultivating community of practice: a guide to managing knowledge. Harvard Business School, Press, Boston
Yamamoto K (2005) Sangyo shuseki no keizaichirigaku (Economic geography of industrial agglomeration). Hosei University Press, Tokyo. (J)
Yamamoto K (2014) The agglomeration of the animation industry in East Asia. Springer, London
Yeung HW-C (1998) Transnational corporations and business networks. Routledge, New York
Yeung HW-C (2005) Rethinking relational economic geography. Trans Inst Br Geogr 30:37–51
Yeung HW-C (2016) Strategic coupling: East Asian industrial transformation in the new global economy. Cornell University Press, Ithaca
Zhu CJ (2012) Human resource management in China: past, current and future HR practices in the industrial sector. Routledge, New York
(J) denotes literature in Japanese.

Japanese/International Managerial Practices Around the World

Performance Analysis of Boundary Spanners in Multinational Enterprises Through the Lens of Management Geography

Rolf D. Schlunze

Abstract The lens of management geography as applied here focuses on managerial preferences and interactions of boundary spanners in MNEs. Expatriates of MNEs play the role of boundary spanners, gathering market information while bridging internal and external organizational contexts. A review of the theory of boundary spanning in the context of expatriate managers showed that contextual management appraisals are still scarce. Therefore, a contextual model was designed to investigate the performance of expatriate managers. This study investigates the performance of boundary spanners through their preferences and interactions in the corporate, market and living environments. Hypotheses for preferences and interactions in each environment guided the analysis. The results infer that a small population of locally embedded managers existed capable of cultural synergy creation. The results of the regression analysis showed that boundary spanners sustaining the firm's market success have strong preferences in the corporate environment. Explanations for the success of boundary spanners in MNEs were given pointing out their role in the global value chain focusing on internal embeddedness.

Keywords Boundary spanners · Preferences · Interactions · Performance · PIP model

1 Introduction

Dicken (1971) puzzled about the underlying organizational mechanism that ensures the survival of the firm, but it was Aldrich and Herker (1977) who uncovered the internal power struggle to make correct inferences and provide information vital for the organizational survival as a mechanism of filtering information from the environment. When geographers still perceived the firm as a black box, social scientists studying organizational behavior shed light on boundary role personnel within the

R. D. Schlunze (✉)
College of Business Administration, Ritsumeikan University, Osaka 567-8570, Japan
e-mail: rolf@mangeo.org

A. Taira and R. D. Schlunze (eds.), *Management Geography*, International Perspectives in Geography 19, https://doi.org/10.1007/978-981-19-4403-1_2

firm. They saw the power position of boundary spanners as evident in the discussion of information-processing. According to Aldrich and Herker (1977), it is the manager who has a role as boundary spanner, paying attention to environmental and technological sources. In geography, the cultural turn has given credibility to new methods including actor-centered research that shifts to the focus to those actors who are managing corporate entities (Taylor et al. 2002; Gertler 2004). Thus, Thrift (2000) addressed managers as "fast subjects" showing the need to investigate decision-makers directly to grasp new practices transforming the global economy and local workplaces. In economic geography, management emerged as a new subfield which focuses on the nexus of managerial decision making and practices in a globalizing corporate world. Management geography targets managerial subjects as a research objective and analyses their behavior in real, relative, relational, and topical space (Scott 2010; Suwala 2012: 295). The research objective of this chapter is to analyze the management of cognitive realms influencing the managerial performance in relational space. The research question addressed here is: for managers with boundary spanning functions in MNEs, what kind of cognitive orientation in terms of preferences and interactions is important for the managerial and firm success?

1.1 Review of Relevant Literature on Boundary Spanning

Expatriate managers play the role of boundary spanners, gathering market information and bridging internal and external organizational contexts (Aldrich and Herker 1977). Scholars of organizational change have long recognized the important role that social networks play in change processes. For example, Kotter (1996) argued that a vital task of managers is using their networks to implement their agendas. Cultural, emotional and social intelligence is a critical aspect of the manager's ability to operate in different sociocultural situations (Elenkov and Pimentel 2008) and/or interpersonal networks influence managerial success (Schlunze et al. 2015). Managerial networks are part of global managers' social capital that can become valuable for the firm if they succeed in overcoming structural holes and winning the function of a broker within the network (Burt 1992, 1997). From an institutional perspective, Ramsey (2005) showed cultural distance and expatriate adjustment matters. Based on a meta-analysis of relationships, several inputs to success have been confirmed by Black et al. (1991). The following factors are counted as inputs: anticipatory factors (experiences, language ability), individual factors (self-efficacy), job factors (role clarity and conflict), organizational factors (co-worker support), and non-work factors (spouse adjustment). Managers act as boundary spanners and actively bridge the different cultural and institutional systems between the countries where headquarters (HQ) and subsidiaries of multinational enterprises (MNEs) locate (Williams 2002; Saxenian 2006). Williams (2011: 27) defines such boundary spanning as highly complex, particularly when multiple and overlapping boundaries created by different agencies, sectors and professions are involved and when these often shift in time and space. Supporters in the intercultural workplace and market environment play a crucial role in the managerial success of such managers. Global managers need to bridge cultural differences within the workplace by diversity management as they facilitate market opportunity by applying new practices. Accordingly, Yagi and Kleinberg (2011) showed boundary spanning as a process of cultural learning leading to increased intercultural competence. Reiche (2011) found that manager boundary spanning positively relates to individual efforts to transfer knowledge from, and acquire subsidiary knowledge for, the headquarters. According to Bathelt and Henn (2014), boundary spanners are agents that create durable corporate linkages based on personal and professional relationships. Boundary spanners are in place to secure both predictable and reliable knowledge and production flows across the corporate value chain. Their management and leadership role is based on high professional trust in capabilities (Bathelt and Henn 2014: 1417). Kleinbaum and Stuart (2014) identified dynamic capabilities through network responsiveness. Trustful co-leadership has been observed by Schlunze et al. (2014), documenting how co-located managers succeed in overcoming cultural differences by sharing their network information creating cultural synergy. Schlunze et al. (2013, 2014, 2015) showed that a typology of preferences spanning from globalizing to localizing could be used to explain the networking patterns of international managers. Facilitating conjoint analysis, a set of preferences constituting certain types of networking strategies, such as *globalizing* vs. *localizing* and *global networking* vs. *embedding* could be differentiated. Liu et al. (2014) shed light on relational risks taking over the role of transnational business networkers. Boundary spanners are gatekeepers of information on intra- and interfirm levels through their many activity dependencies. Andersen and Kragh (2015: 788) critiqued that most literature on boundary spanning focuses on information processing rather than management. Although our knowledge has improved through transnational studies, there is a lack of research addressing the global manager as a boundary spanner. Despite its importance, systematic research into the functioning of the boundary spanner as a core unit of decision-making in relation to his/her managerial preferences and interactions in the corporate, market, and living environment is scarce.

2 Theoretical Background

A model of managerial behavior that includes predictors is needed to grasp the reality of expatriate managers who are under pressure to perform simultaneously in various business environments. Dicken (1971) suggested that it is in the study of perception and information flows that progress can be made in understanding the organizational adjustment processes in respect to the changing business environment. Geographical location plays a role in this *thought model* [Denkmodel], but physical distance is not necessarily the most important characteristic. Referring to Torsten Hägerstrand's observations (Hägerstrand 1966), Dicken found that the spatial mobility of the individual [manager] and the extent of action space are closely related to variables such as the socio-economic status, cultural affiliation, personality-personal attributes, education and aspiration.

According to Adler and Gundersen (2008: 70) every communication has a message sender and a message receiver. Flows of information signals of or from the environment are shown in the Fig. 1. Strait arrows mean information accepted by the receiver which can be an individual actor and/or a team or group within the firm. Zigzag arrows stay for information rejected or filtered out by the encoding and decoding mechanism. Encoding describes the production of a symbol message. Decoding describes the receiving of a meaning from a symbol message. Message sender must encode their meaning into a form that the receiver will recognize. Accordingly, Yagi and Kleinberg (2011: 630) found that the boundary spanner's function involves information processing and acting as an agent of influence in the relational sphere of the MNE. As seen in figure below, the corporate, market and living environments are perceived as major components of the behavioral environment in this study. Within these environments, the manager codes the information flows and makes decisions based on given preferences. Managers rarely act alone, as individuals, rather, participative decision-making managers work, collaborate, and implement major tasks of the firm together (Kleinbaum and Stuart 2014: 353). The information flows derive from specific local or global spaces that are part of an objective environment. However, the information flow does not have perfect coverage and is itself an interpretation made by the individual managers' contextual sense making activities. The perception of the business environment is devised by the abilities of the boundary spanners within the MNEs. Boundary spanners are in charge of codifying and decoding information. They filter or screen the data according to their preferences and communicate their strategic intent within their network, respectively the global value chain of the multinational firm. It is impossible to observe all information processed but preferences important for filtering the data and interactions important for managerial decision-making can be investigated and analyzed in detail. For boundary spanners in MNEs, preferences in three basic sectors corporate, market and living environment can be distinguished. They can be perceived as internal and external, local and global, close and distant environments. Coping with internal and external stress, the manager has pressure to innovate new processes and/or product solutions in order to stay competitive in terms of managerial and/or firm performance. Stress may be generated by changes within these environments involuntarily through changes not anticipated but perceived by the boundary spanners as they occur, and voluntarily as they act as change agents (Czinkota et al. 1999). Therefore, the manager needs to invest in his own and the organization's learning. The manager's cognitive knowledge enables that creativity is perceived within the given environment. Here, the mental maps of action space determined by the preferences and interactions of the boundary spanner become crucial. Thus, it is important to ask what kinds of preferences managers have in particular environments and how their networking practices contribute to their personal managerial and firm performance.

Instead of treating space as a container, nowadays, geographers provide a conceptualization of space as a perspective (Bathelt and Glückler 2011). They refer to this conception as the geographical lens. In this conception, economic exchange

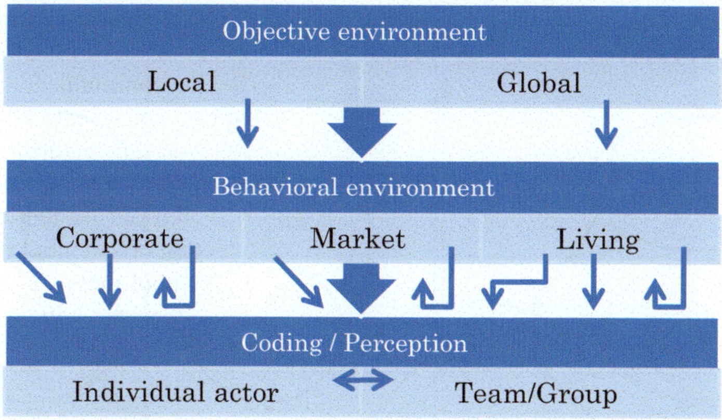

Fig. 1 Information flow in the corporate, market and living environment: important components of the behavioral environment
(*Source* Based in part on Dicken [1971: 429, Fig. 1])

rather than space, becomes the main focus of analysis. The focus of the geographical lens is precisely the spatial overlap of different social and economic processes. The management geography approach opens the black box for those interested in studying behavioral aspects of management in the internal and external contexts of the firm (Schlunze et al. 2012). I arrived at an interactive model where managers with boundary spanning functions actually modify the behavioral environment. Environment complexities increase organizations' need to differentiate boundary spanners' preferences and interactions including their networkability. They are powerful gatekeepers and become even more powerful if they act as change agents. The role of an interpreter and modifier of the behavioral environment makes routinized work impossible. Encoding and interpreting various aspects in the behavioral environment of their business activity, managers propose new strategies and measures to influence changes pro-actively. However, we still need to ask the following questions: What are the preferences that are typical for the intercultural competent boundary spanner able to contribute to the success of the firm?

2.1 Research Framework

In contrast to the research works above that only pursue particular aspects of the managerial performance such as information and knowledge transfer, here an original, systematic concept is deployed that helps to explain the managerial performance through the preferences and networkability of expatriated managers. The research objective is to analyze the preferences and interactions in the corporate, market and living environment at the level of expatriate managing directors and to relate their behavior to managerial and corporate success.

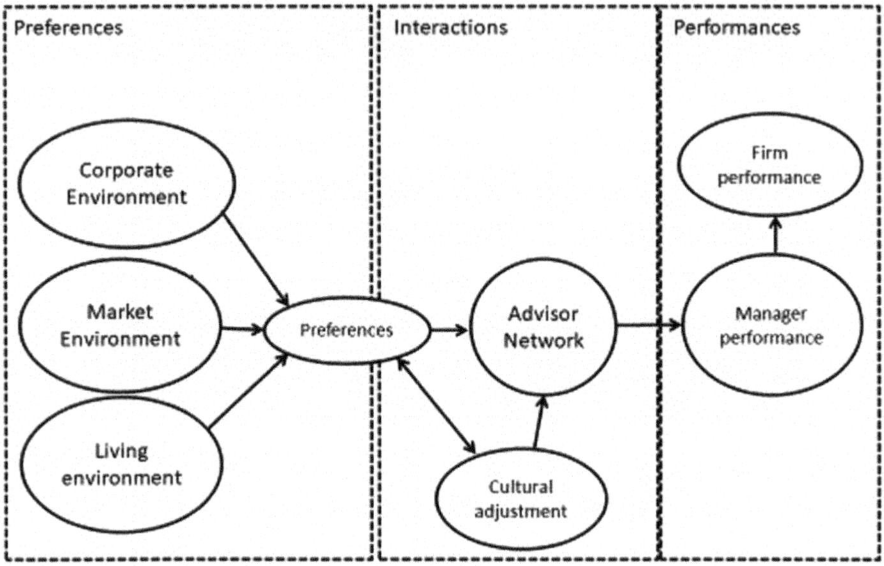

Fig. 2 PIP model—a lens of management geography (*Source* Author's survey)

Discovering the important sources of their effectiveness, I will draw upon a set of preferences, their interactions, and personal attributes in order to work successfully with people from different national cultural backgrounds. A model was developed that includes the above-mentioned factors to grasp a realistic picture of what really matters for boundary spanning by the global manager. The aim was to analyze to what extent preferences and interactions in the corporate, market and living environment sustain the impact of the boundary spanners' managerial and firm performance. It can be assumed that certain preferences in the corporate, market, and living environment impact positively on managerial performance and firm performance. In Fig. 2, the model for the contextual management appraisal is shown. Investigating Preferences, Interactions and Performance (PIP), this model constitutes the lens of management geography designed to answer the research questions above.

2.2 Hypotheses

Dynamic capabilities of adjustment and network responsiveness by actors with a boundary spanning functions would lead to better performance outcomes (Kleinbaum and Stuart 2014: 364). Boundary spanners with high cultural intelligence show better managerial performance because they adjust quicker to the host country (Lee and Sukoco 2010) and are better at creating intercultural synergy (Elenkov and Manev 2009). The acculturation and strategic intent of managers with boundary spanning functions are important for managerial success such as synergy creation (Schlunze 2012, 2016). Since cultural adjustment contributes to the network ability of the boundary spanner, the recruitment of a local advisor should be perceived as an element of successful interactions. Baber (2012) conducted deeper interviews and found that for conflict resolution within Japanese workplace, an interculturally fluent advisor is needed. Meshing with diverse and informed actors in action spaces appears to become an important information source. These interpersonal connections will also help to interpret the code mechanism and/or perceive the objective environment as it is. Thus, it was assumed that certain cross-cultural skills and trustful interactions in the workplace result in a better performance of the boundary spanner. Therefore, I propose the following hypothesis.

H1 The better the cultural adjustment and interactions, the better the managerial performance is.

Based on empirical observations at the level of intercultural workplaces, three success attributes were distinguished in each environment. As a result of previous research facilitating conjoint analysis, the number of variables has been reduced to the three most important ones (see Table 1) The relation between the variables is linear and regression analysis can be formulized for calculating the overall preference of a boundary spanner: According to Schein (2005), the corporate environment is defined by three cognitive levels of organizational culture. To analyze the performance of the boundary spanners in relational space of MNEs, I distinguish here three key components of the corporate environment: the collaboration in the multinational enterprise, the human resource access, and working atmosphere.

H2.1 The stronger the manager's focus is in the corporate environment, the better the managerial and firm performance are.

The market environment consists of market opportunities, cooperation with suppliers and customers in the value chain, and governmental supports (Håkansson and Johanson 1993; Zhang et al. 2015). A market is an institution that links information to buyers and sellers to allow the exchange of goods or services. The boundary spanner has an important role in satisfying customers and clients (Hald 2012).

Table 1 Variables to distinguish preferences in three distinguished environments

Environment	Variables		
Corporate	Collaboration within the multinational enterprise	Human resource access	Working atmosphere
Market	Cooperation with suppliers and customers in the value chain	Market opportunities	Governmental supportive setting
Living	Livable local environment	Local information network	Manifold city life

Source Schlunze et al. 2015, Tab. 1, p.51.

H2.2 The stronger the manager's focus is in the market environment, the better the managerial and firm performance are.

The key elements of the living environment consist of a livable local environment, manifold city life, and the local information network. I assume that a good work-life balance is important when managing abroad. Granovetter (1985) shows that weak ties can inspire new activities and behavioral change. This assumption implies that managers need to cope with the new challenges in the overseas environment. They might seek ideas and inspirations facilitating their personal network in their former and recent living environment. Their efforts lead us to assume that preferences in the living environment might impact managerial performance as well. Thus, the final hypothesis was formulated as follows.

H2.3 The stronger the manager's focus is in the living environment, the better the managerial and firm performance are.

3 Method and Material

With the support of the EBC, European managers were surveyed by questionnaire and interview. Those European managers registered with the EBC received our original questionnaire that was developed to investigate the research model above. A questionnaire survey of 230 European managers based in Japan and another questionnaire survey addressing 330 Japanese managers expatriated to Germany were conducted. Those international managers who indicated their willingness to provide deeper insights by cooperating with our interview survey were contacted after the questionnaire survey was completed. A sample was created that focused on evaluating the hybrid type of international managers who are bilingual and perform with cultural competence. The questionnaire consisted of the following set of questions: (a) preferences in the corporate, market and living environment and additionally general locational preferences indicating workplace and living place; (b) cultural adjustment including particular adjustment practices; (c) trust network to discuss workplace and problems with clients in the market; and (d) managerial performance in term of synergy creation. To evaluate firm performance, the sales figures have been used provided by Toyo Keizai database and correlated with the above-listed factors (a–d). The sample of the first survey included all 230 foreign executive managers listed in the directory of the European Business Council in Japan (EBC). Analysis was conducted with 60 executive managers who fill out a questionnaire in advance of the interviews. For the questionnaire survey, the reply rate of 18%. Half of the replying managers indicated that they were willing to collaborate with the interview survey. A questionnaire was used to prepare for the interviews and to gather data for later database analysis. The questionnaire collected information about the locational preferences, behavioral orientation and networking of the European executive manager. The results from the database analysis and interviews have been double checked by comparing them against the original data. In cases where there was a deviation, I deepened the investigation through follow-up interviews. Finally, 56 valid cases were used for statistical analysis.

A comparative study was carried out on Japanese managers in Germany based on a sample including 330 managers listed in the Toyo Keizai database. A Japanese version of the previously used English questionnaire was sent out in January 2011 to survey Japanese managers based in Germany about (a) their cultural adjustment strategies, (b) locational preferences, and (c) networking behavior. Additionally, 33 Japanese managers met at social gatherings, like a New Year's Party in Düsseldorf and a Hakuba meeting in Hannover, were asked to support the questionnaire survey. In contrast to the up-to-date list of EBC, the Toyo Keizai database is not very reliable. Although Toyo Keizai conducts a telephone survey annually to update the database, some subsidiaries move to new locations and managing directors changing their positions relatively quickly. To update the information given by Toyo Keizai, it became necessary to check web pages and meet managers on various occasions. In total 98 managers replied. The reply rate was 27% because the follow-up strategy was successful and the questionnaire was designed to be filled out in less than ten minutes. Using questionnaire surveys, I evaluate the managerial and firm performance by examining (a) the managers' preferences, and (b) the interactions or cultural adjustment in the context of their trust relations.

For the preference analysis, the number of variables was reduced to the three most important ones. These nine key variables also appeared in the questionnaire which was used to collect data for the database analysis below.

For the interactions and cultural adjustment following questions were used to evaluate the quality and context of trust relations. Since the questionnaire uses a five-point Likert type scale, ordinal data were obtained for each variable. For (h) a set of questions was used. The data obtained from the related answers were transformed into proximity variables showing the geographical distance and frequencies of interactions.

(a) Do you prefer to maintain the business, or do you like to initiate change?
(b) Do you prefer to apply your home country practices, or do you adjust to the practices of the host country?
(c) Do you prefer to participate in activities, or do you like to contribute to the international business community pro-actively?
(d) Do you feel integrated into or excluded from the host community?
(e) My command of the local language is good. I try to use it as much as possible in the workplace.
(f) My partner is understanding and supportive of my work-life abroad.
(g) I am actively involved in the decision-making of the local subsidiary.
(h) Who gives you (where, how often) good advice on how to be successful in the intercultural workplace?
(i) I succeed in creating cross-cultural synergy in my recent workplace (cultural exchange promoting innovation etc.).

Both databases have been matched and multivariate statistics could be performed investigating the hypothesis above. The data of both groups could be matched because not the cultural differences but the preferences and interactions of boundary spanners in MNEs have been the research objective. Descriptive data analysis showed that European managers usually are expatriated with open assignments to Japan and Japanese managers get usually assigned for five years to work in Europe; both populations are expected to have in common a long-term perspective on their overseas assignment. Almost all managers had been on the job for more than one year when surveyed by questionnaire. Since a conservative mindset often prevails and even dominates internal corporate environments, I assumed that for Japanese managers but also for Japan-based European managers, that Japanese management practices function as a reference for human interaction and/or power relations in the relational space. The analytical framework investigating preferences, interactions and performance of the boundary spanners in MNEs was facilitated for the quantitative analyses. First, correlation analysis was conducted with the joint database consisting of 150 valid cases. Following the line of the hypotheses, regression analyses were conducted to investigate the potential contribution of boundary spanners to the firm performance. Only 43 valid cases were used since sales data was not available for all 150 overseas subsidiaries. Due to the limitations of this chapter the results of the quantitative analysis will be discussed only, although qualitative research has been carried out through interview surveys following each questionnaire survey (Table 2).

Table 2 Overview of both samples showing assignment characteristics

	Sample (A)	Sample (B)	Total
Content	Foreign executive managers listed in the directory of the European Business Council (EBC) in Japan	Japanese executive managers in Germanylisted in the Toyo Keizai database plus Japanese managers met on occasion	Managerial directors and presidents of overseas subsidiaries of MNEs
Size of sample	330	363	693
Valid cases	56	94	150
Duration: >1 year	98%	83%	89%
Assignment type	Open	Five years	($n = 78$)
Return (Return rate)	60 (18%)	98 (27%)	158

Source Author's own survey

4 Results

4.1 Results of Correlation Analysis

Correlations have been discovered that show to what extent managerial performance is indeed impacted by the managers' preferences and interactions. The results advertised were usually at a significance level of 0.01 indicated by two stars (**) or at 0.05 indicated by one star (*). It was found that in the corporate environment preferences for workplace harmony and the support of an advisor in the workplace correlate weak but positively for those with good managerial performance (0.242**). This implies that the boundary spanners capable to create synergy skillfully focuses on workplace harmony. In the foreign cultural setting, it is advisable to recruit a local advisor helping to implement workplace practices that keep local staff members and subordinates motivated. It appears that preferences in the market environment such as collaborative development with clients (0.207*) and a relative independency from governmental support (−0.242**) promote the managerial performance. Strong preferences for information networking (−0.759**) and manifold city life (−0.404**) in the living environment appear to have a negative relation with the performance of the manager, but a positive on human resource access was found (0.489**). This could imply that boundary spanners are using weak linkages indeed to improve managerial and firm performance. The analysis shows us that the better the cultural adjustment in terms of language (0.217**), decision-making involvement (0.331**) and integration in local business community (0.333**) equipped with a supportive partnership (0.367**) the better the performance of the boundary spanner. Frequent interaction with an advisor (0.242**) who cares about workplace harmony can promote the managing director in his boundary spanning role. These results suggest that boundary spanners' understanding and attention towards the actors in the workplace nurture their own managerial success in the form of cultural synergy creation which would confirm the hypothesis (H1) that preferable interactions and cultural adjustment contribute indeed to good managerial performance.

4.2 Results of Regression Analysis

It appears that the preferences in the corporate environment were most important for the boundary spanner to succeed overseas. As seen in Table 3, the model 4 showed a good value (R Square = 0.712), explaining the sales performance of the firm by certain preferences and aspects of networking behavior. A preferable firm performance was observed at the level of those boundary spanners who (a) were actively involved in the decision making of the local subsidiary, (b) collaborated in the MNE network, (c) built a good working atmosphere, (d) ensured human resource access, and (e) frequently interacted with a co-located advisor (see Table 3, model 5). To conclude, the preferences, or focus, of successful boundary spanners was on their empowerment by home country HQ, but their gatekeeper function also included maintaining workplace relations (Fig. 3).

Table 3 Regression analysis results—preferences and network

Model summary					
Model	*R*	*R* Square	Adjusted *R* Square	Std. Error of the Estimate	Durbin-Watson
1	0.662[a]	0.438	0.420	104.75023	
2	0.754[b]	0.569	0.539	93.34383	
3	0.811[c]	0.658	0.622	84.56848	
4	0.844[d]	0.712	0.670	79.00524	
5	0.869[e]	0.755	0.708	74.34486	2.094

Source Author's survey
[a]Predictors: (Constant), involved
[b]Predictors: (Constant), involved, MNE Collaboration
[c]Predictors: (Constant), involved, MNE Collaboration, WORK
[d]Predictors: (Constant), involved, MNE Collaboration, WORK, HUMAN
[e]Dependent Variable: 'Relative Sales Performance'

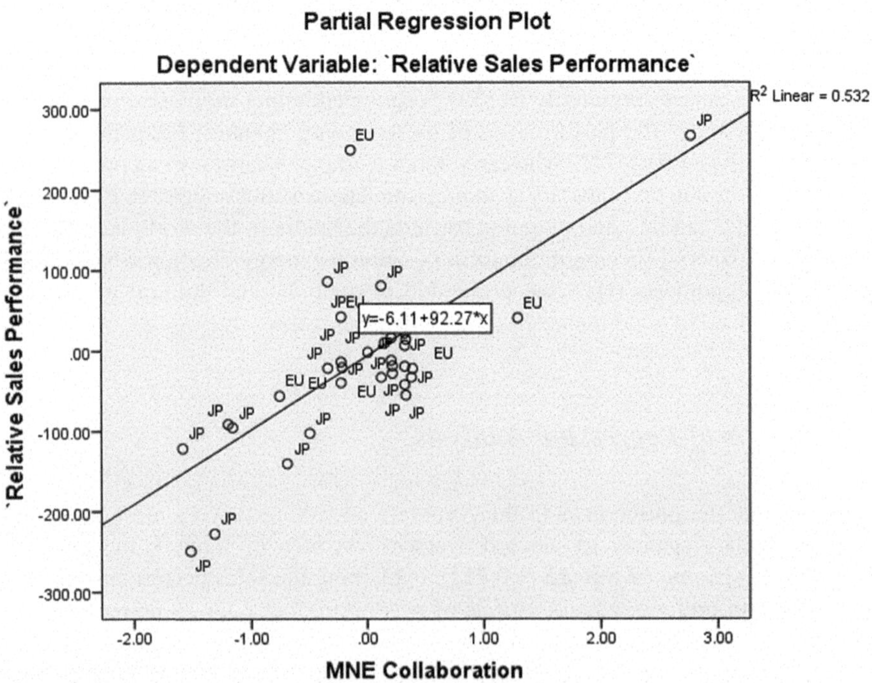

Fig. 3 Preference for the collaboration in the MNE network (*Source* Author's survey)

4.3 Preferences in the Workplace

Collaboration within the MNE network can be viewed as a global integration effort. Global integration becomes effective through local responsiveness and therefore needs to be nurtured by good leadership and effective team building in the local workplace. Collaboration within the MNE network appears to be an important task of the boundary spanner, but this task includes the obligation to negotiate the position and promotion of the overseas subsidiary in the interest of the local employees. In this aspect, local responsiveness is an important part of the global integration efforts of the boundary spanner, but global managers clearly have a preference to ensure their gatekeeper position. The strong impact of this variable indicates that the globalizing function of the boundary spanner in charge to transfer knowledge and other resources from the HQ to the subsidiary is foremost important (Fig. 4).

Boundary spanners in MNEs appear to be ambitious to access and to lead global talents. Human resource access cannot be enabled by the empowerment of the HQ only but needs to nurture by good leadership for the local staff and team members. It appears that an important role of boundary spanners is to select the right people for the right job. Human resource access is not only focusing on talents but also includes

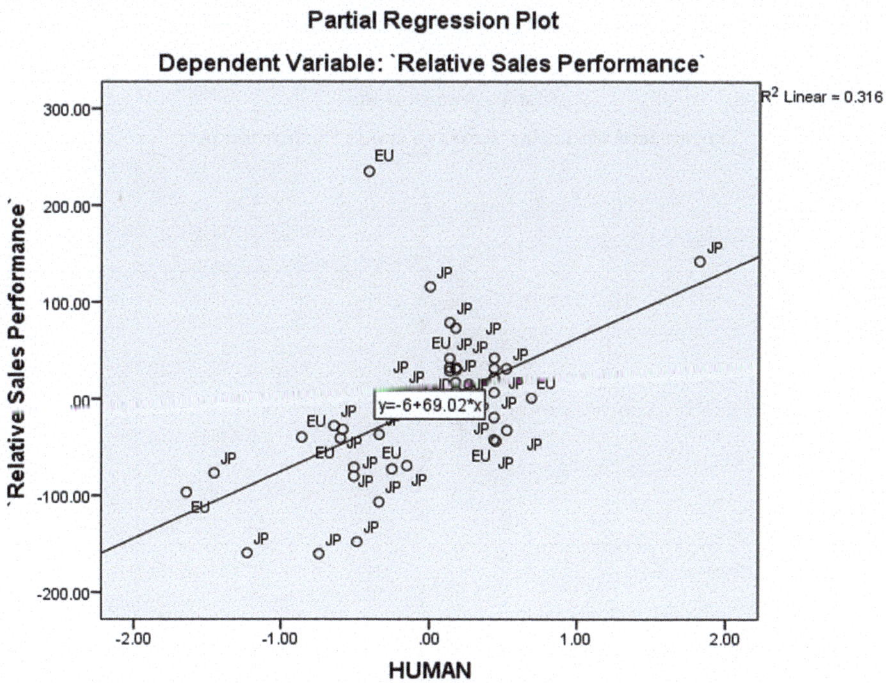

Fig. 4 Preferences for human resource access (*Source* Author's survey)

a trust-building process with local staff members. The second strongest impact in the corporate environment shows that the successful boundary spanner needs to get networked locally with actual and potential staff members in the intercultural workplace.

Workplace harmony that leads to an effective team building is important for managing directors who act successfully as boundary spanners. This can also include the moment of conflict and change. From Fig. 5, it is obvious that Japanese managing directors heading German workplaces who do not have preferences on workplace harmony often failed to show a good sales performance. One reason could be that these Japanese managers believe that within the German workplace, this harmony is not needed. However, successful boundary spanners understand that workplace harmony is always important even it is shaped differently by the cultural values of the particular workplace. The concept of workplace harmony is meaningful for both Japanese expatriated managers and Japan-based managers not only because they are both in charge of managing an intercultural workplace with Japanese subordinates and co-workers. Paying attention to workplace harmony should be perceived as an embedding effort for both groups of boundary spanners.

Since expatriate managers operate in a foreign business environment, they need advice from local managers to perform their boundary spanner roles properly. Figure 6 suggests the trend that boundary spanners who interacted with local advisors frequently were heading firms with good sales performance. To achieve a good sales

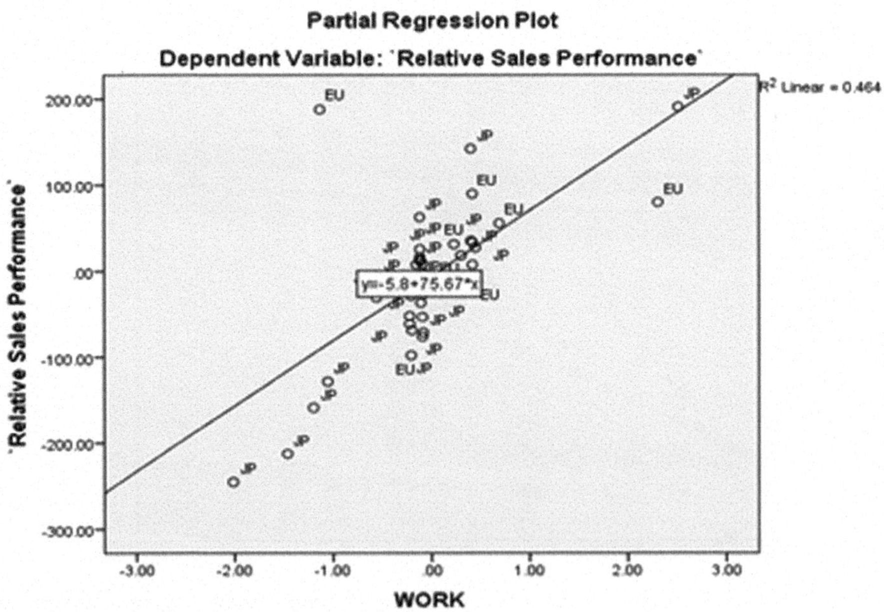

Fig. 5 Preference for workplace harmony (*Source* Author's survey)

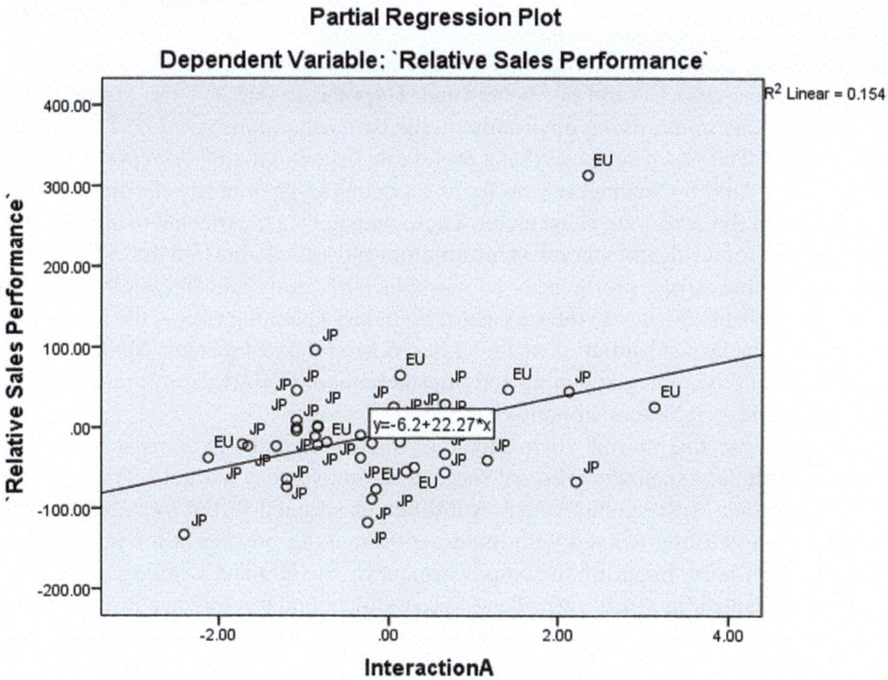

Fig. 6 Frequent interaction with co-located advisor in the workplace
(*Source* Author's survey)

performance, the existence of a co-located advisor able to consult about strategies for how to lead local staff members and customers is helpful. This variable again shows that workplace issues matter most to the boundary spanner and the firm success. The vision and mission of the firm that may include the strategic intent of the boundary spanner needs to be communicated with local advisors and co-workers (Fig. 6).

5 Discussion

The discovery made here was that independent from the national culture of the boundary spanners in MNEs, preferences and interactions in the corporate environment provide the best explanation for the managerial and firm performance. The results let us assume that boundary spanners capable of producing cultural synergy make an effort on cultural adjustment foremost by interactions with a local advisor who cares about the workplace harmony and helps to build trust relations within the workplace. This appears to confirm the first hypothesis. The regression results shown above clearly verified the hypothesis (H2.1) "The stronger the manager's focus in the corporate environment, the better the managerial and firm performance." Hypothesis (H2.2) "The stronger the manager's focus in the market environment, the better the firm performance" could not be verified. Hypothesis (H2.3) "The stronger the manager's focus in the living environment, the better the managerial performance" was falsified. The result suggests that a preferable firm and managerial performance are foremost valid for managers who focus on boundary spanning activities such as networking in the corporate value chain. These managers are expected to aim first on command and control, and second on information and knowledge transfer. The results also assume that strong preferences on workplace harmony and frequent exchange with local advisers are key to the success of boundary spanning role of the managing director in overseas subsidiaries of Japan-based MNEs and Japanese MNEs. These preferences and boundary spanning activities help them to embed corporate strategy and their managerial intent smoothly.

In conclusion, the internal environment of the firm appears to be most important for those boundary spanners who are succeeding in overseas markets. The analysis implies that one of the greatest responsibilities to succeed in the overseas market is to focus on getting involved with the decision-making process at the level of the overseas subsidiary. Ensuring the empowerment by the HQ and winning support in the overseas subsidiary are jobs of the successful boundary spanner in the MNE. Choosing talented people and consulting trustable and experienced advisors in the local workplace are the boundary spanners' success practices. These practices make it possible to achieve cultural synergy. Clearly, the findings of the analyses showed that managing directors with their boundary spanning role are more focused on management issues in the corporate environment rather than the market environment. Nevertheless, their ability to assess the market information provided by local staff members appears to be crucial. It became clear through the above analysis that the successful managers with boundary spanning functions in MNEs should be perceived as global managers who exploit global network relations in workplaces at home and overseas.

Following the findings, I observe that boundary spanners have foremost a globalizing function when leading overseas subsidiaries successfully, but they need to perform localizing functions within the intercultural workplace simultaneously. Global managers are working across cultural boundaries searching for partners in the intercultural workplace able to advise them about accessing local talents while establishing a harmonious and efficient workplace atmosphere through the provision of resources from HQ and within the MNE network.

I summarized the role of the boundary spanner by a model that illustrates the most important findings in Fig. 7. The most important preference of the successful boundary spanner is the collaboration within the MNE, second workplace harmony, and third access to human resources. Obviously, empowerment by the HQ is most important for the expatriate manager but building a network of talented and trustful partners in the intercultural workplace also appears very important. These partners need to be addressed as culturally fluent advisors when managing relations with clients and customers in the foreign market. Communication with supporters provides the feeling of being integrated into the cultural workplace which is a prerequisite for

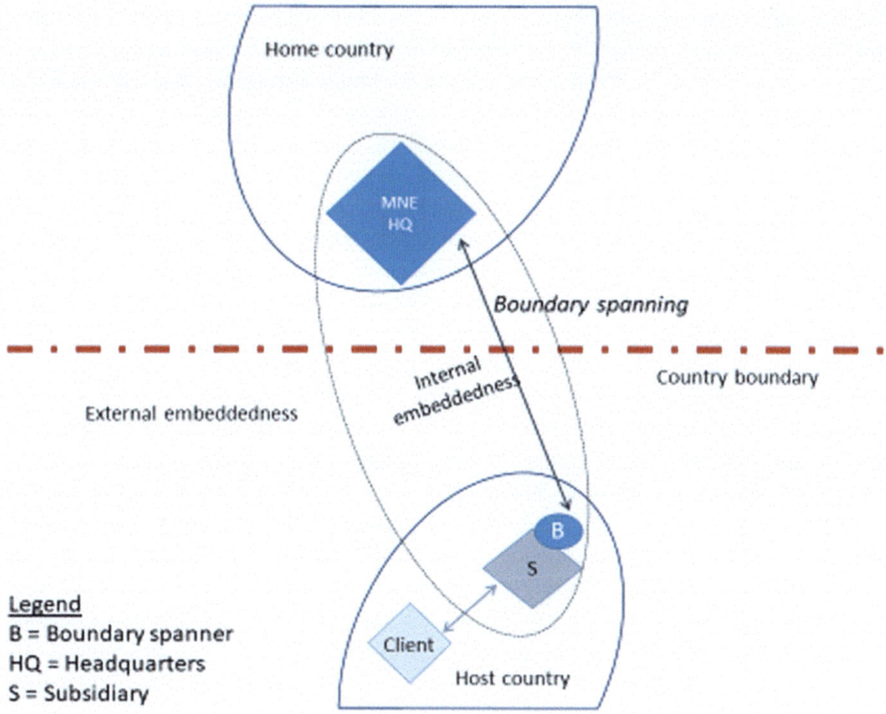

Fig. 7 Boundary spanners' internal embedding of the MNE
(*Source* Author's survey)

effective involvement in decision-making with the team of the overseas subsidiary (S).

The results suggest that managers functioning in an MNE facilitate the firm's internal environment connections when performing their boundary spanning role across borders. Relations to suppliers and clients within the overseas market do not need to be facilitated directly by the managing director but may be delegated to trusted staff members and partners in the overseas workplace. To conclude, for the successful boundary spanner within MNEs, not the embeddedness in the external environment, but the networking in the internal corporate environment appears to be important. To succeed with multiple embeddedness, the boundary spanner based at the overseas subsidiary transfers knowledge, as firm-specific advantages, which is re-combined with existing assets in the local, external business environment (Rugman 2014: 9). Clearly, the Global Value Chain (GVC) theory often ignores that the boundary spanner in the MNE acting as a global manager relies on local staff members when it comes to localizing activities aiming for external embeddedness in overseas markets. This result is in the line of Andersson and Forsgren (2000: 488) who stated that MNE embeddedness is shaped and developed through the successful interactions and cooperation with external stakeholders. They found that external embeddedness exists through external stakeholder relationships with customers, suppliers and other entities but did not indicate who actually builds and sustains these external relations. External relationships develop in long-term exchange are often made possible by local co-workers building and sustaining trust relations. To make my point clear, the "black box" of the firm can only be opened by actor-centered research. I found that the expatriated global manager appears to have foremost an important role as boundary spanners in terms of internal MNE embeddedness. This means that successful boundary spanners tend to focus on the headquarters' activities and relations with internal stakeholders bridging domestic and international contexts. Their role is to develop these internal relationships in the context of financial and administrative power, to balance control and autonomy within the GVC by implementing corporate strategy and hierarchy. These interactions can dominate external stakeholders but depending on the cooperative or competitive character of stakeholder relations the boundary spanner seeks help from local co-workers and subordinates implementing the corporate strategy to achieve internal and external embeddedness of the MNE (Ratajczak-Mrozek 2017).

It became obvious that the cognitive orientation of these boundary spanners is focused on the internal embeddedness while performing globalizing activities in the relational space of the MNEs. It is likely that boundary spanners embed their subsidiary in the market environment by facilitating the capabilities of local staff members who actually help to achieve external embeddedness. Their practices focus on implementing global standards and practices of the MNE harmonizing within governmental settings facilitating market niches or breaking up market restrictions as found previously by Faulconbridge (2008). Referring to our typology of preferences, the results showed clearly that the globalizing and global networking activities are the most important characteristics of a successful boundary spanner at the level of MNEs. The results infer that boundary spanners who are capable to manage the GVC of the MNE dominate the picture of the successful global manager.

Nevertheless, in a globalizing world, we need to draw more attention to the exceptional work of those able to facilitate communication between different communities in different cultural settings with the intercultural competence. Concerning tasks beyond sales performance—such as community building by international social capital—there is need of setting up intercultural training and exchange programs for global managers to embed and localize businesses successfully (Henn 2012).

This research followed an original approach nurtured by original data fed by two questionnaire surveys. To my knowledge, it was shown for the first time that boundary spanners' preferences and interactions matter for managerial and firm success. A shortcoming of course, is that the rich information of the interview survey could not be added to the findings because of the limited space provided for this chapter. Case study research that follows Rugman's call (2014: 15) to take into account the full range of managerial interactions might show, for example, that Japanese expatriate managers at leading automotive multinational firms are directly and proactively involved in external embeddedness. Such cases could also show that this might be precisely because their supplier system shift to the region is not really localized but still managed by Japanese expatriate managers. However, the results of the quantitative analyses showed what successful European and Japanese boundary spanners have in common. This quantitative research showed that MNE managers with boundary spanning functions are usually in charge of internal embeddedness. From the additional interview survey, Japanese managers expatriated overseas were often centered on the headquarters in Japan regarding their decision making but also Japan-based European managers appear to focus more on internal embeddedness because of existing cultural and/or language barriers. Thus, it would be beneficial to investigate in detail how Japanese and European managers build and facilitate their social networks in particular cultural settings. In order to win a better understanding about similarities and differences in decision-making for embedding the MNE, research drawing more on the contextual aspects of doing business overseas is needed. Therefore, I suggest that the lens of management geography introduced here should be applied to qualitative research. The question here is how managers with boundary spanning functions facilitate not only the institutional but also the social network to achieve internal and external embeddedness of the MNE. Actor-based research that applies a contextual model mapping preferences, interactions and managerial performance appears to be promising and will contribute with new insides to the development of the Theory of Management Geography.

Acknowledgements This research was supported by Grant-in-Aid for Scientific Research from the Japanese Ministry of Education, Science and Culture (2007–2009) *Research on the decision making process and spatial behavior of foreign managers in Japan*; and (2010–2012) *Research on firm success and Japanese managers' locational preferences in Germany*. I am grateful for the support by the European Business Council providing a letter of support and a mailing list. I feel deeply indebted to all international managers of European and Japanese overseas subsidiaries who were willing to cooperate with my questionnaire and interview survey. Many thanks go to the anonymous reviewers of the 2016 EAMSA conference and to the discussants at the 16th SIEM research group meeting at the 2017 AJG conference at the University of Tsukuba. Finally, I am grateful for opportunity to present this research results at the Japan Academy of Multinational Enterprises on 19. September 2020. Special thanks go to Professor Noriko Yagi for her qualified critiques and useful recommendations helping to improve this book chapter. Last not least I am grateful for the kind support of my good colleagues Professors Atsushi Taira and William Baber.

References

Adler NJ, Gundersen A (2008) International dimensions of organizational behavior. Thomson South-Western, Mason

Aldrich H, Herker D (1977) Boundary spanning roles and organization structure. Acad Manag Rev 2(2):217–230

Andersen, PH, Kragh H (2015) Exploring boundary-spanning practices among creativity managers. Manag Decis 53(4):786–808

Andersson U, Forsgren M (2000) In search of centre of excellence: network embeddedness and subsidiary roles in multinational corporations. Manag Int Rev 40(4):329–350

Baber WW (2012) Adjusting to a distance space: cultural adjustment and interculturally fluent support. In: Schlunze RD, Agola NO, Baber WW (eds) Spaces of international economy and

management: launching new perspectives on management and geography. Palgrave Macmillan, London, pp 254–268
Bathelt H, Glückler J (2011) The relational economy: geographies of knowing and learning. Oxford University Press, New York
Bathelt H, Henn S (2014) The geographies of knowledge transfers over distance: toward a typology. Environ Plan A 46:1403–1424. https://doi.org/10.1068/a46115
Black JS, Mendenhall ME, Oddou G (1991) Toward a comprehensive model of international adjustment: an integration of multiple theoretical perspectives. Acad Manag Rev 16(2):219–317
Burt R (1992) Structural holes. Harvard University Press, Cambridge
Burt R (1997) The contingent value of social capital. Adm Sci Q 42(2):339–365
Czinkota MR, Ronkainen IA, Moffett MH (1999) International business. Harcourt Brace, Orlando
Dicken P (1971) Some aspects of the decision making behavior of business organizations. Econ Geogr 47(3):426–437
Elenkov DS, Pimentel JRC (2008) Social intelligence, emotional intelligence, and cultural intelligence: an integrative perspective. In: Ang S, Van Dyne L (eds) Handbook of cultural intelligence: theory, measurement, and applications. M.E.Sharpe, New York, pp 289–305
Elenkov DS, Manev IM (2009) Senior expatriate leadership's effects on innovation and the role of cultural intelligence. J World Bus 44(4):357–369
Faulconbridge JR (2008) Managing the transnational law firm: a relational analysis of professional systems, embedded actors, and time: space-sensitive governance. Econ Geogr 84(2):185–210
Gertler MS (2004) Manufacturing culture: the institutional geography of industrial practice. Oxford University Press, Oxford
Granovetter M (1985) Economic action and social structure: the problem of embeddedness. Am J Sociol 91:481–510
Hägerstrand T (1966) Aspects of the spatial structure of social communication and the diffusion of information. Papers and Proceedings of the Regional Science Association 16:27–42
Håkansson H, Johanson J (1993) The network as a governance structure: Interfirm cooperation beyond markets and hierarchies. In: Grabher G (ed) The Embedded Firm. Routledge, London, pp 35–51
Hald KS (2012) The role of boundary spanners in the formation of customer attractiveness. Ind Mark Manage 41(8):1228–1240
Henn S (2012) Transnational entrepreneurs, global pipelines and shifting production patterns: the example of the Palanpuris in the diamond sector. Geoforum 43(3):497–506
Kleinbaum AM, Stuart TE (2014) Network responsiveness: the social structural micro foundations of dynamic capabilities. Acad Manage Perspect 28(4):353–367
Kotter J (1996) Leading change. Harvard Business School Press, Boston
Lee L-Y, Sukoco BM (2010) The effects of cultural intelligence on expatriate performance: the moderating effects of international experience. Int J Hum Resour Manage 21(7):963–981
Liu AH, Gould AN, Rollins M, Gao H (2014) Role conflict and ambiguity confronting transnational business networkers: contrasting social stigma and relational risks for Chinese and Western boundary spanners. Ind Mark Manage 43(6):911–919
Ramsey JR (2005) The role of other orientation on the relationship between institutional distance and expatriate adjustment. J Int Manag 11(3):377–396
Ratajczak-Mrozek M (2017) Network embeddedness: examining the effect on business performance and internationalization. Palgrave Macmillan, Cham
Reiche BS (2011) Knowledge transfer in multinationals: the role of inpatriates' boundary spanning. Hum Resour Manage 50(3):365–389
Rugman AM (2014) Subsidiary specific advantages and multiple embeddedness in multinational enterprises. MNE Acad J 7:1–18
Saxenian A (2006) The new argonauts: regional advantage in a global economy. Harvard University Press, Cambridge, MA
Schein EH (2005) Organizational culture and leadership. Jossey-Bass, San Francisco

Schlunze RD (2012) "Hybrid" managers creating cross-cultural synergy: a systematic interview survey from Japan. In: Schlunze RD, Agola NO, Baber WW (eds) Spaces of international economy and management: launching new perspectives on management and geography. Palgrave Macmillan, London, Basingstoke, Hampshire, pp 24–45
Schlunze RD (2016) Hybrid-manager in Japan: Weg zum interkulturellen Erfolg [Hybrid manager in Japan: path to intercultural success]. In: Chiavacci D, Wieczorek I (eds) Japan 2016—Politik, Wirtschaft und Gesellschaft. IUDICIUM Verlag (VSJF), München, pp 166–190
Schlunze RD, Agola NO, Baber WW (2012) Spaces of international economy and management: launching new perspectives on management and geography. Palgrave Macmillan, Basingstoke, Hampshire
Schlunze RD, Plattner M, Ji, W (2013) Co-leadership success by sharing local and global information networks. In: Schönhuth M, Gamper M, Kronenwett M, Stark M (eds), Visuelle Netzwerkforschung. Qualitative, quantitative und partizipative Zugänge. Transcript Verlag, Bielefeld, pp 161–178
Schlunze RD, Baber WW, Ji W (2014) Preferences and intercultural networking for globalizing practices of successful leaders in the intercultural workplace. In: Alvstam CG, Dolles H, Ström P (eds) Asian inward and outward FDI: new challenges in the global economy. Palgrave Macmillan, London, pp 115–136
Schlunze RD, Ji W, Mori M, Li M (2015) Does Chinese managers' guanxi networking matter to their managerial success? A multiple-case study from Japan. Ritsumeikan Bus J 9:1–17
Scott AJ (2010) Cultural economy and the creative field of the city. Geogr Ann B Hum Geogr 92(2):115–130
Suwala L (2012) Kreativität, Kultur und Raum: Ein wirtsschaftsgeographischer Beitrag am Beispiel des kulturellen Kreativitätsprocesses. Springer, Wiesbaden
Taylor PJ, Walker DRF, Beaverstock JV (2002) Firms and their global service network. In: Sassen S (ed) Global networks—linked cities. Routledge, New York, pp 93–115
Thrift N (2000) Performing cultures in the new economy. Ann Am Assoc Geogr 90:670–692
Williams P (2002) The competent boundary spanner. Public Adm 80(1):103–124
Williams P (2011) The life and times of the boundary spanner. J Integr Care 19(3):26–33. https://doi.org/10.1108/14769011111148140
Yagi N, Kleinberg J (2011) Boundary work: an interpretive ethnographic perspective on negotiating and leveraging cross-cultural identity. J Int Bus Stud 42:629–653
Zhang C, Wu F, Henke JW Jr (2015) Leveraging boundary spanning capabilities to encourage supplier investment: a comparative study. Ind Mark Manage 49:84–94

Changes in the Locational Conditions of the Japanese Machinery and Instrument Industry in China: A Case Study of Dalian Economic and Technological Development Zone

Yasuhisa Abe

Abstract The study aimed to clarify prevailing changes in the locational conditions of the Japanese machinery and instrument industry in Dalian, China. According to a survey of 26 companies in 2008, political and social factors such as government policies aimed at attracting Japanese investment had been crucial for those that had expanded before the 2000s, while from 2000, for example, the existence of business partners became more important. However, the business environment of Japanese companies went into decline from 2006. The influence of rising wage levels and prices was especially negative. Moreover, politico-economic problems affected Japanese companies badly. Most of them had taken advantage of the preferential tax relief offered by the central government which by 2010 was no longer available. Meanwhile, a combination of political and economic incentives was tempting companies to establish new factories in Southeast Asian countries to produce their goods. Nevertheless, survey findings showed most companies had decided to remain in Dalian as the advantages of investing there outweighed the disadvantages. For example, in addition to the effects of accumulation of existing partner companies, replicating the high number of well-trained Dalian workers would be very difficult elsewhere.

Keywords Japanese companies · Wage level · Localization of human resources · Local government · Dalian

1 Discussions on the Arrival of Japanese Companies in China and the Status Quo

Economic geography had devoted a lot of its research of multinational companies to locational patterns, or emphasized the resulting influences on their catchment areas (Matsubara 2006: 85–88),[1] a trend which had been encouraged in preceding years by the relocation of production bases to developing countries in Asia. Japanese

Y. Abe (✉)
Graduate School of Social and Cultural Studies, Kyushu University, Fukuoka 819-0395, Japan
e-mail: snc11960@nifty.com

A. Taira and R. D. Schlunze (eds.), *Management Geography*, International Perspectives in Geography 19, https://doi.org/10.1007/978-981-19-4403-1_3

companies noticeably began to move to other Asian countries in the 1970s, starting in South Korea/Taiwan, etc., and then shifting their labor-intensive industries to ASEAN countries in search of "low-cost and sufficient labor." In the mid-1980s, concomitant with the economic development of these countries and regions, the production bases were moved to China, which inherited the low-cost and generous supply of labor mantle (Seki 1997: 39–50; Seki and Fan 2003: 12–15).

Entering the 1990s, more Japanese companies located their production bases in China. According to Wei et al. (1999), low labor costs, infrastructure improvements, high economic growth, and the various preferential policies of local governments attracted multinationals, with direct foreign investment concentrated in coastal areas. However, inland areas, with cheap labor, and bolstered by the government's investment initiatives, were expected to attract more foreign capital. Suzuki et al. (2001) analyzed the geography of the fiber and electrical machinery sectors—in which Japanese manufacturing was ubiquitous—and indicated that these sectors were concentrating in the Yangtze River Delta, the Bohai Rim region, south China and other coastal areas, while expanding production bases inland. The study by Ehara and Hakozaki (2009: 113–148) also found that in the northeastern and mid-western regions, with the promulgation of preferential investment policies by the government and rising consumption levels, the aforementioned regions attracted more foreign-funded enterprises and urged future research to observe their environmental impact closely.

From a geographical analysis of the locational characteristics of Japanese manufacturing companies vis-a-vis variable functions, Suzuki et al. (2005a) had concluded that, in the coastal cities, Shanghai boasted many production, sales/market, research and development, and overall management bases. In contrast, Jiangsu and Zhejiang Provinces, close to Shanghai, had a large proportion of production bases, while cities in the Yangtze River Delta region varied greatly in terms of the activities Japanese companies engaged in.

The above referred to research indicated that the Japanese companies which arrived in China before 2000 were dominated by export processing enterprises in the manufacturing industry. Most of these companies chose coastal areas for export, imported part, and raw material logistical efficacy. However, after 2000, with the rise in per capita income, China was no longer just a huge production base. It was beginning to be appreciated as the world's largest consumer market (Minami and Makino 2005: 16–17). Therefore, companies that moved to China to target domestic sales had to consider establishing bases in the large cities of mid-west China. After 2005, with the wage increases caused by economic expansion, it was widely believed that many companies were considering moving factories to inland areas or Southeast Asia, in particular Vietnam, to capitalize on the cheaper labor there (Ehara and Hakozaki 2009: 62). What environmental impact did the arrival of these companies have?

Since companies had instinctively adapted to regional environmental changes, to examine the decision-making and behaviors of the companies from entrance to evacuation, Clark and Wrigley (1995, 1997a, b) introduced the concept of sunk cost[2] in economic geography. Schoenberger (1997) meanwhile analyzed why American manufacturing industry had failed to cope with corporate culture changes. With various restrictions on relocating a factory, multinationals often just remained. They did not relocate. In addition to these explanations, many discussions have emphasized the fact that (i) the location of companies is inextricably linked to social, cultural, and political systems as well as economic conditions and (ii) those companies are "embedded" in such systems (Aoyama, Murphy and Hanson 2010). As a result, as Matsubara (ed.) (2009) points out, there may be cases where "inertia" plays a part in the location of various facilities (such as factories) of companies; thus, it is necessary to examine the changes in the internal functions and roles of companies and factories that remain in their current locations.

In addition, since how multinationals expanded overseas had been attracting interest, such as with the localization of enterprises, or transfer of production systems (Matsubara 2006: 87), this paper focused on the labor force, recruitment, wage levels, and the role of local government in relation to changes in locational conditions faced by Japanese companies in China. With Japanese companies accounting for a high percentage of the foreign-funded enterprises, Dalian Economic and Technological Development Zone (DETDZ) provided the requisite conditions to carry out the survey. Moreover, the author analyzed the machine makers that constituted the largest Japanese presence in DETDZ.

The questionnaire survey and interviews with the companies targeted in this paper were conducted in August 2008, and related statistical data were also collected during this period. The results of the survey conducted during this period are introduced in this paper because in Dalian, the target region, wage levels and other corporate costs began to rise markedly during this period, and the city's advantage as a manufacturing base began to decline. The companies in the study area have therefore been taking certain measures to cope with the rising production costs so they can continue their business operations, and it can be considered that this situation has remained basically unchanged since the 2010s. Accordingly, this section mainly presents the situation as of 2008, when the field survey was conducted, and the subsequent situation is explained in Sect. 4.3 whenever possible.

2 Profile of Dalian and DETDZ, and Survey Methods

Located at the southern tip of the Liaodong Peninsula, Dalian is one of the most important cities in northeast China. As of the end of 2007, the city of Dalian had a registered population of 5.782 million. The development of harbors had been the catalyst for gradual improvements to other infrastructure such as international airports, railways, highways, power stations, and postal communications services.

Dalian's machinery, shipbuilding, petroleum, metal and light industries, including textiles and food, had developed over a long period of time to serve and complement the city's powerhouse chemical industry. Moreover, 14 universities taught Japanese, headed by the world- renowned Japanese Language Department—the world's largest—at Dalian University of Foreign Languages. Although overseas

Table 1 Number of foreign investments in Dalian by country/region (Unit of investment: billion dollars)

	Number of investments (%)	Amount (%)
Japan	3,711(29.3)	80.6(31.7)
Hongkong, Macao, Taiwan	3,262(25.8)	65.4(25.7)
The United States	1,510(11.9)	26.4(10.4)
Korea	2,242(17.7)	24.6(9.7)
Else	1,936(15.3)	57.1(22.5)
Total	12,661(100.0)	254.1(100.0)

Note Cumulative from 1984 to 2007
Source Mizuho Corporate Bank Dalian Branch (2008: 5)

companies had recently chosen to reduce their presence in Dalian, as a business outsourcing outpost of Japanese companies (mostly engaged in communications and the software industry) Dalian had made remarkable progress (Friedman 2007: 55–60), with ICT enterprises agglomerating around the software industry park in the urban area.

In the early 1990s, the city was attracting both the highest proportion of Japanese investment and companies (Suzuki et al. 2005a), and even in 2006 was one of the few areas in China still doing so.[3] Japanese companies accounted for 31.7% of foreign investment in Dalian—from 29.3% of the foreign investors (Table 1). Unlike Shanghai, where companies from Hong Kong, Taiwan, Europe and the United States also abounded, Dalian was characterized by a high percentage of Japanese companies.

Across Dalian, the DETDZ was renowned as a destination for Japanese companies. The DETDZ, nestled in Jinzhou District, 27 km away from downtown Dalian, was established in 1984 as one of the earliest economic development zones in China. DETDZ accounted for about 30% of Dalian's total industrial output.[4] The arrival of foreign investment—especially Japanese—was particularly significant. As of March 2007, 184 of the 651 companies that had joined the Japanese Chamber of Commerce and Industry in Dalian[5] were located in the DETDZ, and nearly 80% of them were manufacturing companies. The number of locally recruited Japanese nationals working for Japanese companies was about 2,000, representing about half of the city's resident Japanese population.[6]

As classified by the Japanese Chamber of Commerce and Industry in Dalian, more than half of Japanese companies were engaged in manufacturing, most of which specialized in electrical information and communication equipment, electronic components, mechanical manufacturing tools, electrical and electronic machinery, a number which was supplemented by their parts suppliers (Table 2). Specific examples included, Panasonic, Toshiba, Mitsubishi Electric, Canon, Konica Minolta, Omron and Nidec Corporation.

The reasons for moving to Dalian and subsequent operational problems experienced by 40[7] of the 90 companies located in the DETDZ were published by Toyo

Table 2 Industry breakdown of Japanese Chamber of Commerce and Industry, Dalian (As of April 2007)

Breakdown by major classification	Breakdown by manufacturing industry classification
Agriculture and fishing industry 13(0)	Food, beverages, tobacco, feed 25(6)
Construction industry 12(7)	Textile and textile products manufacturing 40(15)
Manufacturing industry 360(146)	Wood, wood products, furniture, decorations 20(2)
Information and communication industry 69 (3)	Pulp, paper, processed paper products 5(4)
Electricity, gas, heat supply, water industry 5(1)	Printing 7(2)
Transportation industry 39(4)	Chemistry 7(5)
Wholesale and retail business 67(9)	Plastic and rubber products 32(13)
Finance and insurance business 14(1)	Metal and metal products 53(20)
Real estate business 7(1)	General equipment 18(5)
Restaurant, accommodation business 7(1)	Electrical, information and communication equipment, electronic parts, devices 64(34)
Government affairs, medical care, welfare, education 13(1)	Transportation equipment 11(5)
Combined and other service businesses 65(9)	Precision mechanical equipment 64(34) 17(9)
Unclassified 15(1)	Unclassified/Other 73(31)
Total 651(184)	Total 360(146)

Note The number in parentheses was the number of companies located in the development zone. The totals did not match because there were companies that operated across multiple fields
Source Japanese Chamber of Commerce and Industry, Dalian (2007): [2007 Dalian Japan Chamber of Commerce & Industry Member List], Japanese Chamber of Commerce and Industry, Dalian, counted by author

Keizai Inc. (2008): [Overview of the Overseas Companies in 2008 (by country)], for which the firms that co-operated completed questionnaires or participated in material interviews. In the paper, the predominance of the machinery and equipment manufacturing enterprises had been analyzed, with about 60 machinery and equipment manufacturing companies named, from whom the author would receive 26 responses for our survey (a further 14 interviews were also conducted) (see Table 3).

The survey was carried out in August 2008, when performances frequently began to deteriorate due to the financial crisis. The HO financial reports of the first half of 2008 showed declining yields were common, even if companies were still profitable.

In addition to support networks for the above-stated businesses, the author also conducted interviews with the Dalian Representative Office of Japan External Trade Organization (JETRO), the Dalian branches of the Japanese Chamber of Commerce and Industry, and Bank α (Company β, Company γ, etc.),[8] etc. Next, the author

Table 3 Overview of the surveyed companies

Company	Year of entry	Local staff	Japanese staff	Industry and business overview
A	1981	5,200	20	Acoustic products such as dot printers, microphone receivers, etc. M & S of CNC automatic mediation
B	1988	500	4	M & S of carbon brushes for motors, etc.
C	1989	1,050	7	M & S of precision castings, purchase and export of casting machinery and equipment, tools, molds, etc.
D	1989	800	4	M & S of wristwatch parts, parts for electronic control ABS systems parts, etc.
E	1991	1,602	8	M & S of small industrial motors, video components
F	1992	8,911	27	M & S of small precision DC centers, medium-sized precision DC motors, DC fan motors and their components
G	1992	48	1	M & S of sewage treatment equipment and water purification equipment (for Japan), etc.
H	1993	1,900	3	Health equipment manufacturing
I	1993	21	2	Non-ferrous metal processing, international trade
J	1993	2,047	1	Manufacture of electronic components
K	1994	280	2	M & S of control valves, mechanical switches, etc.
L	1994	4,500	10	M & S of optical related products, etc.
M	1994	290	6	Processing and sales of steel materials (shearing and punching of electrical parts), etc
N	1996	630	4	Manufacture of stamping dies, car audio, etc.
O	1996	774	9	Electrical equipment manufacturing
P	1997	87	2	M & S of various precision forged products
Q	2002	37	1	Molding and assembly of resin, metal, etc.
R	2002	27	1	M & S of water treatment membrane products
S	2003	140	2	Manufacture of cylinders for photosensitive drums
T	2003	88	1	Manufacture of precision metal parts (springs)

(continued)

Table 3 (continued)

Company	Year of entry	Local staff	Japanese staff	Industry and business overview
U	2003	50	0	Processing and sales of precision steel materials
V	2003	48	3	Manufacture of general fine chemicals
W	2005	1,300	8	Information and communication equipment development and manufacturing
X	2005	1,900	9	M & S of power tools, gardening equipment, etc.
Y	2005	193	5	Manufacture and sale of automotive parts, etc.
Z	2006	237	1	Manufacture and sale of carrier tape

Notes M & S = Manufacture and Sale. Because company E had multiple subsidiaries in the development zone, the information given was for the one with the most employees
Source Toyo Keizai Inc. (2008): [Overview of the Overseas Companies in 2008 (by country)], Toyo Keizai Inc., Japanese Chamber of Commerce and Industry, Dalian (2007): [2007 Dalian Japan Chamber of Commerce & Industry Member List], Japanese Chamber of Commerce and Industry, Dalian. Edited by author)

would outline what the main attraction of the DETDZ was and transitions made in different periods before examining the prevailing locational changes at the time of the study.

3 Reasons for the Arrival of Japanese Companies in Dalian

Mutations from previous surveys, 18 options to explain company arrivals in Dalian were available, as seen in Table 4. For each option, the companies were required to make an evaluation based on their experience,[9] and tick 1 for "totally agree" (2 points), 2 for "slightly agree" (1 point), and 3 for "not agree" (0 points). The means were calculated later. The companies were divided into two groups according to their date of arrival: one comprised 16 companies that had arrived before 1997 (hereinafter referred to as "Period 1"); and the other, 10 companies whose arrival was post-2002 (hereinafter referred to as "Period 2").[10] Then, for analysis, the author selected the options of which the average scores were 1.00 or higher in Period 1 or Period 2, and between which there were significant disparities.

Table 4 Reasons for Japanese Company Entry into Dalian

Reasons for Japanese company entry into Dalian	Period 1 average scores (Number of responses)	Period 1 average scores (Number of responses)	Overall average scores (Number of responses)
Dalian Municipal Government's active investment promotion activity	*1.56(16)*	*1.40(10)*	*1.50(26)*
Well-equipped port	*1.44(16)*	*1.40(10)*	*1.42(26)*
A preferential area for foreign investment designated by the central government	*1.40(15)*	*1.22(9)*	*1.33(24)*
Short time spent on the round trip due to the proximity to Japan	*1.27(15)*	*1.40(10)*	*1.32(25)*
Complete infrastructure outside the port	*1.27(15)*	*1.30(10)*	*1.28(25)*
Strong intention of presidents	*1.13(15)*	0.70(10)	0.96(25)
Dalian City has its own preferential policies	0.93(15)	*1.00(9)*	0.96(24)
Friendly atmosphere for Japanese	0.71(14)	*1.20(10)*	0.92(24)
A galaxy of talent which is proficient in Japanese	0.94(16)	0.90(10)	0.92(26)
Business partners have already arrived in Dalian	0.53(15)	1.50(10)	0.92(25)
Many companies other than business partners have also arrived in Dalian	0.67(15)	1.20(10)	0.88(25)
Labor costs are lower than **elsewhere** in China	0.67(15)	0.80(10)	0.72(25)
Easy to procure raw materials and parts	0.20(15)	*1.00(10)*	0.52(25)
Deep historical relationship with Japan	0.47(15)	0.60(10)	0.52(25)
Prices are lower compared to elsewhere in China	0.36(14)	0.70(10)	0.50(24)
Dalian and northeast China are very attractive markets	0.20(15)	0.30(10)	0.24(25)
Suitable for manufacturing products in a cool climate	0.00(14)	0.30(10)	0.13(24)

(continued)

Table 4 (continued)

Reasons for Japanese company entry into Dalian	Period 1 average scores (Number of responses)	Period 1 average scores (Number of responses)	Overall average scores (Number of responses)
Information on other cities is scarce	0.07(15)	0.20(10)	0.12(25)

Source Edited from questionnaire survey

3.1 Politico-economic and Socio-economic Factors

Table 4 demonstrated why companies had moved to Dalian, with "Dalian Municipal Government's active investment promotion activity" topping the list, averaging 1.5, convincing Japanese companies they were valued highly. It was thus necessary to carefully consider the contribution of local governments that had adopted such policies to attract investment. Specifically, the then mayor, Wei Fuhai, mapped drafts and plans to establish a "Sino-Japanese Dalian Industrial Park." This industrial base was established in the DETDZ in 1992, signaling the first large-scale development project in China to be jointly undertaken by the Chinese government (20% of the investment came from the Dalian Municipal Government) and Japan (80% of the investment came from governmental financial institutions and trading companies, banks and other private companies). For the convenience of Japanese companies, land transactions were in yen. A total of 77 Japanese companies had moved into the park by 2007.[11]

The Dalian Municipal Government's zeal to attract investment to this industrial park was noted by its resident companies. For example, one of the important reasons for the large-scale electric company E's decision to locate in Dalian was how accommodating the mayor and other senior leaders had been. The then mayor, Bo Xilai (in office from 1993 to 2000), spent lavishly in meeting with presidents and senior management of large companies in pursuit of foreign investment in Dalian. A large-scale home appliance company, W, cited the same reasons for its arrival. Mayor Xia Deren (in office from 2003 to 2009) hosted meetings with the president of company W for the express purpose of winning the company's signature. However, there was disquiet at first that the city was only attracting assembly plants, with an agglomeration of small and medium-sized enterprises conspicuous by its absence (Seki 2000: 151–152; 2003: 113–115). However, in Period 2, the Dalian government courted companies of relatively small scales more zealously, e.g. of 100 staff,[12] as they had with the large companies.

A tailor-made infrastructure for the transportation of manufactured products and raw materials, and the short distance to Japan were two further Dalian selling points. To be precise, the options including "the well-equipped port" (1.42 points), "the complete infrastructure outside the port" (1.28 points), and "the short time spent on the round trip due to the proximity to Japan" (1.33 points) were rated highly.

"This is a preferential area for foreign investment designated by the central government" scored 1.33 points, with respondents impressed by the intention to develop export-driven industries that had exempted enterprises from income tax for the first 2 two years of profit since 1984 in the DETDZ, and by half for the following three (i.e., the "2-year exemption and 3-year reduction" policy); and there was further tax respite still (JETRO 2008: 45).

However, companies that came to the industrial park after 2002 lowered the rating for this option. This was because, since 2000, economic and technological development, bonded and preferential foreign zones such as for export processing, etc., had been established in alternative locations in China. There had only been 14 national economic and technological development zones nationwide when DETDZ opened, but, by 2007, the generic number of national economic development zones, including, foreign investment preferential treatment ones, had grown to 182.[13] Therefore, Dalian was no longer an automatic choice for foreign investment.

On the other hand, the companies that arrived in Period 2 increased the rating for the "welcoming socio-political climate" (1.20 points), at a time when, since 2001, Sino-Japanese political relations had deteriorated at national government level. In the spring of 2005, anti-Japanese demonstrations occurred throughout China, which posed a political risk for Japanese companies. Even the international cooperation bank JBIC and JCIPO (2007: 1) noted, "It is undeniable that the tension between the two peoples will have an impact on business activities." However, in contrast to other regions, Dalian was renowned for its "hospitality to Japanese people," making it a place where Japanese companies could invest in relative safety. Many respondents spoke highly of this option. For example, "when working in the factory in Guangdong Province, (Respondents) encountered anti-Japanese demonstrations, but this did not happen in Dalian. It is very important for foreign resident staff to live with peace of mind" (Company W. For corresponding company names, see Table 3), and others mooted that "Dalian is the most suitable city on the Chinese mainland for Japanese people to live in" (Company γ).[14]

"A galaxy of talent which is proficient in Japanese" received the fairly high score of 0.92, which indicated that such socio-political factors impacted perceptions of locational conditions. Political reforms opened the door to foreign investment in China, but remaining fundamental ideological differences with the mechanisms of socialist countries and their interpretations of historical issues still concerned companies. In conclusion, in the early stages of foreign tenure in the Chinese market, the cooperation and support of the local governments, the hospitality afforded to Japanese nationals and the rich local pool of proficient Japanese speakers greatly contributed to the decisions of many companies to invest in Dalian.

3.2 Production/Selling Cost Factors

Economically speaking, options including "business partners have already set up operations in Dalian" and "many companies other than business partners have also set up operations in Dalian" scored highly, while "the labor cost is lower than elsewhere in China," "the price is lower compared to elsewhere in China," and "Dalian and northeast China are very attractive markets" and other options received low scores. Especially for menial labor, despite the importance of production costs in attracting Japanese companies to China, this was rated lowly in their selection of Dalian over other cities.

Regarding the influence of the timing of arrival, the aforementioned five options averaged below 1.00 for surveyed Period 1 companies. During this period, most of the arrivals were labor-intensive export processing branches of companies, and their demand for cooperation with local enterprises was relatively low. These operations imported parts from Japan and elsewhere, only assembled them in Dalian, and then re-exported the products or semi-finished products either back to Japan or onwards to third countries. Their purpose was not domestic parts distribution or product sales.

However, in respect of Period 2 companies, the mean for "business partners have already arrived in Dalian" was 1.50, 1.20 for "many companies other than business partners have also arrived in Dalian," and 1.00 for "the dispatch of raw materials and parts is convenient," significantly higher than the responses from Period 1 companies, with the average for the first option, in particular, indicating companies were beginning to treat factors related to production and selling costs more rigorously, such as the proximity to suppliers and the availability of raw materials.

Electronic component manufacturers S and T were representative of the companies that emphasized "close association with business partners." For example, Company S followed Canon (did not participate in the survey) to Dalian because of the sharp increase in order volume from Canon, its largest target market. Moreover, Company T stated that proximity to business partners was the biggest reason for transferring production to Dalian, and it planned to establish a second factory to cope with the consequent increase in orders. As well as parts suppliers, Company β (introduction and maintenance of production facilities), and Company γ (wrapper manufacturing) cited the same reasons for their relocations. A large number of large companies had arrived in Dalian in Period 1, leading to the emergence of many suppliers and other dependent firms by Period 2.

Furthermore, many respondents remarked that since many Japanese companies had congregated in the DETDZ, "It is very convenient for visiting business partners (company F, company K), and "It is easy for Japanese companies to exchange valuable information."[15] Together with the remarkably high score for "many companies other than business partners have also arrived in Dalian" among Period 2 companies, it may therefore be deduced that the agglomeration of Japanese companies generated external economic value. For example, companies previously based in the same province as R and β had been, albeit from different industries, followed the pathfinders to Dalian, as it represented, not least, a safe investment. In short, it was thought the presence of embedded Japanese companies would encourage other Japanese companies to follow.

4 Changes in the Locational Conditions in Latter Years

In this chapter, upon company arrival, the author explored the changes in locational conditions by referring to the evolution of company motivations discussed in the previous chapter. In order to analyze them, the author conceived nine operational scenarios that correlated with locational condition variables, and required the surveyed companies to answer whether the presented problems existed, and finally summarized the results in Table 5. In addition, the company comments and interviews were used as references.

Table 5 Operational problems of the surveyed company in Dalian

Operational problems	Period 1 average scores (Number of responses)	Period 1 average scores (Number of responses)	Overall Average (Number of responses)
Increased prices	1.60(15)	1.10(10)	1.40(25)
Rising labor costs	1.60(15)	1.00(10)	1.36(25)
Several shutdowns due to frequent power outages	1.60(15)	0.90(10)	1.32(25)
Difficulty in securing labor	1.21(14)	0.70(10)	1.00(24)
Weakening of government preferential policies	1.14(14)	0.70(10)	0.96(24)
Local procurement rates of raw materials, spare parts and components are low	0.64(14)	0.80(10)	0.71(24)
Local government response is conservative or inconsistent	0.64(14)	0.50(10)	0.58(24)
Poor handling during customs clearance, etc., delaying the transportation of products, raw materials and parts	0.50(14)	0.50(10)	0.50(24)
Away from the main market in China, high transportation costs	0.40(15)	0.60(10)	0.48(25)

Notes The average score was calculated by selecting from three choices: very applicable (2 points), slightly applicable (1 point), and not applicable (0 points)
Source Edited from questionnaire survey

4.1 Changes in Prices and Wage Levels, and Localization of Human Resources

According to the findings of the survey, the main operational problems companies had highlighted in the 2008 survey included "increased prices (including raw materials)" (1.40 points), "rising labor costs" (1.36 points), and "difficulty in securing labor" (1.00 point). The gradual upgrade in the minimum wage that there had been in preceding years supported survey evidence of wage level increases (Table 6).

Although China's wage levels had risen since 2003 (Beijing Weekly 2008), this trend became more pronounced from around 2005, and the inability to retain new staff intensified, making it difficult for many factories to increase productivity. In particular, the vacancies to applications ratio for menial jobs in the start-up period in the late 1980s had been 1:10. In the period leading up to the survey however, even with the assistance of labor agencies searching as far afield as Jilin province, the number of applicants did not meet expectations. In some cases, only 20 out of 30 positions could be filled. Particularly in the 15–25 age group, there were fewer applicants, among who, of those recruited, there was also a high turnover rate, which inevitably hurt productivity. "It takes time for workers unfamiliar with the business to become the backbone of the force (Company B)."

It was suggested that the increasing wages in competing service industries such as the catering sector—where the workload was lighter for basically the same pay—had made it more difficult to retain employees in the previous few years. Urban residents were particularly reluctant to work in factories. It was said that "there are only a few locals in Dalian, and many of the workers are from rural areas in Liaoning Province (Company X)". Moreover, as the Chinese government developed new farmer cooperatives, more employment opportunities arose in rural areas. Thus, the migrant workers from rural areas of Liaoning or other provinces did not necessarily have to go to Dalian for work. "The death knell for recruitment was the one-child policy (Company F, Company γ, etc.)."[16] Compared with post-2002 arrivals, the companies that arrived before 1997 tended to score the options more highly (Table 5), which suggested that they were more aware of the problems caused by changes in locational conditions.

Table 6 Trends in minimum wages in major cities in China

City/Year	2005	2006	2007	2008
Beijing	580	640	730	730
Shanghai	690	750	840	960
Shenzhen	690	810	850	1,000
Guangzhou	684	780	780	860
Dalian (Development zone)	500	650	700	700

Notes 1 yuan = 15.79 yen (August 1, 2008)
Source Edited from the data of Mizuho Corporate Bank, Fujitsu Research Institute, Nikkei Inc. etc.

On the other hand, many companies stated that, other than in menial positions, there was a relatively low turnover of personnel, such as of managers, white-collar workers and technicians, and staff development was progressing smoothly. For example, from a wage level perspective, "Dalian is very attractive for its relatively cheap labor compared with its counterparts in south and east China," especially "sometimes you only need to pay half the salary of a comparative job in a southern city to hire a well-educated white-collar worker" (Company O). As shown in Table 6, although the minimum wage in Dalian was also rising yearly, the growth rate was still very low compared with Shenzhen and Shanghai.

Furthermore, the Japanese language level of the employees was very high. "Because there are many people who can speak Japanese, you can use Japanese as the official language in-company" (Company O), and some Chinese employees could even "exchange views with Headquarters by email" (Company B). Some companies "promote competent, hardworking workers to be managers," and that was because "although the remuneration is relatively low, due to age concerns, the job security trumps the temptation to look for something more immediately lucrative" (Company B). And in other companies, of 9,300 employees, more than 10% had more than 10 years of service. Many of the management positions were filled by Chinese staff, 1 at department, 3 at associate department, and 26 at the section manager level (Company F). The company invested heavily in staff who showed potential. At that time, there were only 3 Japanese employees out of a workforce of 1,900, but it operated smoothly nevertheless (Company H).

Overall, many companies noted a stability in management positions. It was said that this was because "there is a gentleman's agreement between Japanese companies in Dalian not to poach each other's personnel" (Company F). Hence, it was difficult for managers to hop from one Japanese company to another. Problems also existed if they tried to find a job in other foreign-funded enterprises. "American companies usually hire local high flyers with a bachelor's degree or better and strong English-speaking skills, so Japanese employed staff - due to a below average English level - are unlikely to be qualified" (Company O). Also, in terms of wage levels, Dalian's Japanese companies seldom paid a particularly high salary to their employees, instead weighting it according to rival Japanese company pay scales.[17]

Table 3 showed, on average, Japanese nationals only accounted for 0.4% of the workforce. According to an interview with a large textile company in August 2008, the cost of Japanese employees (incorporating housing subsidies and overseas working allowances) amounted to 7 or 8 million yen. On the other hand, even if the industries and sizes of the companies were different, the annual income of Chinese managers at the department manager level in such a large company as company F was not much more than 120,000 yuan (about 1.9 million yen, based on an exchange rate of 1 yuan = 15.79 yen at the time of the survey). Not only that, in Company B, the annual income of managers at the department manager level was only 54,000 yuan (about 850,000 yen, net of various allowances and social security obligations). Many companies believed that the localization of management was necessary to reduce production costs. In general, the successful step-up of locally sourced sub-management to veritable management was at a "satisfactory level" (Company F,

Company L, Company W, Bank α, etc.). Some companies also stated that "labor disputes are rare" (Company F, Company N, Company X).

National survey results illustrated the average working shift of employees of Japanese companies in Liaoning Province (including Dalian) was longer than in other regions (Table 7). Compared with major cities in other provinces, high school graduates and newly recruited administrative and technical staff worked the longest average shifts. Some management positions were also ranked first, and remaining grades second. On the other hand, the pay scale averages in Liaoning Province were second from bottom (Table 8).

Since Tables 7 and 8 were statistical results for all companies in Liaoning Province, they may not have accurately reflected the situation in Dalian. However, the responses during interviews suggested vindication. For example, "Northeastern employees are simpler, more diligent, and of higher quality than those in south China" (Company I), "The high quality of Dalian employees is an advantage, and because the employees have a sense of belonging in their hometown, they have highly stable lives, and many are very diligent and work hard to complete the tasks designated. Although they will not take the initiative to do things not designated, in general they are better than southern employees" (Company H). The author can surmise employees in Dalian were both enthusiastic about work and had highly stable lives.

In a world where wages and turnover rates were increasing everywhere else, that the training of managers and white-collar workers, skilled workers and other

Table 7 Average years of employee service by region and job category

	Average for all job categories	Senior Manager	Manager (DM)	Manager (WM)	Mid-career A & T	New graduate A & T	High school graduate staff
Tianjin City	6.4	7.8	8.1	7.6	5.2	3.4	3.6
Liaoning Province	5.9	7.6	9.0	7.0	4.5	4.1	3.8
Beijing City	5.0	6.3	6.8	5.0	4.2	3.1	3.3
Jiangsu Province	4.9	6.3	6.1	5.6	3.3	2.2	2.2
Guangdong Province	4.6	6.3	6.8	5.0	2.9	3.0	2.3
Shanghai City	4.4	6.9	6.1	5.1	3.5	2.5	2.5
National	5.2	7.2	7.1	5.8	4.0	3.1	2.8

Notes DM = Department Manager WM = Workplace Manager, and A & T = Administrative/Technical Staff

The survey was as of November 2006, with the author compiling data for regions with more than 25 responding companies

Source Edited from JBIC/JCIPO (2007): [The 9th Japanese Company Questionnaire Survey Results of Aggregation and Analysis], JBIC/JCIPO, p. 50

Table 8 Average monthly salary by region and job category

	Average for all job categories	Senior Manager	Manager (DM)	Manager (WM)	Mid-career A & T	New graduate A & T	High school graduate staff
Tianjin City	3,859	10,726	6,018	3,466	1,612	1,800	1,272
Liaoning Province	5,008	13,886	6,541	3,594	1,795	1,853	978
Beijing City	8,850	24,171	10,871	7,494	3,771	2,977	1,647
Jiangsu Province	5,700	17,357	8,430	4,663	1,988	1,965	1,165
Guangdong Province	6,279	21,188	11,169	4,577	1,703	2,666	1,251
Shanghai City	7,820	19,651	10,788	6,158	2,880	2,886	1,335
National	6,677	17,824	9,372	5,187	2,362	2,500	1,257

Notes DM = Department Manager WM = Workplace Manager A & T = Administrative/Technical Staff
The survey was as of November 2006, with the author compiling data for regions with more than 25 responding companies
Source Edited from JBIC/JCIPO (2007): [The 9th Japanese Company Questionnaire Survey Results of Aggregation and Analysis], JBIC/JCIPO, p. 50

local assets was bringing positive results kept production in Dalian. Particularly in the manufacturing industry, due to the regional characteristics of booming Japanese language education, there were many local people who could assist the Japanese personnel, i.e. realizing the potential of the factory only required a minimal Japanese presence (Bank α).[18] Besides that, pay scales for these staff rose more slowly than for the average worker,[19] meaning Japanese companies could secure the employment of suitable staff for relatively low wages.

4.2 *Politico-economic and Socio-economic Narratives, and Local Government Countermeasures*

Generally speaking, Japanese manufacturing companies that moved to China had strong concerns about changes in the political and economic conditions that had been fostered in preferential central government foreign investment policies they had thitherto benefitted from in the DETDZ.

By the time of the survey, not only were they only effective for approximately five years, a score of 0.95 (Table 3) for "it has been watered down" (JETRO 2008: 41) indicated a perceived change in locational conditions that raised concerns regarding the instability of Sino-Japanese political relations referred to in the Sect. 3.1. Although this did not pose an obvious problem on a local scale in Dalian, at a national level, it still represented a huge political and social risk.

One of the politico-economic issues that had a profound impact on companies in Dalian was "several shutdowns due to frequent power outages (1.32)." This was because, at the time of the survey, due to power shortages, since 2006, various regions in China had been implementing a mostly summer "power rationing" policy that targeted factories and other facilities, which became a serious problem in Dalian. As Dalian was not the provincial capital (the seat of the provincial government), it was not in a position to dictate its allocation. It therefore suffered from a wide range of "power rationing," often with late or even retrospective notice of power cuts.

Although not directly because of "power rationing", most large companies nevertheless established factories in Vietnam and elsewhere that produced the same products (bridge production) for lower wages, with politico-economic weighting a factor in relocation choices. For example, Company W, in addition to establishing factories in Vietnam, Malaysia, and the Philippines, also set up a factory that duplicated Dalian production in the city of Zhuhai, Guangdong Province. Companies F and H emulated Company W in Vietnam. It was believed these complementary lines of production intended to diversify the risk were established at the behest of corporate clients.[20]

Although there were unresolved politico-economic issues in Dalian, as examined above, in general, the attitude of local government in Dalian to Japanese companies was much more amicable than in other cities, and this was the big advantage of Dalian. The returned questionnaires suggested there were few companies that believed the attitudes of local government and the customs office were problematic (Table 5).

For a foreign company to set up business in China, it faced issues that could not be foreseen in its homeland. These included the need to build relationships with governments and business partners as well as grasp complex and non-transparent business procedures. As for attracting companies to a socialist country like China, if the PR activities of local governments could reassure foreign companies about the local political situation, local business etiquette and other socio-political factors, it would influence where companies located. Although the central government had constrained foreign-funded enterprises with various regulations, ultimately, whether or not to implement and how to apply them lay with local governments. In this sense, having a good relationship with local governments had become an important issue (Company X).

Upon moving to China, where the relationship between companies and local government officials was very important, Company L also noted that, "because of the complicated formalities, the support of the municipal government has become one of the reasons to choose Dalian. Compared with major cities like Shanghai and Beijing, in provincial cities like Dalian, companies enjoy more face-to-face opportunities with local government officials." In addition, when Company S arrived in Dalian, the municipal government gave guidance on obtaining a business license, and introduced it to government executives, whose recommendations shepherded the company's local recruitment of management. Moreover, the company was located far from the center of the DETDZ, where the infrastructure was incomplete at that time, which it was said the local government had made a promise to improve.[21] The same was true for labor disputes. "In 2005, when large-scale labor disputes occurred in the DETDZ, the local government quickly appeased the laborers, and since then there have been few" (Company N). Furthermore, many large companies benefitted from more direct local government support policies, such as preferential local tax relief. Many companies thought highly of the welcome and assimilation policies of the local government.

Even though the needs of the Japanese companies which accounted for a high proportion and absolute value of foreign-invested enterprises in Dalian were undoubtedly catered to, while the number of non-Japanese foreign companies was stable, with fewer new Japanese arrivals, the proportion of Japanese-funded enterprises gradually declined. It was therefore suggested that Japanese companies engaged in more frank dialogue with the local government and strengthened ties with non-Japanese foreign enterprises.

4.3 Stability of the Newly Arrived Enterprises

As for Table 5, "local procurement rates of raw materials, spare parts and components are low" was scored as low as 0.71. As mentioned in Sect. 2, the suppliers in Dalian had not been concentrated enough, which caused frustration with the local supply chain of spare parts and components. However, at the time of the survey in 2008, since the local procurement rates were upward and the transportation routes from Japan, South China and East China to Dalian had been established, this problem was gradually abating (according to Bank α and the JETRO Dalian Office). For example, Company K stated that "upon arrival in Dalian, most of our spare parts and components were imported from Japan, or procured from manufacturers in South and East China, respectively. However, since we rigorously trained the local suppliers, trade with them has been increasing in recent years."

On the other hand, the surveyed companies did not deem "away from the main market in China" (0.48 points) a problem. It may be because the main markets for their merchandise were overseas, such as in Japan.

In the above context, the author discussed the factory configuration that Japanese enterprises adopted to respond to the changes in locational conditions. In the survey interviews many enterprises stated that because of price and wage rises in Dalian, there was a huge risk in opening new offices and factories there (according to Company B, Bank α, etc.). In fact, the numbers and sizes of investments by Japanese enterprises had been in decline since the peaks of 2005 (Fig. 1), with a significant drop in large factory investment particularly noticeable (Bank α, etc.). Conversely, none of the enterprises with factories established in Dalian considered relocating to rural coastal areas or anywhere inland, both where prices and wages were low. Some Bank α customers considered moving their factories to another city in Jilin Province, but none pursued it because they had noticed the prevailing rise in prices and labor costs in these potential alternative Chinese locations, and considered that inflation in these places was much faster than in Southeast Asia, such as in Vietnam.

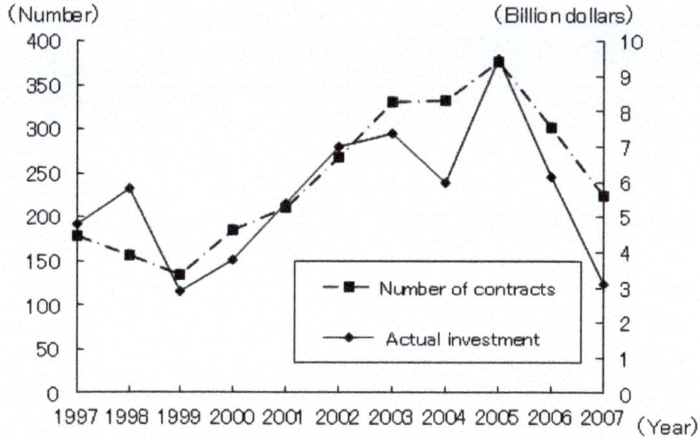

Fig. 1 Changes in Numbers and Amounts of Investments made by Japanese Enterprises in Dalian (*Source* Mizuho Corporate Bank Dalian Branch [2008]: [Overview of Dalian, Version: 2008–07] Mizuho Corporate Bank Dalian Branch)

No enterprise considered relocating its entire factory operation elsewhere at that time, such as to Vietnam, where bridge production had already commenced. That was not only as there were still many advantages to having established factories in Dalian, such as accelerated job familiarization, fewer labor disputes, an amenable local government, etc., but also because considerable wage rises and local labor disputes were so frequent in Vietnam. Consequently, there was still nowhere able to viably replace China's labor supply. Many enterprises were particularly concerned that "huge losses would be incurred as skilled personnel would have to be cultivated from scratch after relocation" (Company B). It therefore appeared many resident enterprises would be embedded to Dalian for a further, undetermined, period.

Looking at the situation from 2009, when this survey was conducted, statistical data to 2018 shows that wage levels in China have continued to rise markedly in this period. The wage level in terms of annual income of Dalian increased from 34,304 yuan in 2008 to 87,592 yuan in 2018 (Table 9). Cheap labor has certainly not been a factor in the arrival of manufacturing firms. Moreover, if the exchange rate is considered, the dollar-yen exchange rate tended to appreciate from 2009 to 2013, and it is thought that the cost increase could be absorbed; however, since 2014, the exchange rate has been at a stable level, in the range of 100–120 yen to the dollar, which is not a level at which the cost increase can be absorbed (Table 9). As a result, although the amount of foreign capital invested in Dalian increased significantly to over $10 billion in 2010, it has decreased noticeably since 2015, staying around $3 billion (Table 9).

On the other hand, the data also show that as of 2020 some of the companies surveyed in 2008 are still located in Dalian, and the factories that have been moved into the city continued to survive by changing their roles and functions. Of the Japanese enterprises that have set up operations in China as of 2020, 36.6% responded

Table 9 Changes in average wages of incumbent workers in Dalian, investment amount by foreign capital, and exchange rate for yen (2008–2018)

	2008	2009	2010	2011	2012	2013
Average annual salary of incumbent workers	34,304	38,765	44,615	49,728	54,821	59,063
Dollar-Yen exchange rate	103.4	93.6	87.8	79.8	79.8	97.6
Investment amount by foreign capital	5.00	6.02	10.03	11.01	12.35	13.60

	2014	2015	2016	2017	2018
Average annual salary of incumbent workers	63,609	69,390	73,764	81,884	87,592
Dollar-Yen exchange rate	105.9	121.0	108.8	112.2	110.4
Investment amount by foreign capital	14.00	2.70	3.00	3.25	2.68

Note The unit of wages is Chinese yuan, the unit of investment amount is billions of dollars, and the exchange rate is yen to the dollar
Source China City Statistical Yearbook (each year edition) and IMF data

that they are seeking to "expand" as the direction of their business development in the next one to two years (JETRO 2021). This percentage shows a trend of decline from the peak of 66.8% in 2011 (JETRO 2017). Companies choosing to "downsize" or "withdraw" made up 7.7% together, while the majority of companies (55.6%) chose to "maintain the status quo" (JETRO 2021). This trend can be interpreted as the enterprises' being in a stage where they are maintaining the location in which they have established overseas operations, regardless of changing conditions in the location. The phenomenon of businesses continuing in their overseas location amid changing locational conditions, discussed in this paper based on 2008 data, can be observed at present in Dalian. The result of survey was that the companies had advanced into the country could absorb the increase in production costs and maintain the balance of payments of their factories, due to the concentration effect of the presence of client companies and the skilled workforce resulting from the presence of local middle managers with long service years.

5 Outlook for Embedded Enterprises

As detailed above, this paper mainly discussed the impact of changes in the locational conditions on embedded Japanese machinery and equipment manufacturing enterprises before 2008, in terms of wage levels, the labor force, satisfying the labor demand, role of local government, etc.

In the early 1990s, Dalian had been home to the largest number of Japanese enterprises in China, especially manufacturing factories. Looking at the factors behind the growth of Japanese businesses, at first, with attractive Japanese language education policies and both a welcoming socio-political and politico-economic climate, some local governments enthusiastically courted Japanese companies. While historical links to Japan were a major driver in Japanese commitment to areas, the companies that had expanded since the 2000s stressed the proximity to other Japanese companies and expanding business partners, i.e. the "economic geographical factor" had become more important for them.

Since the late 2000s, locational condition changes such as pay rises for menial work and the consequent difficulties in securing a labor supply had impacted enterprises profoundly. Especially since 2006, the rate of employee resignations had increased, particularly of only recently recruited employees, which many enterprises believed would stifle production efficiency. However, this problem could be seen everywhere in China, including in the inland areas, and thus did not justify a domestic relocation of factories from Dalian. Many enterprises believed that the growth rate of wages—the explanation of which could partially be tempered by the increase in the minimum wage—in Dalian was lower than in Shenzhen and Shanghai, yet the quality of local labor was better than in big cities, and the turnover rate low. Further to that, wages inland and in all rural areas were increasing, which most of the enterprises believed would be close to matching those in coastal urban areas in the future. As for management and white-collar labor, the author received evaluations indicating that the rise in wage levels was small and the stability high. To augment the benefits to job familiarization that the suitability of Dalian's labor market offered, most of the enterprises trained and cultivated personnel in-house. An added challenge was a shift in national politico-economic policy that, for example, toughened the thitherto favorable conditions for foreign investment. Most of the embedded enterprises had availed of the preferential taxation policies of the central government. However, most of the relief only lasted for five years, and, as previously stated, it had shrunk in preceding years.

In contrast, by Dalian being an outlier, Japanese companies could solve most problems by meeting with more accommodating local administrations, with whom they had a big influence on policy implementation. Many large enterprises enjoyed the more direct local support policies, such as specially tailored preferential local tax relief, with the welcome and assimilation policies of the local government highly appreciated.

Even though a consequent bridge production had already been attempted, such as in Vietnam, these third countries also presented challenges such as rising wage levels and frequent labor disputes, meaning China still had not been replaced as the regional go-to labor resource, e.g. in terms of the size of the labor pool.

In the course of rapid changes in the prevailing locational conditions in Dalian, in addition to the shortcomings of the possible alternatives, another undeniable reason for the stability shown by the machinery and equipment manufacturing enterprises was the 'sunk' costs, which were highlighted by Clark and Wrigley in a series of studies. In particular, the initial cost of arriving in Dalian, training new staff, and the capital required to withdraw from the local market in accordance with the laws and practices in China constituted a heavy burden for an enterprise.

The other reasons included: the localization of human resources in management departments was accelerated by dynamic staff development; the agglomeration of the supply chain had streamlined transactions in recent years; the increase in the number of new arrivals advertised the financial injections into the local economy that they brought, such as to both management and non-management salaries, and therefore gradually strengthened the negotiating positions of enterprises with local government. It was of importance that the enthusiasm for in-house employee training and the "localization" advanced by means of employing local managers made a great contribution to the stability of Japanese enterprises. Select recruits who had been honed in-house were important resources for running businesses.

Nevertheless, from 2006, the number of manufacturing enterprises moving to China (including Dalian) fell drastically, consequently requiring Dalian to reinvent itself. In particular, it was imperative to overhaul the infrastructure and revitalize preferential tax policies in order to attract research and development (R&D) departments of foreign-funded enterprises. Some of the companies which were interviewed and surveyed established their own development departments in the preferential tax parks in Dalian, e.g. Planning, Design, and Software Design (Company H), as in Software Park. Company W had arrived in Dalian in 2005 with the idea of installing a development department. This company stated "there is a large well of talent in Dalian proficient in Japanese which is conducive to the establishment of development departments, such as in product design, which is in line with our vision. If we just produce export processed merchandise, South China is a better choice than Dalian." It would be interesting to see how many enterprises would subsequently set up their R&D departments in Dalian.

However, it should be pointed out that as of 2008, when the survey was conducted, due to the concentration effect of the presence of client companies and the skilled workforce resulting from the presence of local middle managers with long service years, the companies that had advanced into the country could absorb the increase in production costs and maintain the balance of payments of their factories. In the case of the BPO businesses targeting Dalian discussed in Chap. 8, new business opportunities have emerged in recent years through the use of ICT in business processes instead of call-center operations; in contrast, in the case of the manufacturing factories discussed in this chapter, it is unclear whether the factories will be able to absorb rising costs and maintain their operations in the future.

In recent years, in the field of economic geography, it has become an important theme to discuss the changes in the roles and functions of factories in a region during the process of location, from the time a company moves into the region to the time it shuts down or relocates to another region (Matsubara 2009). For this reason, the author believes that this would be an important topic for further study and that management geography will play a key role.

Acknowledgements This paper was based on (1) the contents of the Japanese paper "Chuugoku niokeru Nikkei-Kikaikiguseizougyou no Ricchikankyou no Henyou," published in "Geographical Science (Chiri-Kagaku)" Vol. 65, No. 4 in 2010), (2) a post-2010 addendum found in the final section. I was also sincerely grateful to Ms. Fang Jing, a graduate student at Kyushu University, for her cooperation in conducting this research.

Notes

1. Suzuki et al. (2005b) and Taira (2005) papers on the locational strategies of multinationals.
2. The expense an enterprise invested in its undertaking and could not be recovered when the undertaking was cancelled or shrunk. According to the documentation of Tsuchiya (2002: 48–49), the sunk costs fell into three categories, dependent on the business phases of an enterprise: (1) sunk cost of starting a business; (2) sunk cost of deposit; (3) sunk cost of withdrawal. Taking labor expenses as an example, the sunk costs in the three categories were, respectively: (1) the cost of employee training for the purpose of starting a new business; (2) salaries based on seniority; (3) severance settlements.
3. In terms of economic and development zone total regional production volume (measured by GDP), 2006 statistics ranked Dalian Economic and Technological Development Zone fourth in China (Peng 2007: 541).
4. Development and Reform Bureau of Dalian Economic and Technological Development Zone (2005: 7).
5. This association was founded in 1983 and its main purposes were to strengthen business activity coordination between member enterprises, develop Sino-Japanese economic exchanges, and promote Sino-Japanese friendship. 651 enterprises had become members by March 2007. (Affairs Department of Dalian Japanese Chamber of Commerce and Industry 2007: 243–255).
6. Dalian Branch of Mizuho Corporate Bank (2008: 22).
7. The interviewees were all Japanese employees, i.e. local presidents and managers.
8. Company β was engaged in wrapping paper, and Company γ the supply and repair of production equipment. Both the companies had been serving the machinery and equipment manufacturing companies in Dalian which had been interviewed.
9. The Chinese employee replies were initially considered, with options limited to three, where possible.
10. There was a boom of Japanese company arrivals in China in 1995, an adjustment period from 1996 to 1999, and a second boom from 2000 (Suzuki et al. 2005a, 48). In this paper, the stationing periods of the subject enterprises were classified according to the second stationing boom from 2000.
11. With a total number of nearly 2,000 participants, from 1993 to 2002, about 30 investment briefings for this industrial park were held in Japan (including in Tokyo, Osaka, Nagoya, Kitakyushu, etc.), with Mayor Bo Xilai present for several in striving to attract businesses. During that period, 700 enterprises expressed interest and a further 500 tentative inquiries were recorded (Dalian Industrial Park Development Management Co., Ltd. 2007: 22–86).
12. Enterprises embedded in Dalian also replied: "The Dalian Mayor actively invites investment and we received an enthusiastic welcome with the purpose of attracting businesses" (according to Company S) and "The Deputy Mayor attended our ceremony to celebrate the completion of the construction of our factory" (according to Company γ).
13. China Association of Development Zones (2009).
14. Note that "strong intention of presidents" (0.92 points) was also highly evaluated, possibly because the respondents could not articulate the specific reasons for moving to the area. However, Dalian had been a Japanese colonized foothold for 40 years (from 1905 to 1945). More than 200,000 Japanese nationals had lived there at the height of the occupation. Some presidents in financial circles in the 1990s had spent their childhoods in Dalian, and consequently had deep feelings for it. According to interviews conducted by the Dalian Office of the JETRO in August, 2008, Mitsubishi Electric, Mitsui & Co., Nisshin Oillio, Onoda Cement, and Daiwa Real Estate, etc. had employees who had lived in Dalian before.
15. "Competitors in Japan exchange information and even trade with each other" (according to Company L). "Even if you are a competitor, you can communicate on business issues; cooperation rather than competition has been strengthened, which is unimaginable in Japan" (according to Company K).

16. Though the impact of the new *Labor Contract Law* that had come into effect (Yamashita and Gong 2009) in January 2008 was noteworthy, the majority of survey respondents replied that there had been "no effect.".
17. Large enterprises generally curbed wage rises, with 800 yuan per month for menial jobs at Company W and Canon the nadir pay scale for the new graduate intakes, while elsewhere cases of 1,000 yuan per month in factories of 200 to 300 employees could be found. If a new arrival paid higher wages, it had a domino effect on overall wage levels in Dalian. Therefore, although Company W paid low wages, to retain employees, not only were there social security safeguards, there were also perks such as free meals and accommodation.
18. Some enterprises believed that "local personnel are more suited to dealing with the local government and Chinese customers" (Company N).
19. Except for proficiency in Japanese, this was the prevailing tendency in China as a whole, including in Dalian. The underlying reason was that the number of college students who could assume these positions in China had soared in preceding years. As a consequence, the supply exceeded demand. From 2001, the employment rate of Chinese college students dropped to a low of 70%. In Guangzhou for example, the average monthly salary of the year's college graduates in their first jobs was about 1,500 yuan in 2009, and in the same year, the average monthly salary of migrant workers from rural areas was 1,811 yuan (China Economic News, November 15, 2009: 19).
20. Small and medium-sized enterprises alike recognized the risk of the excessive concentration of production bases in Dalian. However, these enterprises did not have the capital or manpower required to decentralize them (Company B).
21. For example, because the company's bachelor quarters that most of the employees lived in were inconveniently located for shopping on foot, the government set up a bus stop near the company.

References

Affairs Department of Dalian Japanese Chamber of Commerce and Industry (2007) 2007 Member List of Dalian Japanese Chamber of Commerce & Industry. Dalian Japanese Chamber of Commerce & Industry, Dalien

Aoyama Y, Murphy JT, Hanson S (2010) Key concepts in economic geography. Sage, Thousand Oaks

Beijing Weekly (2008) Changes in China's payroll income. http://www.pekinshuho.com/jj/txt/2008-04/14/content_110170.htm. Accessed 15 Apr 2010

China Association of Development Zones (2009) China Development Zone Website. http://www.cadz.org.cn/. Accessed 10 Jan 2009

China National Bureau of Statistics (2019) China city statistical yearbook 2019. China Statistic Press, Beijin

Clark GL, Wrigley N (1995) Sunk cost: a framework for economic geography. Trans Inst Br Geogr 20:204–223

Clark GL, Wrigley N (1997a) The spatial configuration of the firm and the management of sunk cost. Econ Geogr 73:285–304

Clark GL, Wrigley N (1997b) Exit, the firm and sunk costs: Reconceptualizing the corporate geography of disinvestment and plant closure. Prog Hum Geogr 21:338–358

Dalian Branch of Mizuho Corporate Bank (2008) Dalian Profile (July 2008 Edition). Dalian Branch of Mizuho Corporate Bank, Dalian

Dalian Industrial Park Development Management Co., Ltd. (2007) 15-year history of Dalian Industrial Park jointly operated by China and Japan. Dalian Industrial Park Development Management Co., Ltd., Dalian

Development and Reform Bureau of Dalian Economic and Technological Development Zone (2005) 2005 Development Report on Dalian Economic and Technological Development Zone. Development and Reform Bureau of Dalian Economic and Technological Development Zone, Dalian

Ehara N, Hakozaki D (eds) (2009) China's economic frontline: The reality of inward and outward Investment Strategies. JETRO, Tokyo

Friedman TL (2007) The world is flat: a brief history of the twenty-first century, 3rd edn. Holtzbrinck Publishers, Stuttgart

JBIC and JCIPO (2007) The 9th Japanese company questionnaire survey results of aggregation and analysis. JBIC and JCIPO, Tokyo

JETRO (2008) How the 11th five-year plan will change China? Overseas Research Series 374. JETRO

JETRO (2017) Survey of Japanese Companies in Asia and Oceania 2017. JETRO

JETRO (2021) Survey of Japanese Companies in China 2021. JETRO

Matsubara H (2006) Economic geography. University of Tokyo Press, Tokyo

Matsubara H (ed) (2009) Economic geography of location adjustment. Hara Shobo, Tokyo

Minami R, Makino F (eds) (2005) Introduction to the Chinese economy, 2nd edn. Nihon Hyoronsha, Tokyo

Mizuho Corporate Bank Dalian Branch (2008) Dalian City Overview, July 2008 Edition, Mizuho Corporate Bank Dalian Branch, Dalian

Peng S (ed) (2007) 2007 China development zone yearbook. China Financial & Economic Publishing House, Beijing

Schoenberger E (1997) The cultural crisis of the Firm. Blackwell, Cambridge and Oxford

Seki M (1997) The new phase of Japanese companies' expansion into China. Organizational Science 30–4:39–50

Seki M (2000) A new era of entering China on Japanese companies. Shinhyoron Publishing Inc., Tokyo

Seki M (2003) 'A field scholar' walks through China. Nihon Keizai Shinbunsha, Tokyo

Seki M, Fan J (eds) (2003) Localization of Japanese companies in China. Shinhyoron Publishing Inc., Tokyo

Suzuki Y, Sakurai Y, Yu J, Shu J, Sato A (2001) The siting of Japanese manufacturing corporations in China. Bus Rev (Osaka City University) 52–3:1–23

Suzuki Y, Li H, Jiang T (2005a) On the new trend of the locational activities of Japanese corporations in China. Bus Rev (Osaka City University) 55–3:47–72

Suzuki Y, Sakurai Y, Sato A (2005b) The location theory of multinational corporations. Hara Shobo, Tokyo

Taira A (2005) Overseas locations and strategies of Japanese companies. Kokon Shoin, Tokyo

Toyo Keizai Inc (2008) Overview of the Overseas Companies in 2008 (by country). Toyo Keizai Inc., Tokyo

Tsuchiya J (2002) Geographical studies of chain store development and its cost structure in UK retailing. Japan J Hum Geogr 54:40–55

Wei Y, Liu X, Parker D, Vaidya K (1999) The regional distribution of foreign direct investment in China. Reg Stud 33:857–867

Yamashita N, Gong M (eds) (2009) The Transformation of China's Labor Laws. Kyushu University Press, Fukuoka

Management Issues in Global R&D of Japanese Chemical Companies

Natsuki Kamakura

Abstract In recent years, Japanese chemical multinational companies (MNCs) have tended to expand their research and development (R&D) abroad, mainly to other Asian countries. It is important to understand these changes to build a functional division of labor that takes locational advantage of the strengths of domestic and overseas R&D. To examine this issue, we conducted data analysis and interviews with 16 major Japanese chemical MNCs between 2012 and 2015 and found that 12 of them had overseas R&D. The four main reasons for establishing overseas R&D are as follows: (1) to respond quickly to the local market and customer service, (2) mergers and acquisitions (M&A), (3) acquisition of talent, and (4) collection of technical information. The majority of overseas R&D sites of the case study companies in Asia are for talent acquisition and market expansion. Although Japanese chemical MNCs still concentrate their core R&D functions in the home country, analysis from a location and organizational perspective suggests a new direction with a more decentralized organization and decentralized location.

Keywords Research and development (R&D) · Multinational company (MNC) · Globalization · Chemical industry

1 Introduction

With the emphasis on creating new value-driven innovations in the manufacturing industry, the acquisition of globally dispersed superior knowledge and technology is becoming increasingly important for manufacturing companies. Against this background, the strategic deployment of research and development (R&D) functions by multinational companies (MNCs) has attracted worldwide attention (UNCTAD 2005; OECD 2008).

How knowledge moves from one place to another and how it is combined is one of the most important phenomena in terms of understanding the geography of

N. Kamakura (✉)
Graduate School of Arts and Sciences, The University of Tokyo, Tokyo 153-8902, Japan
e-mail: kamakura@frs.c.u-tokyo.ac.jp

A. Taira and R. D. Schlunze (eds.), *Management Geography*, International Perspectives in Geography 19, https://doi.org/10.1007/978-981-19-4403-1_4

innovation (Feldmanm 1994). Much attention has been paid to these knowledge flows in relation to the global division of labor of MNCs and the associated new location developments (e.g., OECD 2004; Malecki 2010). In particular, the importance of facilitating internal and external knowledge flows in each location has been pointed out in international management studies (von Zedtwitz et al. 2008; Meyer et al. 2011). More specifically, Meyer et al. (2011) stressed the importance of "multiple embeddedness," which implies the need to exploit diverse home country strengths at the multinational level and the need to strike a balance between intra-firm networks and embedding them in the region where they are located at the subsidiary level. However, in management studies, the focus on the context and unique institutions of the location with its research resources has been insufficient (McCann and Mudambi 2005).

In geography, which is more interested in the context of location than in management studies, studies of specific large firms have been conducted under the research trend called "the geography of enterprise" (Hayter and Watts 1983; Walker 1989; Dicken 1990; Goda 2009). Goda (2009) divides "the geography of enterprise" into two main types of research: multi-plant enterprise research and production system research. According to him, research on the spatial division of labor within a firm is a research area that straddles both the study of multi-plant enterprises and the study of production systems in order to analyze the hierarchical structure and logistical relationships between establishments and the position of the establishments as a prerequisite for that.

However, the spatial division of labor within a firm focuses on regional disparities in the hierarchical structure of business establishments, as exemplified by Massey (1984); thus, the division of labor between products and processes in the domestic manufacturing industry has been the main topic of discussion. In other words, R&D functions are generally considered to be concentrated in large cities and establishments where headquarters are located, and there has been little understanding of the "spatial division of labor in R&D."

R&D activities have many aspects that differ from production activities because of their long-term and uncertain nature, their dependence on chance, and their need for high-level human resources (Huchzermeier and Loch 2001). In addition, as corporate R&D activities have expanded and diversified both domestically and internationally, a division of labor, which is difficult to explain by a simple hierarchical structure, has been formed between domestic and overseas R&D locations (e.g., Asakawa 2001).

In analyzing the phenomenon of the "spatial division of labor in R&D" as an extension of the spatial division of labor theory in geography, it is useful to pay attention to the knowledge that is important in R&D activities and to analyze the spatial flow of that knowledge, rather than the production system. Zeller (2004), for example, takes a large Swiss pharmaceutical company and analyzes in detail the process of increasing access to the knowledge base in regional innovation arenas such as the San Francisco Bay Area, Boston, and San Diego. This study also refers to the division of labor between R&D activities in the home country, where oligopolistic rival firms compete for access to knowledge-based research institutions concentrated in a particular region and supplement their R&D activities in the home country by deploying them in multiple regions.

Japanese MNCs have invested less in R&D overseas than Western firms (Niosi 1999; Odagiri and Yasuda 1991), and have developed their R&D centers mainly in Japan. This may be welcomed from the perspective of the need to maintain the domestic industry in the face of the increasing offshore transfer of production functions. However, as symbolized by the phenomenon of "Galapagosization," in which companies develop products that are in demand only in Japan (see Mizukoshi 2014), there is a limit to the extent to which they can conduct R&D activities only domestically in order to expand into overseas markets that are expected to grow further.

As the domestic market is expected to shrink in the future due to declining birthrates and an aging population, it is clear that Japanese MNCs are facing an urgent need to further develop their overseas markets. To develop products that are in demand in overseas markets and to attract talents from abroad, they should consider expanding their overseas R&D activities. To deal with these issues, it is necessary to reexamine the role of domestic locations where R&D functions have been concentrated, and to build a strategic division of labor both domestically and internationally, while taking advantage of overseas locations.

To study this issue, we conducted a data analysis and interview survey with 16 major Japanese chemical MNCs (Kamakura 2018). There are four reasons for using the chemical industry for our analysis. The first is that (1) the industry has undergone a dynamic geographical shift, particularly in the production function (Murmann 2003). In the long history of the chemical industry, its location has changed from Europe to the United States, then to Japan, and more recently to China and other Asian countries (Verbeek and Mah 2020). The second reason is that (2) the industrial characteristics of chemical R&D are unique, as the chemical industry is one of the manufacturing industries with a relatively high R&D expenditure. It is important to deepen the process technology to increase the scale of mass production, and cooperation with companies that will become users is also necessary for product development (Cesaroni et al. 2004). The third reason is (3) the complexity of the organizational structure of chemical companies. They produce a large proportion of materials and intermediate products, and their organizational structure is more complex due to the wide range of users compared to other industries. Furthermore, they are frequently engaged in mergers and acquisitions (M&A) (Weston et al. 1999). Finally, (4) the chemical industry in Japan has been reevaluated for their user-focused functional materials and improved profitability since the 2000s (Itami 2009; Kikkawa 2011) and it is essential for the industry to expand into overseas markets and to strengthen relationships with user companies located overseas.

The analysis of Japanese chemical MNCs was carried out by interviewing the managers and members of R&D departments of headquarters in Japan as well as analyzing the company history, articles, IR reports, and other materials. We also conducted interviews with representatives of local subsidiaries or the head of the R&D department at the overseas locations. The interviews were conducted between May 2012 and November 2015 and the length of each interview was roughly one to two hours. In this chapter, we focus on the overseas R&D sites of the case study companies in Asia for talent acquisition and market response, in order to discuss management issues in global R&D.

In the following section, we review the macroscopic changes in the chemical industry from the perspective of both production and R&D, and the overseas expansion of R&D by the case study companies. In Sect. 3, we focus on talent acquisition and market-oriented type R&D in Asia to understand the actual situation. Finally, Sect. 4 discusses the main subject of this chapter and concludes briefly in Sect. 5.

2 Geographical Changes and Globalization of R&D in the Chemical Industry

2.1 Geographical Expansion of the Chemical Industry

The modern chemical industry emerged in the 1850s in England, where the textile industry was flourishing at the time. The British hegemony did not last long, however, and by the 1880s, Germany had become the center of the chemical industry. However, with the outbreak of World War I in 1914, Germany's dominant position in the chemical industry was broken and the American chemical industry grew dramatically. The U.S. continued to dominate the chemical industry during the interwar years and after World War II, especially as petrochemicals became mainstream instead of coal chemistry, it became the technological leader of the chemical industry (Murmann and Landau 1998; Murmann 2003).

After World War II, the chemical industry grew in Japan, and there was a growing momentum for domestic production of petrochemical products in particular. In 1970, Japan surpassed Germany and the United Kingdom in terms of share of production in the chemical industry by country (Murmann 2003).

In the 1980s, the chemical industries in Europe, the U.S., and Japan faced structural recessions due to the oil shock, and the chemical industry in Japan began to deal with their excess capacity (Togashi 1986). In contrast, the petrochemical industry in the oil-producing countries of the Middle East, especially Saudi Arabia, and in Asian countries and regions such as Korea, China, Taiwan, and Singapore, began to grow.

Figure 1 shows the value of chemical industry shipments by country and region in the 2000s. It shows that the value of global chemical shipments has been growing rapidly over the past decade or so, with growth particularly strong in Asian countries outside of Japan. In particular, China has come to account for the largest share of growth. However, data for the same regional category were not available and therefore could not be added to this figure. Data as of 2018 from another source show that China accounts for 35.8% of global chemical shipments, with a growing gap between China and the EU as a whole and the U.S., which ranks second on a country-by-country basis (Cefic 2020).

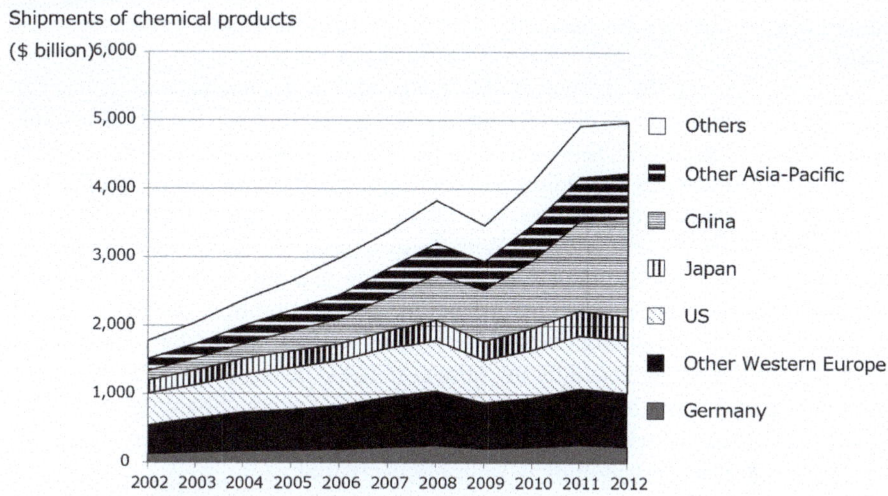

Fig. 1 Shipments in the chemical industry (2002–2012)
(*Source* American Chemistry Council 2013)

As described above, the chemical industry has been expanding from Europe to the U.S., but after growing in Japan during the period of rapid economic growth, China and other parts of Asia have become the center of production and consumption. In response to these changes, there has been a change in the power structure and location of MNCs. In the 2019 rankings of companies producing chemical products comparing sales in the chemical sector, companies from emerging economies have grown through joint ventures with chemical companies in developed countries, such as Sinopec of China in second place and SABIC of Saudi Arabia in fourth place, which topped the list of companies in 2019.

2.2 *Geographical Changes in R&D of the Chemical Industry*

Next, we focus on R&D in the global chemical industry and review the geographical changes therein. Historically, Europe and the U.S. have been at the core of R&D activities and the establishment of technology in the chemical industry, with Japan gradually making its presence felt. In 2017, in terms of the share of patents related to the chemical industry, excluding pharmaceuticals, by country (based on the European Patent Office), the U.S. accounted for approximately 30%, Japan and Germany each accounted for approximately 15%, and these three countries together accounted for approximately 60% of the total. If European countries such as France and Switzerland are included, the percentage of the total is approximately 80%. However, the share of other countries, such as China, has been increasing since the early 2010s, while the share of major countries has been on a downward trend (Germany Trade and Invest 2020).

We then examined the changes in R&D expenditure in the chemical industry in major countries and regions for 2003 and 2018 (Fig. 2). In 2003, the EU as a whole had the largest expenditure, followed by Japan and the United States. Between 2003 and 2018, while the R&D expenditures of each region and country grew significantly, China's R&D expenditure increased more than tenfold, giving it the largest expenditure as of 2018 (Cefic 2014, 2020). With the exception of South Korea, the ratio of R&D costs to sales has declined slightly, indicating that although R&D costs have increased, they have not reached the growth in sales. In addition, the ratio of R&D expenditure to sales is higher in Japan than in other countries. The chemical industry in Japan has been strengthened by investment in R&D because Japan is a resource-poor country and is not highly competitive in terms of production costs. However, compared to other countries, the amount of R&D expenditure has not increased much and the ratio of R&D expenditure to sales has decreased.

As mentioned above, an overview of the data at the country level shows that Europe (e.g., Germany), the U.S., and Japan still have technological advantages in the chemical industry. However, a comparison of R&D expenditures between the early 2000s and late 2010s shows that China is catching up rapidly in terms of R&D, with a remarkable growth in both R&D and sales.

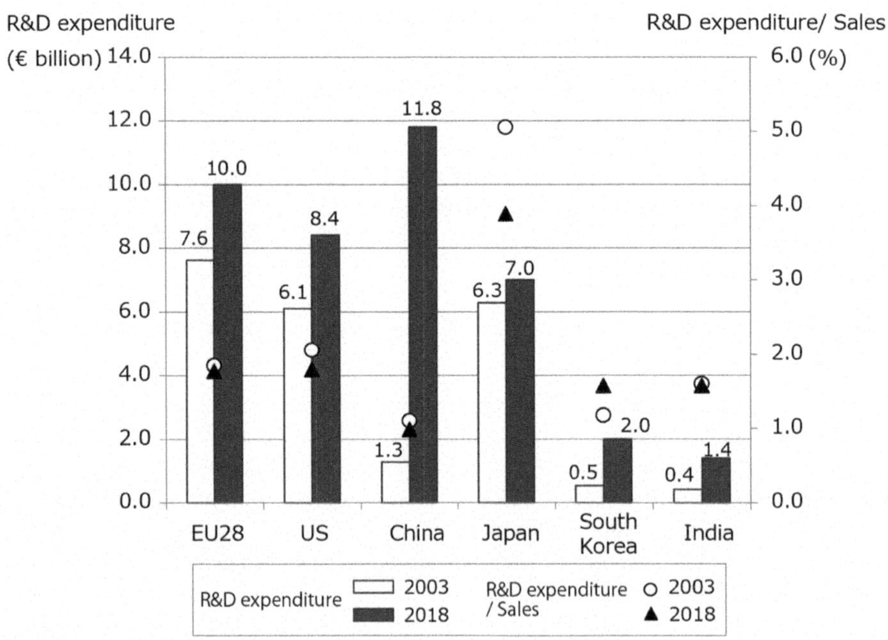

Fig. 2 R&D expenditure in the chemical industry in 2003 and 2018 (*Source* Cefic 2014, 2020)

This qualitative change in the chemical industry in China is related not only to the enormous R&D expenditure of Chinese companies with enormous financial resources, but also to the movement of MNCs from developed countries to establish research laboratories in China, which is a growing market and rich in human resources. In fact, many chemical MNCs from developed countries have established R&D centers in the Yangtze River Delta region centered in Shanghai, China. In particular, some of the world's leading chemical MNCs, such as DuPont and Dow Chemical of the U.S. and BASF and Bayer of Germany, have established R&D facilities in Shanghai, as well as the R&D facility of Toray, one of the case study companies in this chapter.

2.3 *Location and Function of Overseas R&D Sites of the Case Study Companies*

Lastly, the case study companies in this study are reviewed in terms of the location of their R&D sites overseas. The case study companies are Sumitomo Chemical, Mitsui Chemicals, Mitsubishi Chemical, Teijin, Toray, Kuraray, DENKA, Showa Denko, JSR, Asahi Kasei, Shin-Etsu Chemical, Tosoh, DIC, ZEON Corporation, Ube Industries, and Kaneka (16 companies in total), all of which are listed on the first section of the Tokyo Stock Exchange, and whose sales are large among Japanese chemical companies. At the time of the survey, 12 companies, excluding Asahi Kasei, Shin-Etsu Chemical, Tosoh, and ZEON, were found to be engaged in overseas R&D activities. The four main reasons for establishing overseas R&D are as follows: (1) quick response to the local market and customer service, (2) M&A, (3) acquisition of talents, and (4) collection of cutting-edge technical information.

Table 1 and Fig. 3 show the main overseas R&D sites of the case study companies. Most of the sites located in Europe and the U.S. were acquired through M&A, when the existing R&D site of the local company became one of the sites of a Japanese company as a result of business integration with a Western company. In particular, DIC is mainly engaged in the paint business, but in the 1980s it acquired an American paint manufacturer, which is larger than DIC, so that four of its five sites, excluding the one in Qingdao, China, were the former sites of the acquired company.

Many of these sites are located in Asia, but this change has mainly occurred since the 2000s. Particularly prominent in Asia are Shanghai and Singapore, where both production and R&D functions of chemical companies are concentrated. Many of these sites are located within production sites to respond quickly to changes in the growing Asian market. This type of overseas R&D is typical and is called market-oriented R&D (Håkanson and Nobel 1993).

Some companies cited access to rich and talented human resources and advanced R&D as one of the reasons for locating R&D sites in Asia. Emerging countries such as China and India are becoming the main destinations, particularly for talent acquisition purposes (UNCTAD 2005).

Table 1 List of overseas R&D locations of case study companies

Sales rank	Company	Location of overseas R&D (Country) M&A
1	Mitsubishi Chemical	Tessenderlo (Belgium), Santa Barbara (US), Dalian (China)
2	Sumitomo Chemical	Cambridge (UK), Barcelona (Spain), Saint-Didier eau Mont d'Or (France), Walnut Creek, Libertyville (US), Seoul, Iksan, Pyontek (South Korea), Shanghai (China), Tainan (Taiwan), Singapore, Seremban (Malaysia), Mumbai (India), Sao Paulo (Brazil), Arusha (Tanzania), Pretoria (South Africa)
3	Mitsui Chemicals	Hanau (Germany), Emilia Romagna (Italy), San Jose, Los Angeles, Irvine (US), Daejeon (Korea), Shanghai (China), Singapore
4	Toray	Abid (France), Seattle (US), Seoul (Korea), Shanghai, Nantong (China), Singapore
5	DIC	St. Mary's Cray (UK), Frankfurt (Germany), Cincinnati, Carlstadt (US), Qingdao (China)
6	Showa Denko	Preston (UK), Hsinchu (Taiwan), Singapore, Kedah (Malaysia)
7	Teijin	Middlesbrough (UK), Arnhem (Netherlands), Heinsberg (Germany), Chester, Auburn Hills, Milpitas (US), Shanghai, Nantong (China)
8	Kuraray	Zwijndrecht (Belgium), Frankfurt (Germany), Pasadena, Portage (US)
9	DENKA	Suzhou (China), Singapore
10	JSR	Leuven (Belgium), Sunnyvale (US), Ochang (Korea), Yunlin (Taiwan)
11	Kaneka	Westerlo (Belgium), College Station (US), Seoul (South Korea)
12	UBE	Valencia (Spain), Rayong (Thailand)

Source Company documents and our own interviews

In addition to these types, many of the sites, such as JSR, Kaneka, Toray, Teijin, and Sumitomo Chemical, emphasized their proximity to specific customers and research institutions. Among them, JSR had established R&D sites in Europe, the U.S., and Asia for semiconductor and display materials, respectively, and had established a division of domestic and overseas R&D functions. Due to space constraints, we will save this user-oriented type expansion for another paper.

In the following section, we describe in detail the talent acquisition and market-oriented R&D sites in Asia, which are characteristic of the global expansion of the R&D function in the case study companies.

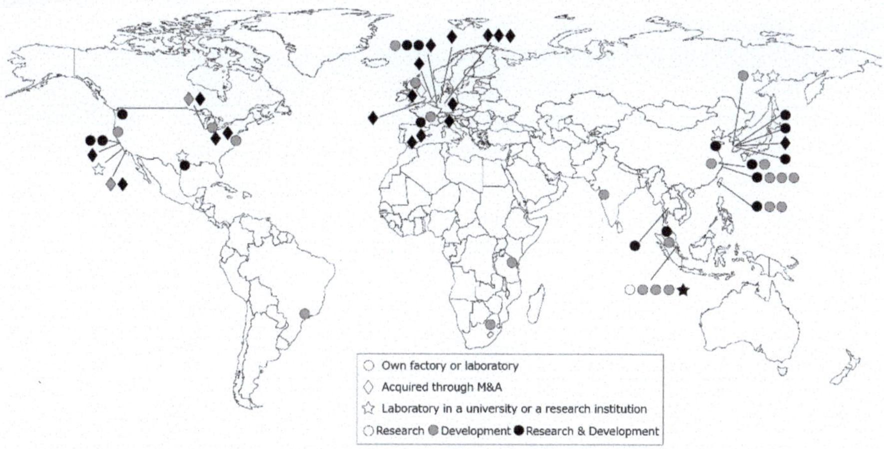

Fig. 3 Map of overseas R&D locations of case study companies
(*Source* Company documents and our own interviews)

3 Cases of Talent Acquisition and Market-Oriented R&D in Asia

3.1 DIC Qingdao Fine Chemicals

DIC (formerly Dainippon Ink and Chemicals) was founded in 1908 as a printing ink company. Today, it has not only captured the top share of the global market for various inks, but also produces liquid crystal materials, organic pigments for color filters, synthetic resin-related products, and other products derived from the technologies accumulated in their printing ink business.

DIC Qingdao Fine Chemicals was established in 1996 in Qingdao, China. It is located in the Hi-Tech Industrial Park in the southeast of Qingdao City. There are many reasons why the company chose to locate in Qingdao, but it is believed that the local government was cooperative and supportive in terms of infrastructure and licensing, and that Qingdao was not too large compared to Shanghai and Beijing, making it a "sturdy" place for DIC to expand their R&D abroad.

The initial goal of this site was to recruit top-level talent from all over China (DIC 2009: 178). At the time of its opening, it was relatively easy to recruit personnel because the facilities were better than those of the surrounding universities in Qingdao. However, in recent years, the competition for talent has become fierce in China, and although Qingdao does attract talent, it is more difficult to attract top-level personnel than in large cities such as Beijing and Shanghai.

At the time of its opening, most of the work was related to resin research, a research theme that had been carried out at the company's Sakai Plant in Japan, partly because of the proximity of Qingdao City to Kansai International Airport. However, at the time of the 2014 interview, it was partially responsible for almost all research areas related to DIC's elemental technologies, such as organic and polymer design, optics and color, dispersion, and application evaluation, making it a "microcosm of DIC," so to speak.

In addition, the Chinese market has grown substantially since the establishment of the company, so the role of product development in the local market has become more important than simply acquiring talent. However, the policy to strengthen the development of products for the Chinese market had already been announced in approximately 2000, and the number of employees did not increase as planned at that time.[1]

With regard to the division of labor with Japan, DIC Qingdao Fine chemicals does not specialize in a single field and does not have any particular strength in any one field, so it basically works on behalf of the Japanese R&D.

3.2 *Teijin Product Development China*

Teijin has historically been a textile company, producing high-performance fibers and carbon fibers. Teijin also produces a large number of chemical products, and in recent years has been aggressively expanding into the medical field. Teijin Product Development China is located in the Teijin Group's Nantong area (Nantong, China), close to Shanghai. The Nantong area itself opened in 1994, slightly earlier than Toray Group as described below, and was the first Japanese synthetic fiber company to set up a plant in the Nantong Economic and Technical Development Zone.

Teijin Product Development China was itself established in 2012 and opened for business in April 2014. As of 2015, the number of employees had increased from approximately 20 to several dozen. A relatively large number of new graduates, mainly in the fields of textiles and chemistry, apply for the positions and three Japanese employees are dispatched to train young employees in their 20s to 30s.

The company has two main roles: first, to develop textile products, and second, to discover the technical demands of local customers for raw yarns. However, the company does not have the capability to develop yarns at this time.

The company is said to be a development site for "creating products to sell" and not an extension to more basic research functions. Since it was fully opened in 2014 and the training period of the employees had just finished in 2015, the division of labor with Japan was to be established in the future.

3.3 *Toray Fibers and Textiles Research Laboratories China (TFRC) and Toray Advanced Materials Research Laboratories China (TARC)*

Toray is another company that has long focused on textiles and is famous for its carbon fiber for use in aircraft as well as its chemical business. Regarding Toray's overseas R&D activities, there is a clear division of labor in Europe, America, and Asia (Kamakura 2014). The TFRC discussed in this chapter, which was established in 2002, is the first full-scale overseas R&D center in the Toray Group. TFRC is still the largest of Toray's overseas R&D. TARC, which is independent of TFRC, is also engaged in R&D activities in Shanghai.

TFRC is located in the Toray Group's Nantong area, adjacent to the Teijin Group's Nantong area, as mentioned above. There are approximately 3,000 employees in the Nantong area, of which more than 200 work in the TFRC. The average age of workers in the company is young, at around 30 years old, mainly because the company hires new graduates who have completed master's programs at Chinese universities. The language used is mainly Japanese because of the frequent communication with and training in Japan, and mastery of Japanese is a condition for promotion. Turnover rates are in the range of a few percent to 10 percent, and retention rates are higher than those of surrounding local companies.

TFRC was established in 2002 and was the first foreign company to carry out R&D in the textile industry in China; its functions range from basic to product development, with applications in industries ranging from clothing to automobiles. The most important mission is to perform polymer design, polymerization, advanced processing, and product development in the textile field in the Nantong area, including production functions.

The division of labor with Toray in Japan is basically outsourcing from Japan to Nantong. However, cooperation can be divided into two types: first, there are areas for which Toray in Japan is responsible for everything from exploration to full-scale research to perfect the technology. TFRC is responsible for the preliminary stage of development (looking for costs and shortcomings for mass production). The later stages of development (i.e., coordination with business feasibility) are carried out in cooperation with Toray and TFRC. The other type is led by TFRC, which develops products by taking advantage of its location in Nantong and its proximity to customers in China while also taking advantage of the technologies that Toray has accumulated in the past.

TFRC is a one-of-a-kind fiber R&D center, and has become one of Toray Group's most important R&D centers, with strengths in consistency between research facilities and production sites and proximity to customers and contractors.

Next, TARC was established in 2004 as a spin-off of the aforementioned TFRC, and is located in the Zizhu Science Park, a high-tech park in Minhang District, Shanghai. When it was established in 2004, the number of personnel was approximately 25,[2] but it increased to approximately 80[3] in 2012 and to more than 100 in 2015. Less than 10% of these employees are dispatched from Japan, and instead, local personnel in China are employed. Unlike TFRC, which has a larger staff size and a better education system, TARC mainly recruits mid-career workers rather than new graduates because it requires work-ready personnel who can handle a wide range of fields. Since it is located in the city of Shanghai, it is relatively easy to obtain the required personnel.

In TARC, Japanese is the main language. In the past, English was used as the language of communication; however, many local employees switched jobs to Western companies in China. Thus, to avoid being used as a springboard to change jobs to Western companies and to facilitate communication with Japan, the official language of the company was changed.

An example of the division of labor in Japan is water treatment research. For water treatment research, it is important to obtain data on the performance of Toray Group's water treatment membranes in different water qualities in different regions. Therefore, a joint project with Shanghai Jiaotong University, which is also located in the Zizhu Science Park, makes this kind of research possible. The R&D process involves sending the data obtained from the local demonstration study by TARC to Toray in Japan to develop the membranes in Japan.

TARC is allowed to propose new research themes to Toray in Japan. However, it is said that it is difficult to come up with a realistic theme based on a good understanding of Toray's elemental technologies unless one has worked in Toray Group for a certain length of time. The number of personnel and functions is steadily increasing, and it is expected to propose new research topics through Chinese production sites, customers, research collaborators, IP activities, and technical marketing.

3.4 UBE Technical Center (Asia) Limited (UTCA)

Ube Industries was established in 1942 through the merger of a coal mining association, an ironworks, a cement manufacturer, and a nitrogen manufacturer. Ube Industries is a chemical company with a diverse range of products, including chemicals and resins, functional materials such as battery materials and polyimides, pharmaceutical ingredients and intermediates, cement and other construction materials, metal forming machinery, and industrial machinery. The chemical business, the core business of Ube Industries, has been expanding overseas, with major production sites in Spain and Thailand.

UTCA is located in Rayong Province, approximately 3 h by car from Bangkok, the capital, and approximately 2 h south of Suvarnabhumi International Airport in Thailand. It is located in close proximity to the UBE Group's caprolactam, nylon, and synthetic rubber production sites, but at a different location.

The establishment of UTCA in 2004 was strongly motivated by the desire of the managing director of Ube Industries (from Thailand), who was in charge of Ube Industries' Thai operations, to conduct basic research in Thailand. Most of the R&D personnel are local Thais, with many having obtained doctoral degrees in the

U.S., Japan, etc., or graduates of leading local universities such as Chulalongkorn University.

When the center opened, it provided technical services such as material evaluation and defect analysis of nylon products on the premises of the nearby production site, and dispatched trainees to Ube for approximately one year each. However, due to the difficulty of arranging for laboratory equipment locally, it was necessary to import equipment from Japan. In addition, there were strict regulations on reagents, so it took some time to establish the research environment. Therefore, it was not until 2012 that they began experimenting with locally produced caprolactam, butadiene rubber, and nylons.

Since locally hired researchers are not experienced in practical experimental work to deal with customers, they are supervised by experienced engineers who were rehired after retiring from Ube Industries in Japan. Doctorate holders do not try to conduct experiments on their own, and because of the lack of lab assistants in Thailand to support them, they have to specify detailed experimental conditions from Japan, which makes it difficult to conduct experimental research without guidance.

In addition, the UTCA has struggled to instill a research culture without class consciousness, such as that practiced in Japan, where PhDs learn experiments from skilled technicians who have graduated from technical colleges. On the other hand, young local researchers sometimes complain about the lack of freedom, which is different from university research. This highlights the difficulties of communication between different cultures and generations (Ota 2008; Onishi 2014).

Moreover, the Japanese Regional Taxation Bureau has pointed out that the education of research know-how, such as instruction in experiments and how to deal with problems, may be the result of granting technology to an overseas subsidiary. For this reason, it is necessary to pay a considerable amount of money for the work involved in education on a business trip basis from Japan, and there is also an issue of where to bear these costs. On the other hand, the turnover rate is high among the young generation in Thailand, and the resignation of trained personnel can discourage their instructors.

As of the time of the interview in 2014, instructions for the experiment were being sent from Japan via videoconference or email. Rather than a division of labor between Thailand and Japan, UTCA was in the process of training young local researchers. In 2010, it was hoped that the number of employees would increase to approximately 45 in three to five years,[4] but this number was still half the size of the previous plan. However, UTCA is targeted to become an R&D center for the entire Ube Group by 2022.

3.5 *Mitsui Chemicals Singapore R&D Centre (MS-R&D)*

Mitsui Chemicals is one of Japan's leading diversified chemical companies and is engaged in a wide range of chemical businesses from basic chemicals to automotive and healthcare chemicals. Mitsui Chemicals' overseas business can be broadly divided into two categories: large market products and functional products. For functional products in particular, R&D is more important than cost reduction, and the company has also been developing its R&D strategy overseas.

MS-R&D, the first full-fledged overseas R&D center in Mitsui Chemicals, is located at Science Park II in Singapore. The area around Science Park II is densely populated with national universities, university hospitals, and other science and technology-related facilities, and has attracted many R&D sites for MNCs.

Although MS-R&D was established in 2011, Mitsui Chemicals began collaborating with A*STAR (Singapore Science and Technology Research Agency) in 2004 and started R&D in Singapore at the recommendation of the EDB (Singapore's Ministry of Economy, Trade and Industry) and A*STAR, which was co-sponsoring a materials symposium held in Singapore in 2006. Initially, catalytic chemistry research was conducted in the A*STAR facility, with a staff of approximately five people. Since then, the medium-term management plan for fiscal 2011 called for the strengthening of R&D in Singapore, and the number of personnel in Singapore was expanded through the company's spin-off.

MS-R&D has 20 employees (as of October 2014), with 7 expatriates and the remaining 13 comprising multinational talents from all over the world. At the time of its opening, it was planned to increase the number of staff from 14 to 30 by 2013,[5] but at the time of the interview in 2014, the number of staff members had not yet reached that scale.

MS-R&D mainly develop and commercialize advanced materials and technologies based on nanotechnology and biotechnology. It recruits specialists in specific technical fields through academic journals. In addition, there are six manufacturing subsidiaries in Singapore that belong to the Mitsui Chemicals Group, to whom MS-R&D provide technical support, such as dealing with minor technical problems.

In terms of division of labor with Japan, the Sodegaura Research Center, which is Mitsui Chemicals' main site of R&D, is an organization of approximately 1,000 people, so MS-R&D is not considered to be of a scale that would have a significant impact on the overall R&D system. However, Singapore has globally attracted nearly 300 R&D sites of MNCs to the city, making it easier to obtain information on the latest technologies and markets, particularly in Southeast Asia. As a result, it is said to play an increasingly important role as a frontline base for finding business partners from the early stages of R&D.

4 Discussion

4.1 Findings from Talent Acquisition and Market-Oriented R&D in Asia

Based on the above case studies in Asia, we summarize the situation of talent acquisition and market-oriented centers in Asia for Japanese chemical MNCs. First, the case of DIC, which established its R&D center as early as the mid-1990s, shows that it is becoming increasingly difficult to recruit top personnel in China outside of major cities. Similarly, the case of Toray's TARC shows the advantage of its location in Shanghai, where it is relatively easy to acquire talents. On the other hand, in the case of Toray, because some research centers of larger Western chemical MNCs are also located in Shanghai, the official language of the company was changed from English to Japanese to deter employees from leaving the company.

Outside of China, Ube Industries' UTCA has been attracting highly educated people in Thailand, and Mitsui Chemicals' MS-R&D has been successful in attracting people from all over the world. However, in the case of UTCA, it takes a certain period of time for local Thai personnel to acquire the skills required by Japanese chemical companies, and it is not easy to build a relationship with the skilled Japanese instructors due to cultural and generational differences. For MS-R&D, there was also a conflict regarding what role a small center of excellence could play in relation to the large-scale R&D being conducted in Japan.

Overall, the number of recruits at sites other than Toray was less than the planned number at the time of the interviews, suggesting that the process of recruiting, training, and retaining local personnel is not straightforward for the operation of overseas R&D. In particular, as pointed out in the case of Toray's TARC, it is an obstacle for local talents to come up with a realistic theme that utilizes in-house technology unless they have a long history in the company.

As for the progress in the division of labor with Japan, many of the sites were in the startup or training stage of new recruits at the time of the interview, and many had not yet achieved a clear division of labor. However, DIC Qingdao fine chemicals, which celebrated its 20th anniversary in 2017, has seen a change in its division of labor with the domestic sector, as the Chinese market has grown, and it is now working more on product development directly related to its business than when it was first established. In addition, Toray's TARC has been working on research projects that can only be conducted in the local area in collaboration with local research institutions.

In the case of talent acquisition, the time and cost of training local personnel tended to be higher than expected. Regarding the division of labor within and outside of Japan, it has changed from the initial purpose of its establishment, as its scale is smaller than that of the domestic market, and its function of responding to the local market and collecting cutting-edge information has become more important.

4.2 Spatial Division of Labor in R&D of Case Study Companies

The results for all the case study companies are summarized in the following four points. First, among the Japanese chemical MNCs surveyed, there are some relatively large ones that concentrated their main R&D functions in Japan. These firms are considered to be emphasizing the protection of intellectual property by retaining their R&D functions domestically.

Second, the most common reason for Japanese chemical companies to expand their R&D functions overseas was to respond to customers. This is due to the industry characteristics of chemical firms, with most of their activities conducted as suppliers to manufacturing firms in other industries (Cesaroni et al. 2004).

The third point is that some companies that set up an R&D site overseas to conduct future research by acquiring local talents have difficulty accomplishing their first purpose. The Asian cases presented in this chapter show the difficulties involved in mentoring and retaining young researchers in the company due to cultural and generational differences.

Fourth, in several cases, the role of the R&D function changed after it was established; even when it was established for other reasons, such as in the DIC case, where it became marked-oriented, taking advantage of its location in a growing market.

From these results, we conceptualized the spatial division of labor in R&D by Japanese chemical MNCs (Fig. 4). First, we call the division of labor, in which R&D activities are concentrated in Japan and the organizational structure is centralized, the "domestic completion type." As has been noted in the past, many of the companies in the case study fit into this type, concentrating their core R&D functions in Japan.

However, some companies tend to decentralize their global locations due to changes in the functions of existing sites and the location of new R&D sites. Their organizational structures are still centralized, but we can say that they are gradually changing from the "domestic completion type" to the "domestic-centric type."

Although not conspicuous in the case of Asia in this chapter, some companies have partially shifted to the "segregation type," where the core R&D activities are concentrated in Japan but the organizational structure is decentralized, mainly due to business acquisitions.

The "mutual division type," in which R&D is globally dispersed and the organization is decentralized, has not yet been completely applied in case study companies. An example of a MNC with its home country in another country, BASF, headquartered in Germany, have been conducted R&D mainly in Europe and the United States. However, it has been expanding its R&D function in the Asia–Pacific region by establishing a new large-scale innovation campus in Shanghai, China in 2012 and in Mumbai, India in 2017, in order to acquire abundant human resources and markets. In Japan, where the automotive industry is concentrated, it has established an R&D center in Amagasaki to develop battery materials for automobiles and consumer products. Thus, we can observe characteristics of the organization and location of the R&D that match regional strengths. Since the domestic market is not expected to

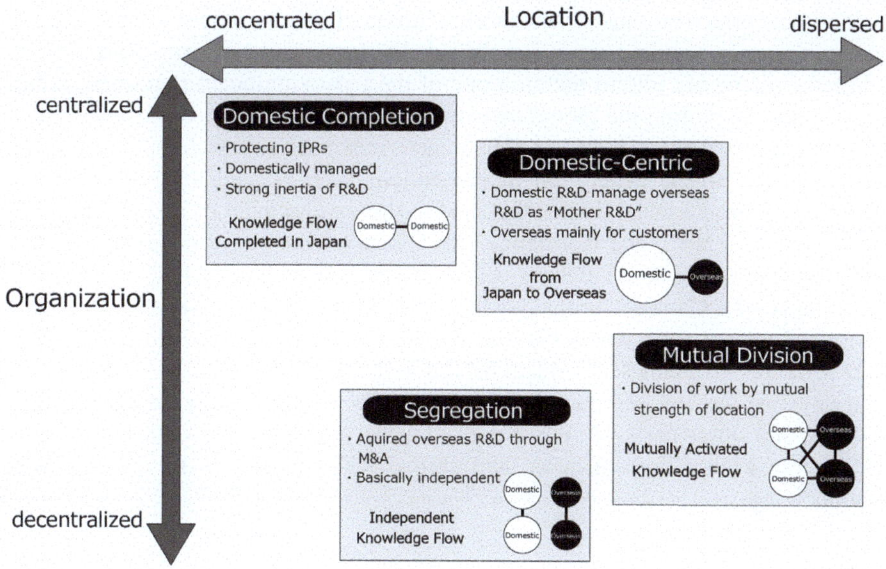

Fig. 4 Changes and direction of spatial division of labor in R&D
(*Source* Author's survey)

grow in Japan, localization and self-reliance of overseas subsidiaries is also important for manufacturing companies to more efficiently capture demand overseas. Although R&D activities are long-term and uncertain, it is expected that new innovations will be generated by a more diverse environment and talents in the future.

5 Conclusion

The R&D system of Japanese chemical MNCs is changing rapidly, especially in Asia where the pace of change is extremely fast. The position of these emerging countries in the chemical industry is still changing in terms of the location of R&D and it may take some years to draw conclusions regarding the future development of the division of labor in R&D.

Business and corporate reorganization is proceeding rapidly worldwide in the chemical industry, and an increasing number of Japanese chemical companies may change to the "domestic segregation type" or "mutual division of labor type" in the future. Given the cases above, general logic and educational systems of management as Japanese MNCs tend to become obstacles to the hiring and retention of competent talent at overseas R&D. One of the reasons for this is an overwhelming difference in scale to domestic R&D. To build a functional division of labor that takes advantage of the strengths of domestic and overseas R&D, it is not sufficient to proceed with simple localization; instead, it might be desirable to build a global R&D system with a more decentralized organizational structure while linking R&D resources accumulated in Japan with newly acquired resources abroad (Mudambi and Navarra 2004).

Finally, we would like to mention one of the most significant remaining issues in this study. Regarding the global division of labor in R&D, there was insufficient analysis of the performance aspects of R&D activities, such as how the spatial division of labor relates to the generation of innovations such as patent applications and innovative ideas and technologies that lead to the development of new products. In previous studies, Nieto and Rodríguez (2011) analyze the performance of overseas R&D activities of the Spanish firms. Also, Schaefer and Liefner (2017) evaluate the performance of a Chinese company which establishes R&D facilities in developed countries. In this regard, we would like to collect examples of the fruits of overseas R&D activities of Japanese chemical MNCs in the future.

In any case, as the chemical industry expands geographically and the growth of China and other parts of Asia peters out, the change in the division of labor by Japanese MNCs both at home and abroad will continue to be a noteworthy phenomenon.

Notes

1. In 2000, the company announced a plan to strengthen its product development function for China, increase the number of employees to 120, and expand the number to 250 in the future (Nikkei Business Daily, February 17, 2000).
2. Nikkei Business Daily, October 19, 2004.
3. Nikkei Business Daily, January 5, 2012.
4. Nikkei Business Daily, July 30, 2010.
5. Nikkei Business Daily, September 13, 2011.

References

American Chemistry Council (2013) Guide to the business of chemistry 2013. American Chemistry Council, Washington, DC

Asakawa K (2001) Organizational tension in international R&D management: the case of Japanese firms. Res Policy 30:735–757. https://doi.org/10.1016/S0048-7333(00)00103-7

Cefic (2014) The European chemical industry: Facts & Figures 2014. http://fr.zone-secure.net/13451/106811/publication/contents/templates/Cefic_F_and_F_2014-Full_report_Blanc_150dpi.pdf. Accessed 30 Oct 2020

Cefic (2020) Facts & Figures of the European chemical industry 2020. https://cefic.org/library-item/the-2020-european-chemical-industry-facts-and-figures/. Accessed 30 Oct 2020

Cesaroni F, Gambardella A, Garcia-Fontes W, Mariani M (2004) The chemical sectoral system: firms, markets, institutions and the process of knowledge creation and diffusion. In: Malerba F (ed) Sectoral systems of innovation: concepts, issues and analyses of six major sectors in Europe. Cambridge University Press, Cambridge

DIC (2009) DIC 100 nen shi (100 year's history of DIC). DIC, Tokyo (in Japanese)

Dicken P (1990) The geography of enterprise: Elements of research agenda. In: Smidt M, Wever E (eds) The corporate firm in a changing world economy: case studies in the geography of enterprise. Routledge, London

Feldmanm MP (1994) The geography of innovation. Kluwer Academic, Boston

Germany Trade & Invest (2020) The chemical industry in Germany 2020. https://www.gtai.de/resource/blob/64542/121894962e5bfeb883a79d3ec6ae44d7/industry-overview-chemical-industry-in-germany-en-data.pdf. Accessed 21 Sept 2020

Goda S (2009) Daikigyo no kukan kozou (Spatial structure of large companies). Hara Shobo, Tokyo (in Japanese)

Hayter R, Watts HD (1983) The geography of enterprise: a reappraisal. Prog Hum Geogr 7:157–181. https://doi.org/10.1177/030913258300700201

Håkanson L, Nobel R (1993) Determinants of foreign R&D in Swedish multinationals. Res Policy 22:397–411. https://doi.org/10.1016/0048-7333(93)90009-7

Huchzermeier A, Loch C (2001) Project management under risk: Using the real options approach to evaluate flexibility in R&D. Manage Sci 47:85–101. https://doi.org/10.1287/mnsc.47.1.85.10661

Itami H (2009) Chemistry-oriented transformation of Japanese industry. Chem Chem Ind 62(2): 114–116. http://www.chemistry.or.jp/opinion/doc/ronsetsu0902-e.pdf. Accessed 21 Sept 2020

Kamakura N (2014) Kenkyu kaihatsukinou no kukanteki bungyo to kigyo bunka: seni kei kagaku kigyo no jirei (The spatial divisions of labor in R&D and corporate culture: the case of chemical fiber firms). Jinbun Chiri (Japan J Hum Geogr) 66:38–59. https://doi.org/10.4200/jjhg.66.1_38 (in Japanese)

Kamakura N (2018) Kenkyu kaihatsukinou no kukanteki bungyo: Nikkei kagaku kigyo no soshiki ricchi saihen to gurobaruka (Spatial divisions of labor in R&D: organizational and locational restructuring with the globalization of Japanese chemical firms). University of Tokyo Press, Tokyo (in Japanese)

Kikkawa T (2011) How Japan's chemical industry can overtake the world. Chem Chem Ind 64(7):559–560. http://www.chemistry.or.jp/opinion/doc/ronsetsu1107-e.pdf. Accessed 21 Sept 2020

Malecki EJ (2010) Global knowledge and creativity: new challenges for firms and regions. Reg Stud 44:1033–1052. https://doi.org/10.1080/00343400903108676

Massey D (1984) Spatial divisions of labour: social structures and the geography of production. Macmillan, London

McCann P, Mudambi R (2005) Analytical differences in the economics of geography: the case of the multinational firm. Environ Plan A 37:1857–1876. https://doi.org/10.1068/a37311

Meyer KE, Mudambi R, Narula R (2011) Multinational enterprises and local contexts: the opportunities and challenges of multiple embeddedness. J Manage Stud 48:235–252. https://doi.org/10.1111/j.1467-6486.2010.00968.x

Mizukoshi S (2014) Is Japan the 'Galapagos Islands' of social media? Global Asia 9(2):36–39. https://www.globalasia.org/v9no2/cover/is-japan-the-galapagos-islands-of-social-media_shin-mizukoshi. Accessed 21 Sept 2020

Mudambi R, Navarra P (2004) Is knowledge power? Knowledge flows, subsidiary power and rent-seeking within MNCs. J Int Bus Stud 35:385–406. https://doi.org/10.1057/palgrave.jibs.8400093

Murmann JP (2003) Chemical industries after 1850. The Oxford encyclopedia of economic history. https://www.alexandria.unisg.ch/255485/1/Murmann_OEEH.pdf. Accessed 21 Sept 2020

Murmann JP, Landau R (1998) On the making of competitive advantage: the development of the chemical industries of Britain and Germany since 1850. In Arora A, Landau R, Rosenberg N (eds) Chemicals and long-term economic growth. Wiley, New York

Nieto M, Rodríguez A (2011) Offshoring of R&D: Looking abroad to improve innovation performance. J Int Bus Stud 42:345–361. https://doi.org/10.1057/jibs.2010.59

Niosi J (1999) The internationalization of industrial R&D: From technology transfer to the learning organization. Res Policy 28:107–117. https://doi.org/10.1016/S0048-7333(98)00107-3

Odagiri H, Yasuda H (1991) Overseas R&D activities of Japanese firms. In: Goto A, Odagiri H (eds) Innovation in Japan. Clarendon Press, Oxford, New York

OECD (2004) Global knowledge flows and economic development. OECD Publications, Paris
OECD (2008) The internationalisation of business R&D: evidence impacts and implications. OECD Publications, Paris
Onishi J (2014) Tai Betonamu shinshutsu nikkei kigyo ni okeru jinteki shigen manejimento no ibunka kan shokuba masatsu he no eikyou ni tsuite (The influence of human resource management differences between Japanese and locals on workplace conflicts at Japanese overseas manufacturers in Thailand and Vietnam). Transcultural Management Review 11:21–37 (in Japanese)
Ota M (2008) Takokuseki kigyo to ibunka manejimento (Multinational companies and cross-cultural management). Dobunkan, Tokyo (in Japanese)
Schaefer KJ, Liefner I (2017) Offshore versus domestic: Can EM MNCs reach higher R&D quality abroad? Scientometrics 113:1349–1370. https://doi.org/10.1007/s11192-017-2533-5
Togashi K (1986) Sekiyu kagaku kogyo ni okeru kouzo fukyo go no saihen to konbinato no ricchi hendo (Restructuring and locational change of the petrochemical industry in Japan after the second oil crisis). Ann Jpn Assoc Econ Geogr 32:163–181. https://doi.org/10.20592/jaeg.32.3_163 (in Japanese)
UNCTAD (2005) World investment report 2005: Transnational corporations and the internationalization of R&D. United Nations, New York, Geneva
Verbeek T, Mah A (2020) Integration and isolation in the global petrochemical industry: multiscalar corporate network analysis. Econ Geogr 96:363–387. https://doi.org/10.1080/00130095.2020.1794809
Walker R (1989) A requiem for corporate geography: New directions in industrial organization, the production of place and the uneven development. Geogr Ann: Series B, Human Geography 71:43–68. https://doi.org/10.1080/04353684.1989.11879586
Weston JF, Johnson BA, Siu JA (1999). Mergers and acquisitions in the global chemical industry. Bus Econ 34(4):23–31. Gale Academic OneFile. Accessed 21 Sept 2020
von Zedtwitz M, Gassmann O, Birkinshaw J (eds) (2008) Management of international research and development. Edgar Elgar Publishing, Cheltenham
Zeller C (2004) North Atlantic innovative relations of Swiss pharmaceuticals and the proximities with regional biotech arenas. Econ Geogr 80:83–111. https://doi.org/10.1111/j.1944-8287.2004.tb00230.x

Small- and Medium-Sized "Global-Niche" Firms in Japan: A Key for the Rejuvenation of Japan's Local Economy?

Atsushi Taira

Abstract Drawing on the concepts of pipelines and buzz, this study argues for the characteristics and strategies of global-niche firms in Japan through case studies in Shikoku. Global-niche firms in Japan (most of which are small- and medium-sized) have the highest expertise and state-of-the-art technologies, and dominate a significant portion of the relevant world market. The global-niche firms in Shikoku analyzed in this study are among them. Local connections with suppliers and customers (buzz) vary from firm to firm. Many firms have worldwide networks for selling their products through global pipelines that they have cultivated through incessant efforts. The results of the study reveal a mixed contribution by global-niche firms to the local socio-economy. In sum, ever-lasting entrepreneurship in management is critical for growth of global-niche firms. The global and cross-cultural minds of managers as boundary spanners are also of importance. A future challenge from a local economic perspective might be on how to embed more global-niche firms in their localities.

Keywords Small- and medium-sized firms · Global-niche firms · Pipeline · Buzz · Japan

1 Introduction

The population of Japan peaked around 2005 at 127 million and began shrinking thereafter due to a decreasing birth rate and an aging population. In 2010, China replaced Japan as the second largest economy in the world following the United States. Even though Japan suffered from a long recession in the so-called "lost decades" following the burst of the bubble economy at the beginning of 1990s, Tokyo continued to undertake a range of downtown development projects during the period such as the Rainbow Bridge project in 1993, Roppongi hills project in 2003, and renovation projects in the Marunouchi district in front of the Emperor Palace in the 2010s, which included the renovation of the Tokyo railway terminal building.

A. Taira (✉)
Faculty of Education, Kagawa University, Kagawa 760-0016, Japan
e-mail: taira.atsushi@kagawa-u.ac.jp

A. Taira and R. D. Schlunze (eds.), *Management Geography*, International Perspectives in Geography 19, https://doi.org/10.1007/978-981-19-4403-1_5

In contrast, most other regions, especially those along Japan's periphery, have been struggling to survive in an increasingly competitive environment coupled with the population decrease.

Despite these difficulties, several firms, most of which are small- or medium-sized, have been increasing their output and building a global reputation for their sophisticated products and services. These firms are called "global-niche" firms; they have recently drawn attention from administrators of the central and local governments of Japan and from researchers in economics, sociology, geography, and other related fields (The Ministry of Economy, Trade and Industry of Japan 2014; Hosotani 2014, 2017). This study examines the spatial features and strategies of "global-niche" firms in Japan, drawing on the concepts of Bathelt et al. (2004) to focus on their pipelines and buzz generation. "Pipelines," in this study, refer to personal connections between intra- and inter-firms and relevant agencies. "Buzz" refers to temporal and coincidental information exchanges mainly for innovation among relevant actors especially both in the local and relational spaces (Taira 2020). In addition, this study examines whether these global-niche firms could play a key role in rejuvenating the local economies where they are located, and discusses policy-related matters for promoting the activities of global-niche firms. Here, global-niche firms refer to those that have a significant share in the relevant world market given their high-quality products and services, based on their state-of-the-art expertise and technology (Hosotani 2014, 2017). Global-niche top (GNT) firms refer to firms that have the following attributes among global-niche firms: realizing both a very high share in the world market and a high revenue, originality of products and independence of the firm, existence of an alternative plan as a risk hedge strategy, and having the potential to maintain a significant share in the world market (The Ministry of Economy, Trade and Industry of Japan 2014).

In 2013, the Ministry of Economy, Trade and Industry of Japan presented an economic recovery plan, which included a measure to assist global-niche firms. Next, in 2014, it announced 100 global-niche-top (GNT100) firms to promote the plan. Interestingly, many of the GNT100 are located outside the major metropolitan areas of Tokyo and Osaka, with the two housing 23 and 18 GNT100 firms, respectively (Fig. 1). Shikoku, the smallest island among Japan's four major islands, sandwiched by Honshu (the main island) and Kyushu (the southern island), is the leading Japanese region in terms of the number of "global-niche" firms in the fields of chemical products, electronics, and acrylic panels for large scale water-tanks, despite its small population.

2 Previous Studies and Their Shortcomings

Economic geographers have long been concerned with the spatial patterns of economic activities performed mainly by firms and industries. The main focus of previous studies has been regional specialization, industrial agglomeration, consumption and retail, work and employment, and state and development policies

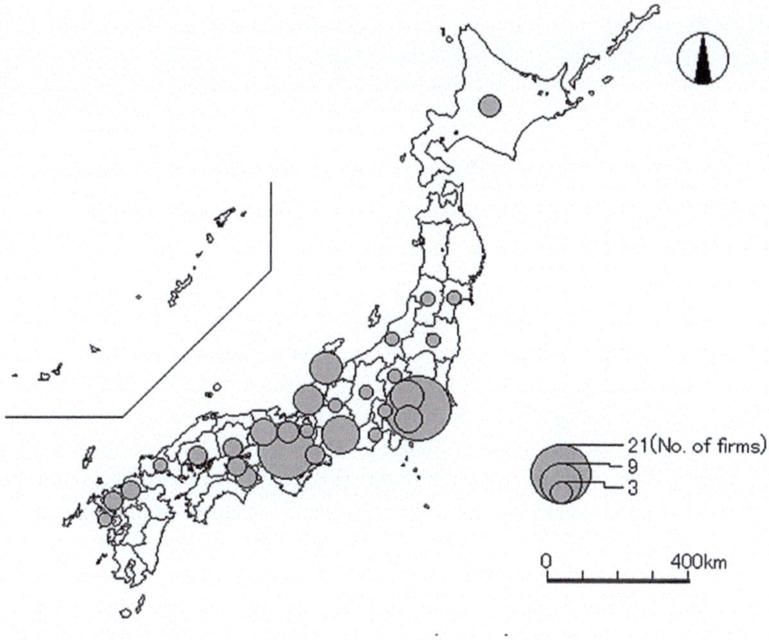

Fig. 1 Global-niche top firms 100 (2014)
(*Source* METI [2014])

(Coe et al. 2007; Aoyama et al. 2011; MacKinnon and Cumbers 2019). Among them, industrial agglomeration has attracted much attention from researchers. Previous studies have tried to explain the factors and mechanisms of agglomeration of firms and related entities in space (Piore and Sable 1984; Granovetter 1985; Scott 1988; Ueno and Nishimura 1990; Storper 1997; Yamamoto 2005). Along with globalization after the Second World War, especially since the 1980s, spatial manifestations of transnational corporations (TNCs), which are the main actors of foreign direct investment (FDI), have also drawn increasing attention from researchers (Vernon 1966; Hymer 1972, 1976; Dunning 1980, 1988; Helleiner 1981; Rugman 1981; Dicken 1992). The study of globalization continued and later expanded to the study of global production networks and global value chains (Peck and Yeung 2003; Yeung 2016).

Taira (2020) claims the necessity to bridge studies of industrial agglomeration and those of multinational corporations through his case study of the glove-related industry in Shikoku, Japan. The author found that innovative leading firms in the industrial cluster actively expand their businesses abroad coupled with efforts to establish their corporate brands, while the manufacturers' association plays a critical role as a facilitator to create a regional brand. Taira (2020) concludes that an appropriate balance between these two branding strategies is key for the survival of local industrial clusters. In this context, to expand businesses within and beyond the country, exploiting pipelines and buzz is considered crucial (Bathelt et al. 2004). Knowledge creation is key to the success of firms.

2.1 What is Knowledge? What is the Difference Between Knowledge and Information? Why Does Knowledge Creation Matter?

Since the 1990s, discussions on the activities of firms, particularly those in industrial clusters, have seen increasing number of researchers paying attention to "knowledge" in corporate management and operations (Nonaka and Takeuchi 1995; Itami 2005; Bathelt and Glückler 2011). Nonaka and Takeuchi (1995) distinguish between knowledge and information; while knowledge involves belief and commitment, information does not. They further point out that previous studies examined knowledge in the context in which they regard organizations as information processing machines; thus, previous studies have failed to pay attention to knowledge creation processes. For example, they claim that Drucker (1993) has argued the importance of tacit knowledge, but has not mentioned the importance of inter-personal relationships and knowledge sharing in knowledge creation. Nonaka and Takeuchi (1995) argue that knowledge creation matters because it enables firms to realize continuous innovation, which lends these firms competitive advantages in the market. According to them, the strength of Japanese firms is in their ability to change tacit knowledge to explicit knowledge, and in the role of middle managers as creators and facilitators of knowledge creation in the "middle-up-down" management structure of the firm. However, Nonaka and Takeuchi (1995) mostly ignored inter-firm relationships, except for an example of an electronic firm, and did not consider the role of the region where the firm is located, which could be a geographical point of analysis.

Itami (2005) introduced the concept of *ba* into organizational studies, defining *ba* as the framework of a situation in which the people participate, consciously or unconsciously observe each other, converse, and understand and stimulate each other. He claims that organizations need not comprise only systems, but also orders born out of processes at the frontline of the business and further highlights that it is *ba* that fills the missing link between the explicit structure of an organization and its invisible processes. According to him, this space is filled with information. His question is: How should the firm be organized to enable its employees to exchange and share information smoothly, and stimulate and motivate each other at work? Itami's concept of *ba* has continued to draw the attention of many researchers in organization studies, business administration, and related fields, such as Ishikura et al. (2003) and Morita (2012). Itami's argument is, however, based on the organizational interaction of people; hence, it would be fair to say that his concept lacked geographical aspects such as the exchange of knowledge and information beyond the *ba* situation, that is, across space and regions.

2.2 How Does Firm Size Affect Knowledge Creation and Its Transfer? What Are the Strengths of Small- and Medium-Sized Global-Niche Firms?

Another shortcoming of the previous studies on firm strategies and knowledge is that their focus appeared to be limited to large companies; for example, all case studies introduced in Nonaka and Takeuchi (1995) cover Japan's leading large firms in the manufacturing sector. Since around 2000, however, increasing attention has been given to the performance of leading small- and medium-sized firms (Watanabe et al. 2001; Inoue 2009), which have shown resilience in the midst of the long recession during Japan's lost decades. A critical strategy for small- and medium-sized firms in Japan to survive in the competitive world is foreign direct investment (FDI). Following large corporations that started FDI in the 1960s and saw intensive FDI growth since the 1980s (Seto 1995; Izawa 1996; Taira 2005), an increasing number of small- and medium-sized firms began FDI since the 1990s. As a result, many researchers, including Kato (2011) and Nakazawa (2012), have begun paying attention to this new movement. Asia, especially East and South-East Asia, has been a major destination for FDI in small- and medium-sized firms. Ono (2015) and Itagaki et al. (2016) discuss the strategies and operational processes of Japanese successful small- and medium-sized firms in Asia. Researchers' attention also relates to the relationship between small- and medium-sized firms and the local socio-economies in which they operate. For example, Kato (2003) argues that there is a close relationship between small- and medium-sized firms and the industrial cluster. Nihon Chusho Kigyo Gakkai (2016) and Nihon Seisaku Kinyu-koko Sogo Kenkyujo (2016) point out that small- and medium-sized firms play a key role in local socio-economies.

What differentiates successful small- and medium-sized firms from others? Tsuchiya et al. (2015) discuss the characteristics of the global management of innovative small- and medium-sized firms. Global-niche firms are leaders among those successful small- and medium-sized firms (Hosotani 2014, 2017). Nonaka and Takeuchi (1995) argue that the ability and capacity of knowledge creation are key for firms to be resilient and successful. Expanding on the concept of Itami's *ba*, we can also hypothesize that exploiting buzz and expanding pipelines over regions and nations is another factor for the success of firms. In other words, knowledge creation is possible both within the firm and over space through buzz and pipelines.

2.3 How Do Global-Niche Firms Operate Locally and Globally? What Are the Roles of Pipelines and Buzz? What Kind of Roles Do Global-Niche Firms Play in the Local Economy?

So far, studies such as Hosotani (2014, 2017) have analyzed the roles of small- and medium-sized firms in either industrial clusters or regional economies. However, these studies lack spatial perspectives. Thus, this study incorporates the concepts of knowledge creation, buzz, and pipelines through a case study of leading small- and medium-sized firms in the non-major metropolitan regions of Japan. We focus on non-major metropolitan regions due to an assumption that small- and medium-sized firms in non-major metropolitan regions have more independent business operations than those in major metropolitan regions where large firms provide more business opportunities for small- and medium-sized firms through hierarchical intra-firm transactions.

Regarding knowledge transfer in space, previous studies in the 1990s (Camagni 1991; Malmberg 1996; Maskell 1998) have argued that while codified knowledge is globally transferred, tacit uncodified knowledge is not so. Later, however, Bathelt et al. (2004) claimed that tacit knowledge is also transferable through global pipelines. As Taira (2020) claims, while theoretical debates are flourishing, empirical evidence on this subject remains limited. This study attempts to fill this gap by investigating the strategies and operations of small- and medium-sized global-niche firms in Shikoku, focusing on their pipelines and buzz generation with a discussion on policy-related initiatives by the central and local governments.

3 Methodology, Hypotheses, and Study Context

3.1 Methodology and Hypotheses

This study is mainly based on fieldwork conducted between 2015 and 2020. Firms included in the case study comprised those that are on the GNT firms list compiled by the Ministry of Economy, Trade, and Industry (METI); these were contacted by the author for interview. Eventually, two firms (Firms A and B) in Kagawa were visited for interviews (Firm A in 2015 and Firm B in 2018) and one firm (Firm C) in Tokushima was contacted by mail in 2018. Additionally, Firm D, which had the potential to become a global-niche firm, was interviewed in 2015. These firms were interviewed about their operational history and current business including characteristics of suppliers and customers, strength of firms, and future agendas. Research interviews were also conducted at the office of the Shikoku Bureau of the METI in 2010 and 2018, and at the Kagawa Industry Support Foundation in 2019, both located in Takamatsu. These institutions were asked measures to assist local firms

Table 1 Basic attributes of sample firms (2017)

Firm	Established	Location	Domestic employees	Annual sales (yen)	Main products
A	1969	Miki, Kagawa	83	1.7 billion (2016)	acrylic panels for large-scale water tanks
B	1947	Marugame, Kagawa	591	44.1 billion	inorganic, organic, fine chemical products; building-related materials
C	2000	Naruto, Tokushima	10 skilled workers	20% of the world share of 288 million dollars	ultraviolet-rays-LED
D	1925	Takamatsu, Kagawa	23	1.3 billion (2016)	internet sales of shoes

Firm	Domestic networks	Foreign operations	International and domestic awards
A	Okinawa, Kobe	USA, Korea	Global-Niche top 100, Guinness world records
B	Tokyo, Osaka, 14 other locations	China	Global-Niche top 100
C	na	na	Global-Niche top 100, awards in Japan
D	na	China	Awards in Japan

Sources Kagawa Keizai Repotosha (2017) and author's survey

in the region and agendas. The author also attended a number of seminars of the Shikoku Bureau of the METI to promote FDI by small- and medium-sized firms in Shikoku during this period. Table 1 shows basic attributes of sample firms.

We hypothesize that "global-niche" firms, which are appropriately managing their pipelines and buzz, would play a crucial role to lead struggling local economies and would have the potential to rejuvenate these economies. Moreover, we hypothesize that governmental institutions help connect global-niche firms with the regions where they are located and with other firms as potential partners, thereby creating pipelines and buzz.

3.2 *Context: Governmental Initiatives, Policies, and Schemes*

In Japan, the Ministry of Economy, Trade and Industry (METI), in collaboration with the regional branches of the Organization for Small & Medium Enterprises and Regional Innovation and the Japan External Trade Organization (JETRO), has initiated a number of measures to rejuvenate economies in local regions outside the main metropolis represented by Tokyo and Osaka. For example, these three governmental and semi-governmental organizations hold a series of seminars in various places in Japan in order to promote the internationalization of business for small- and medium-sized local firms, introducing successful case studies. These seminars not only help local firms to obtain information and knowledge about international operations, but also give them opportunities to build networks with potential partners. The seminars themselves serve as spaces for buzz generation for business opportunities within and beyond the country. Some seminars include a question-and-answer segment and post-seminar gathering over drinks and light meals to help participating firms' network with each other.

Among the three governmental institutions mentioned above, JETRO Shikoku plays a central role in promoting FDI by local firms. The Shikoku branch of the METI has been a back-up facilitator for this initiative. However, considering the number of staff and their expertise, the branch has the potential to play a more significant role in the internationalization of local economies. Other agencies and institutions that promote the internationalization of local business operations also hold similar seminars. Thus, coordination among relevant agencies and institutions is necessary. In order to address the shortcomings of the global-niche initiative (relative lack of buzz), the METI has started a new initiative for selecting leading local firms that have the potential to contribute to the future of the regions.[1]

4 Global-Niche Firms in Shikoku

Shikoku is the smallest island among Japan's four major islands (the others are Honshu, Hokkaido, and Kyushu). Divided into four prefectures (Kagawa, Tokushima, Ehime, and Kochi), Shikoku is the only major island that does not have large cities with a population exceeding a million and is not linked by the shinkansen, the high-speed rail network. However, as mentioned in the introduction, Shikoku is a major region that houses a number of global-niche firms. This chapter draws on the concepts of pipelines and buzz, and explores the characteristics and strategies of leading global-niche firms in Kagawa and Tokushima prefectures, as well as a firm that has the potential to be one amongst them in the future.

4.1 Foundation: Setup and Location

The factors and processes for setting up global-niche firms in Japan vary across firms. A closer inspection, however, reveals some common features that are noteworthy: entrepreneurship, unique ideas, potential products or services, and location, that is, geography. First, entrepreneurship is key (Kishikawa 2017); it stems from the personal motivation to start a new independent business that could bring innovation in the related field and region. It is believed that the Japanese are not so independent-minded (Amino 1999). Indeed, it is a fact that most college graduates in Japan aim to enter large leading firms in the country, although their target industries have changed over time from manufacturing to financial and services. Nonetheless, the other fact remains that although the numbers have remained small over time, there have always been some independent-minded persons who have become entrepreneurs within and beyond the major metropolitan regions and have relentlessly attempted to realize their unique ideas, which have the potential to be successful in various ways. In addition, every new business has a place of origin; entrepreneurs attempt their businesses in a given environment—physical, socioeconomic, political, and cultural (Yasuda 2016). Thus, geography matters.

Firm A was founded in Takamatsu, Kagawa, in 1969, to produce acrylic panels for large-scale water tanks. As a new company, a major challenge was the lack of the reputation and brand name of the firm in Japan. However, the firm had the highest level of expertise in the production of acrylic panels for large-scale water tanks with the founder having worked in a representative firm of the country in the field (i.e., a pipeline). A firm's ability to create state-of-the-art products is critical to appeal to potential customers. Originally, the founder opened a plant near the town of Takamatsu, Kagawa. Later, in order to expand its business, he decided to relocate to a newly built industrial park in the town of Miki (east of Takamatsu) based on the recommendation of a government personnel of the Kagawa Prefecture (i.e., a local buzz).

Firm B was founded in Marugame, located in western Kagawa, in 1947. Firm B chose to locate its facilities in Marugame owing to the existence of fiber-related (rayon) companies and suitable skilled labor in the region. At the time, Firm B was known to successfully make carbon disulfide (the raw material for rayon). The corporate themes of Firm B are "power of originality" and "creating new niches in the world."

Firm C was established in 2000 as the first venture firm in the academic-private collaborative framework in Tokushima Prefecture (a local buzz), based on a collaboration with Tokushima University (one of Japan's national universities). Achieving a global first, Firm C succeeded in mass producing ultraviolet-rays-LED (UV-LED), which had the highest level of radiation efficiency in the market.

Finally, Firm D was founded in 1925 in downtown Takamatsu, Kagawa, as a *geta* (Japanese traditional sandal) shop. Later, it expanded to include the functions of the wholesaler and manufacturer, becoming a leader in the Chugoku-Shikoku region.

4.2 Business Expansion Based on the firm's Strengths

Firms need to expand their businesses to grow. There is a range of strategies to expand business: exploiting new markets within and beyond the country to sell their products and services, produce new products and services, and create related and/or new businesses. Porter (1990) claims that gaining a competitive advantage is critical to be successful in the market and explains this concept through his diamond model, comprising firm strategy, structure, and rivalry; factor conditions; demand conditions; and related and supporting industries. Firms are required to develop appropriate strategies to optimize these conditions and are incessantly asked to arrange and renew their strategies to adapt to changes in the business environment.

Thus far, Firm A has been producing acrylic panels for over 300 large water tanks for zoos and aquariums, not only in Japan but also in overseas markets, most recently in Israel, Portugal, New Caledonia (France), and China. In 2015, the firm held about 70 percent of the world's share in the aquarium water tank-making market. These tanks are produced in four plants in Japan: Miki and Shido, Kagawa (50 employees each), Uruma, Okinawa (commenced operations in 2004 with 25 employees), and Kobe, Hyogo (commenced operations in 2009 with 25 employees).

The first strength of Firm A is the "unique quality"—the special technique for making acrylic panels for a large-scale water tank by gluing together a few centimeters of acryl panels, guaranteeing both strength and transparency simultaneously. This technique is extremely difficult to carry out. Currently, the firm has among the best expertise, globally, in producing acrylic panels for these water tanks.

The second strength of Firm A is a unique employee training system that emphasizes bringing up *Shokunin* (craftsman). *Shokunin* are professionals who are responsible for the whole process (gluing, modeling, grinding, etc.) of manufacturing acrylic panels for water tanks. In order to maintain this craftsmanship, despite the capacity that it needs to realize, the firm maintains a rather small entity size, that is, the power of "compactness" (about 50 employees in each plant). Thus, the firm does not seek economies of scale as in the case of large firms.

The third strength of Firm A is the internationalization of business since 1982. The firm opened its first foreign office in Seattle in the US in 1993, followed by a second office in Seoul, Korea in 1996 (later closed in 2002). In addition, the firm established an affiliate in North Carolina in the U.S. in 1999.[2]

The executive of Firm A points out:

> Locality in large metropolitan areas such as Tokyo is not needed in the situation that the firm performs its business mainly overseas. Only "quality" matters. (Interview 2015)

On the contrary, the manager pointed out that human relationships in the locality (e.g., personal place of origin) affected business operations. At the same time, *glocal* personal human relationships (pipelines) play a critical role in expanding the business overseas (e.g., establishing a U.S. office).

In 2013, Firm A was selected as a Global-Niche top 100 (GNT100) firm by Japan's Ministry of Economy, Industry, and Technology (a major recognition in the home country). The firm has developed state-of-art technology to make acrylic panels (*aquawall*) from acrylic fibers (resin) for large-scale water tanks. The firm was awarded several Guinness world records for its large-scale water tanks. The most recent one was awarded to a water tank in an aquarium park in Macao, which is 40 m wide and 8.3 m high. The acryl panel has a 64.5 cm width. Firm A's annual turnover in 2014 was 2 billion yen (17 million dollars), of which over 80 percent came from its overseas businesses.

Meanwhile, the main expansion strategy of Firm B has been to diversify its business operations. Therefore, its main products range from chemical products (inorganic, organic, and fine chemical products for tires, fibers, and detergents) to building materials (interior, exterior materials for houses, and pavement materials). Originally, Firm B was strong in producing sodium sulfate (synthetic detergent) products, which still commands the top share in the domestic market. Firm B is also strong in manufacturing organic solderability preservatives (preventing oxidation of printed wiring boards), claiming the top shares both in Japan and in the world (about 50% share in the world market). Owing to these achievements, in 2013, Firm B was selected as a Global-Niche top 100 (GNT100) firm by Japan's Ministry of Economy, Industry, and Technology.

As of 2017, Firm B had 591 employees (1,071 employees, including its affiliated firms), of which 60 were working at the headquarters in Marugame and 50 at a nearby R&D center in Utazu as engineers and researchers. Firm B has 13 domestic branches (including Tokyo, Nagoya, Osaka, and Fukuoka), two manufacturing plants (Marugame in Kagawa, and Tokushima), one of the above-mentioned R&D centers in Utazu, Kagawa, and 13 affiliated-firms (11 domestic and two international). In terms of its international intra-firm network, Firm B has six branches (Shanghai, Shenzhen, Taoyuan (Taiwan), Singapore, Los Angeles, and London). *Sogo shosha* (Japan's general trading firm) plays a critical role in selling their products (a global pipeline).

Unlike Firm B, Firm C has focused on a niche to maintain its market leader status. The main products of Firm C are the UV-LED and its related products, such as sterilization machines and air purifiers. Firm C's customers are spread globally through the firm's global pipelines; their products are used in counterfeit bill detectors and medical analysis devices. *Violeds,* an advanced sterilizing technology of the firm, was selected by the National Aeronautics and Space Administration of the United States (NASA) to be applied it to its International Space Station. The world LED market is expected to grow from 166 million dollars in 2016 to 288 million dollars in 2017 and 550 million dollars in 2021. Firm C claims that it has a 20 percent share of the world LED market with its partner firm, emphasizing establishing global patents over manufacturing products.

Firm C boasts its no-plant strategy, that is, outsourcing manufacturing processes through global pipelines while concentrating on the R&D activities at the site in Tokushima. Thus, Firm C' s employment numbers are small, comprising 10 skilled workers (engineers and professionals) who are trained on the job and are required to be multi-functional, responsible for both R&D activities and sales (including patent-related jobs). Firm C's efforts and accomplishments drew attention in the market and in 2013, Firm C was selected as a Global-Niche top 100 (GNT100) firm by Japan's Ministry of Economy, Industry, and Technology.

Lastly, Firm D does not belong in a state-of-art industry; the firm is engaged in a traditional manufacturing sector, that is, the shoes industry. However, through real-world trial and error, Firm D finally endeavored to explore a new market called a "cyber market" in the Internet and succeeded in its operation. From early on, the manager of Firm D recognized increasing competition and challenges in maintaining the traditional shoe business in the market. Thus, the manager decided to engage not only in shoe wholesale business but also in shoe-production and retailing. As of 2015, the major goods of the firm were ladies' shoes (90%) and clothes (10%). The firm (mainly the top manager) is in charge of planning and designing. In the early 1990s, the firm depended on manufacturers in the Nagata area in Kobe, which has been a major shoe-making area in Japan, to make products.[3] However, the expanding online business later drove the firm to find new sub-contractors to make shoes elsewhere; eventually, the firm began importing shoes from Korea and Taiwan. In the mid-1990s, Firm D decided to undertake foreign direct investment (FDI) to expand its business. In 1994, Firm D established a joint venture with Chinese and Korean partners (pipelines) in Shanghai, China, with the aim of expanding the production function, and sold its products to volume sale stores and mail order companies in Japan. The firm, however, closed that plant a few years later due to difficulties faced in joint venture management and, instead, opened a representative office in Shanghai, switching to consignment production with five to six local firms located in the suburbs of the Shanghai metropolitan area. At the same time, the firm opened its retail shops in Okayama and Takamatsu, Japan and in Shanghai, China, but later closed these shops due to difficulties in finding suitable and talented workers.

Another move was to open its shops on major internet shopping sites, beginning with *Rakuten,* the leading online retail firm in Japan, in 2002; such stores gained popularity later because of their good quality and reasonable pricing. The firm's contribution to the online store was highly regarded, earning it the "Shop of the year" award numerous times from *Rakuten.* Currently, the Internet has played a major role in the firm, accounting for a sales target of 1 billion yen (about 9.5 million US dollars). A future agenda is selling its products directly in the Chinese online market from its office in China. The firm emphasizes employing talented workers who are interested in product manufacturing and have the ability to innovate. In addition, the top manager says that the sensitivity of identifying key trends is critical in business. Unlike other successful firms outside the major metropolitan regions, the top manager of Firm D is not considering relocating its headquarters to Tokyo. He considers keeping the headquarters in Takamatsu, Kagawa to be a contribution to his home region.

4.3 Knowledge Creation Through Pipelines and Buzz, and Challenges

In the current competitive business environment, knowledge creation and innovation are fundamental for firm resilience (Nonaka and Takeuchi 1995; Bathelt and Glückler 2011). An entrepreneurial mind is essential for the firm's creativity and innovation (Sakakibara 2002). Thus, it is possible to say that firms need creative and innovative employees, especially in top and intermediate management positions, to enhance firm resilience. For their positive and outward-looking characteristics, creative and innovative personnel have the potential to connect their firms with other firms, related agencies, and customers within and beyond their locality. In other words, they are expected to make pipelines and buzz (both local and relational) and to keep them humming.[4] The expanding web of pipelines and buzz within and beyond the locality provides relevant firms with further opportunities to exploit and expand their businesses. In this way, a positive cycle can occur (Taira 2020).

As Schlunze (2012) argues, among small- and medium-sized firms, the existence of "*glocal*-minded" managers (hybrid managers) in both headquarters and foreign affiliates, who can understand the customers' perspective, is critical for the success of the international business. The "frontier spirit" of *glocal*-minded managers plays a critical role in expanding new markets through direct contacts (making pipelines) with potential partners and customers, without relying on intermediate agencies and consultants such as the Japan External Trade Organization (JETRO) and import–export firms such as *sogo shosha* in Japan. At the same time, managers are required to operate the business locally in order to be able to operate effectively.

Firms face challenges that must be overcome throughout their operations. Success at a specific period is soon obsolete. These challenges stem from both within and beyond the locality. Even a global crisis can occur suddenly, such as the COVID-19 pandemic in 2020. Challenges can also emerge from within the firm; manager-employee relations, succession of top managers, the firm's organizational and bureaucratic structure, and the firm's culture can be sources of challenges. Thus, firms should always be prepared to cope with future challenges. The "knowledge creation" attitude of the firm's managers and employees can help the firm not only in creating new products but also in tackling challenges.

In the case of Firm A, personal connections (pipelines and buzz), which have potential synergistic effects, played a role in determining the location of the headquarters and the plant in Miki, Kagawa. Emphasizing the "made-in-Japan" quality and "craftsmanship" of the top manager himself enabled the firm to embed its business locally and incessantly create knowledge for making acrylic panels for large water tanks. Similarly, continuous knowledge creation in the relevant chemical fields has made Firm B resilient for a long time. This strength stems from the firm's strategy of *glocal* arrangement of organizations in order to exploit knowledge creation synergies through intra-firm networks. While the headquarters, R&D facility, and the main chemical plant are agglomerated in the Utazu area in Kagawa, other plants and domestic sales branches are scattered in Japan, and affiliate and international sales branches are also widespread in the world. Figure 2 shows the domestic supplier and customer networks (pipelines) of Firm B.

Every firm has challenges to overcome to be successful in an increasingly competitive economic environment. Future challenges for Firm B are to continue to identify new niches in the market (for example, in electronics and automobiles) and to produce new products that are suited to those niches. Firm C was confident in its state-of-art products, manufactured based on the firm's distinctive knowledge acquired by the top manager through personal connections in the locality (local buzz). Firm C, however, faces difficulties in selling its products to Japan's large firms due to its lack of an established brand name/value (lack of pipelines). Thus, Firm C decided

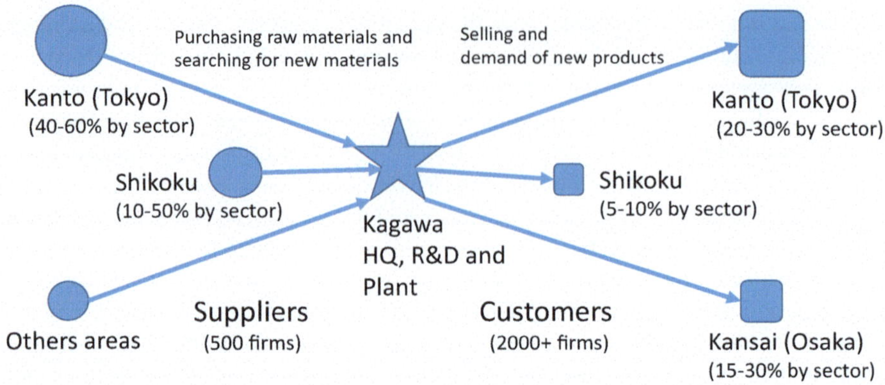

Fig. 2 Domestic supplier and customer networks (pipelines) of Firm B (*Source* Firm B)

to go global, changing its strategy quickly to sell its products abroad through global pipelines built by the firm. In particular, a global pipeline with a Korean firm, which understood the potential of Firm C's products, proved critical. The Korean firm asked Firm C to make its products in exchange for patent fees paid to Firm C. Expanding networks (pipelines) are key for the future; participating in international trade fairs has the potential for the firm to find new suppliers and customers, thereby creating global pipelines (Bathelt et al. 2014). The top manager of Firm C emphasized that "win–win" relations between the firms and suppliers/customers are crucial. Thus, incessant efforts to create new pipelines and buzz are of importance. Such pipelines and buzz are not limited to the real world; cyber space will become increasingly critical for business. Accordingly, Firm D has made efforts to enhance its potential to expand on the Internet and to succeed in Japan. The next step for Firm D will be expanding its marketing sphere beyond the national border.

5 Implications and Conclusions

Drawing on the concepts of pipelines and buzz, this study argues for the characteristics and strategies of global-niche firms in Japan through case studies in Shikoku. While Japan has recently undergone an economic recovery after a long recession since the early 1990s, many local regions are still suffering from a long stagnation. In this context, small- and medium-sized global-niche firms located in these local regions have attracted the attention of researchers and administrators from national and local governments for their potential to rejuvenate the local economy. Global-niche firms in Japan (most of which are small- and medium-sized) have the highest expertise and state-of-the-art technologies, and dominate a significant portion of the relevant world market. The global-niche firms in Shikoku analyzed in this study are among them. Local connections with suppliers and customers (buzz) vary from firm to firm. Many firms have worldwide networks for selling their products through global pipelines that they have cultivated through incessant efforts. The results of the study reveal a mixed contribution by global-niche firms to the local socio-economy. While some firms have strong linkages with other local firms and related agencies, and have contributed to increasing job opportunities in the region (Firms A and B of this study), other firms appear to be rather "stand-alone" firms without strong connections within the regions where they are located (Firms C and D). Thus, a future challenge from a local economic perspective might be on how to embed more (hopefully all) global-niche firms in their localities. The central government has recently begun implementing a relevant policy. Further appropriate policies by both central and local governments to promote such initiatives might be necessary.

Location affects business in terms of local buzz and *ba* that can lead to new knowledge creation and innovation. However, at the same time, firms must expand their business beyond borders. Thus, firms always need to implement *glocal* strategies to perform in a rapidly changing environment. Through the above analysis, it is clear that a positive cycle of business internationalization might be realized by expanding foreign markets to sell these products through pipelines and buzz, and investing the profits into R&D activities and plants to make the most sophisticated, value-added products. To realize this agenda, ever-lasting entrepreneurship is critical. Geographically, "thinking *glocally* and acting *glocally*" is a key. The global and cross-cultural minds of managers as boundary spanners are also of importance.

We need to perform more in-depth analysis of firms that can draw out the potential of the area where they are located (Hosotani 2017). An agenda for future studies might be to examine the "meaning" of locality, identify the role of the "locality" for *glocal* firms, and bridge micro-level and macro-level studies to expand the scope of management geography. Conducting further studies on the characteristics and strategies of local "leading firms" such as global-niche firms from a geographical perspective might be fruitful for bridging this gap.

Acknowledgements I would like to thank the participating firms that I interviewed for their precious time. I am very grateful to Michael Barrett and Paul Batten for their precious comments. This study was supported by grants-in-aid for scientific research of the Japan Society for Promotion of Science (JSPS) (Grant No. 26370926, 19K01187) and a research grant from the Hyakujushi Bank Academic Culture Promotion Foundation in 2017.

Notes

1. For roles of leading firms in the local industrial cluster, see Taira (2020).
2. For internationalization of small- and medium-sized firms' operations, see Sakamoto et al. (2016).
3. About the shoe industry in Kobe in relation with the ethnic minority group, see Yamamoto (2000, 2002).
4. About relational economic geography, see Yeung (2005).

References

Amino Y (1999) Sekai ni hirakareta nihonretto (Japanese archipelago which is open toward outside). In: Ishii Y and Yamauchi M (eds), Nihonjin to tabunka shugi (The Japanese and multiculturalism). Yamakawa Shuppansha, Tokyo: 4–22. (J)

Aoyama Y, Murphy JT, Hanson S (2011) Key concepts in economic geography. Sage, Los Angeles

Bathelt H, Feldman MP, Kogler DF (eds) (2011) Beyond territory: dynamic geographies of knowledge creation, diffusion, and innovation. Routledge, Oxon, Abington

Bathelt H, Glückler J (2011) The relational economy: geographies of knowing and learning. Oxford University Press, Oxford

Bathelt H, Golfetto F, Rinnalo D (2014) Trade shows in the globalizing knowledge economy. Oxford University Press, Oxford

Bathelt H, Malmberg A, Maskell P (2004) Clusters and knowledge: local buzz, global pipelines, and the process of knowledge creation. Prog Hum Geogr 28:31–56

Camagni R (1991) Innovation networks: spatial perspectives. Belhaven Press, London

Coe NM, Kelly PF, Yeung HWC (2007) Economic geography: a contemporary introduction. Blackwell, Oxford, U.K.

Dicken P (1992) Global shift: the internationalization of economic activity, 2nd edn. Guilford Press, New York

Drucker PF (1993) Post-capitalist society. Butterworth-Heinemann, Oxford

Dunning JH (1980) Towards an eclectic theory of international production: some empirical tests. J Int Bus Stud 11:9–31

Dunning JH (1988) Explaining international production. Unwin Hyman, London

Granovetter M (1985) Economic action and social structure: the problem of embeddedness. Am J Sociol 91:481–510

Helleiner GK (1981) Intra-firm trade and the developing countries. Macmillan, London

Hosotani Y (2014) Gurobaru nicchi toppu kigyoron (Global-niche top enterprises). Hakuto Shobo, Tokyo. (J)

Hosotani Y (2017) Chiiki no chikara o hikidasu kigyo (Firms which extract regional power). Chikuma Shobo, Tokyo. (J)

Hymer S (1972) The multinational corporation and the law of uneven development. In: Bhagwati JD (ed) Economics and world order. Macmillan, London, pp 113–140

Hymer S (1976) The international operations of national firms: a study of direct foreign investment. MIT Press, Cambridge

Inoue Z (ed) (2009) Chusho kigyo no senryaku (Strategies of small- and medium-sized firms). Doyukan, Tokyo. (J)

Ishikura Y, Fujita M, Maeda N. Kanai K, Yamasaki A (2003) Strategy for cluster initiatives in Japan. Yuhikaku, Tokyo. (J)

Itagaki T, Sakai M, Hayashi K, Torii Y (eds) (2016) Chusho kigyo no ajia tenkai (Operations of small- and medium-sized firms in Asia). Chuokeizaisha, Tokyo. (J)

Itami H (2005) Ba no ronri to maneijimento (The theory of 'ba' and management). Toyo Keizai Shimposha, Tokyo. (J)

Izawa Y (1996) Nihon kigyo gurobaruka no kozu (Globalization of Japanese companies). Gakubunsha, Tokyo. (J)

Kagawa Keizai Repotosha (2017) Kagawa no kaisha joho, 2018 edition. Kagawa Keizai Repotosha, Takamatsu. (J)

Kato H (2003) Chiiki chusho kigyo to sangyo shuseki (Local small- and medium-sized firms and the industrial cluster). Shinhyoron, Tokyo. (J)

Kato H (2011) Nihon sangyo to chusho kigyo (Japan's industry and small- and medium-sized firms). Shinhyoron, Tokyo. (J)

Kishikawa Z (2017) Keieigaku yoron (Concepts of management science). Dobunkan Shuppan, Tokyo. (J)

MacKinnon D, Cumbers A (2019) An introduction to economic geography, 3rd edn. Routledge, London

Malmberg A (1996) Industrial geography: agglomeration and local milieu. Prog Hum Geogr 20:392–403

Maskell P (1998) Low-tech competitive advantages and the role of proximity: the Danish wooden furniture industry. European Urban and Regional Studies 5:99–118

Ministry of Economy, Trade and Industry of Japan (METI) (2014) "Gurobaru nittchi toppu kigyo 100" o senteishimashita (Announcement of selection of global-niche top 100 firms). News Release (March 17, 2014). Ministry of Economy, Trade and Industry of Japan, Tokyo. (J)

Morita M (ed) (2012) Ba no chikara (The power of "ba"). Hakuto Shobo, Tokyo. (J)

Nakazawa T (2012) Gurobaruka to chusho kigyo (Globalization and small- and medium-sized firms). Chikuma Shobo, Tokyo. (J)

Nihon Chusho Kigyo Gakkai (2016) Chiiki shakai ni hatasu chusho kigyo no yakuwari (Roles of small- and medium-sized firms in local society). Doyukan, Tokyo. (J)

Nihon Seisaku Kinyu-koko Sogo Kenkyujo (2016) Chiiki keizai no shinko to chusho kigyo (Development of local economies and small- and medium-sized firms). Doyukan, Tokyo. (J)

Nonaka I, Takeuchi H (1995) The knowledge creating company: how Japanese companies create the dynamics of innovation. Oxford University Press, New York

Ono I (ed) (2015) Machi koba kara ajia no gurobaru kigyohe (From a small manufacturer in a city in Japan to an Asian global firm). Chuokeizaisha, Tokyo. (J)

Peck J, Yeung HWC (eds) (2003) Remaking the global economy: economic-geographical perspectives. Sage, London

Piore M, Sable CF (1984) The second industrial divide: possibilities for prosperity. Basic Books, New York

Porter M (1990) The competitive advantage of nations. Free Press, New York

Rugman AM (1981) Inside the multinationals. Croom Helm, London

Sakakibara K (2002) Keieigaku nyumon (2nd edn) (Introduction to management science). Nihon Keizai Shinbun Shuppansha, Tokyo. (J)

Sakamoto T, Sakai M, Hayashi K, Torii Y (eds) (2016) Chusho kigyo no ajia tenkai (Operations in Asia by Japan's small- and medium-sized firms). Chuo Keizaisha, Tokyo. (J)

Schlunze RD (2012) "Hybrid" managers creating cross-cultural synergy: a systematic interview survey from Japan. In: Schlunze RD, Agola NO, Baber WW (eds) Spaces of international economy and management. Palgrave-Macmillan, New York, pp 24–45

Scott A (1988) New industrial spaces. Pion, London

Seto R (1995) Nihonkigyo no takokusekika katei (Multinationalization of Japanese firms). Bunchindo, Tokyo. (J)

Storper M (1997) The regional world: territorial development in a global economy. Guilford Press, New York

Taira A (2005) Spatial dynamics and strategies of Japanese-affiliated companies. Kokonshoin, Tokyo. (J)

Taira A (2020) Beyond the cluster: a case study of pipelines and buzz in the glocal relational space of the glove-related industry of Shikoku, Japan. Geogr J 186:45–58

Tsuchiya T, Kaneyama K, Harada S, Takahashi Y (2015) Kakushinteki chushokigyo no gurobaru keiei (Global management of innovative small- and medium-sized firms). Dobunkan, Tokyo. (J)

Ueno K, Nishimura R (1990) A research note on formation of local industrial regions. Annales of the Japan Association of Economic Geographers 36: 47–57. (J)

Vernon R (1966) International investment and international trade in the product cycle. Q J Econ 80(2):190–207

Watanabe Y, Ogawa M, Kurose N, Mukoyama M (2001) 21 seiki chusho kigyoron (Small- and medium-sized firms in the twenty-first century). Yuhikaku, Tokyo. (J)

Yamamoto K (2005) Sangyo shuseki no keizai chirigaku (Economic geography of industrial agglomeration). Hosei Daigaku Shuppankyoku, Tokyo. (J)

Yamamoto S (2000) Reconstruction of the synthetic shoemaking industry in Nagata-ku, Kobe City after Hanshin-Awaji great earthquake disaster. Annales of the Japan Association of Economic Geographers 46: 281–294. (J)

Yamamoto S (2002) "Zanichi Korean" entrepreneurs in the synthetic shoe-making industry district in Kobe. Quarterly Journal of Geography 54: 1–19. (J)

Yasuda T (2016) Kigyo muen shakai niokeru shokibo kigyo no yakuwari (Roles of small firms in non-entrepreneurship-based society). In Nihon Chusho Kigyo Gakkai (ed) Chiikishakai ni hatasu chusho kigyo no yakurai (Roles of middle- and small-sized firms in local communities). Doyukan, Tokyo: 97–108. (J)

Yeung HW-C (2005) Rethinking relational economic geography. Trans Inst Br Geogr 30:37–51

Yeung HW-C (2016) Strategic coupling: East Asian industrial transformation in the new global economy. Cornell University Press, Ithaca

(J) denotes literature in Japanese.

Changing Business Communities in Industrial and Rural Spaces

Industrial Agglomeration and Regional Development Planning Analyzing by GIS in the City of Utsunomiya, Tochigi, Japan

Takahito Niwa

Abstract The purpose of this study is to clarify the spatial nature of the industrial agglomeration that forms the basis of the manufacturing industry in Utsunomiya as a case study. I also consider the possibility of "multi-polarization of industrial agglomeration" from the perspective of area-wide industrial accumulation and inter-firm transaction networks. I then examine the promotion of sustainable manufacturing through "multi-polarization of industrial agglomeration." Spatial autocorrelation using Moran's I statistic was adopted as a method in order to discuss the spatiality of aggregation. There are several industries that have the potential to develop industrial agglomeration in Utsunomiya. As the Japanese central government promotes policies for regional revitalization, local governments must promote more attractive development plans through their own strategic management. It is necessary to search for new industrial promotion measures with an understanding of the industrial structure and trading structure of companies by data analysis. In this regard, the city of Utsunomiya initiated the Utsunomiya Leading Company Support Project in April 2019.

Keywords Industrial agglomeration · GIS · Local Moran's I · Utsunomiya · Japan

1 Aim of This Research

1.1 Research Background

Many studies on Japanese economic geography have focused on the industrial agglomeration of manufacturing and changes in industrial structure (Kagami and Tsuji 2003; Matsuhashi et al. 2013; Hassink et al. 2018). With the ongoing globalization of the economy, however, the internationalization of supply chains as global value chains (GVCs), and integration of financial markets have intensified industrial and inter-city competition at the global level. At the firm level, while some multinational enterprises (MNEs) are reorganizing their production systems

T. Niwa (✉)
Faculty of Economics, Teikyo University, Tochigi 320-8551, Japan
e-mail: niwa@ucre.teikyo-u.ac.jp

A. Taira and R. D. Schlunze (eds.), *Management Geography*, International Perspectives in Geography 19, https://doi.org/10.1007/978-981-19-4403-1_6

globally, small- and medium-sized enterprises (SMEs) that maintain domestic or regional production activities are facing intensified competition related to the global economy. As a result, the hollowing out of industry in Japan's old industrial areas has begun to take a visible form.

In the city of Utsunomiya, which this chapter takes as a case study, the decline of the industrial sector has been particularly severe. As a result, pessimism about the city's future is inevitable (Ukai 2006). The effect of attracting companies in promoting industry remains significant. Recently, the strategic attraction of companies, targeting a specific range of industries and companies, has become a common practice (Ito 2008). However, the withdrawal or downsizing of core companies can seriously affect local SMEs in terms of the industrial agglomeration of a city, as in a company town like a Tochigi Prefecture in Japan, characterized by automobile or home appliance manufacturers (Economic and Enterprise Committee 2012). It is better not to assume that attracting companies will have a permanent effect.

Regarding the manufacturing industry in Utsunomiya, Ukai (1990) stated, "The fact that land prices are relatively low within a radius of 100-km of Tokyo defines the formation process of industrial agglomeration in this region. Since the quantitative accumulation of the attracted companies has progressed beyond the growth rate of local SMEs, local SMEs have not grown up." Ukai (1990) is pointing out the problem of the weak relationship between large companies and local businesses. The formation of a sustainable industrial structure is therefore necessary to maintain industrial competitiveness into the future. Tsujita (2005) argued that specializing in a particular industry is associated with higher economic growth. On the other hand, Malizia and Ke (1993) maintained that regional economies need diversity in order to ensure stability in a global economy. This argument for regional economic diversity is, in other words, a strengthening of the economy of urbanization. The term refers to the fact that the concentration of a wide variety of industries in a particular region reduces the risk of trade contraction and increases the level of economic activity in the region (Ito 2011). It has also been argued that ensuring diversity enhances the resilience of regional economies (Fujii 2013).

These concepts have been widely debated in the context of industrial agglomeration, whether MAR-type agglomeration (Marshall 1890; Arrow 1962; Romer 1986) within the same industry or Jacobs-type agglomeration (Jacobs 1969) in diverse industries (e.g., Henderson et al. 1995; Glaeser et al. 1992; Van der Panne 2004). To date, research on industrial agglomeration has not provided a clear answer as to which type of industrial agglomeration is desirable (Beaudry and Schiffauerova 2009; de Groot et al. 2016). In this context, recent research on industrial agglomeration has focused on the path dependence theory, generalized Darwinism, and complexity theory of evolutionary economic geography (Boschma and Frenken 2006; Boschma and Martin 2010). Related to this, the concept of related variety has been used to focus attention on the degree of relatedness within industrial agglomerations (Frenken et al. 2007; Boschma and Frenken 2011). Although the concept of related variety needs to be measured not by the division of industrial categories but by indicators that show the reality of relatedness (Boschma and Martin 2010), it is not easy to construct analytical data.

What is important here is how to ensure diversity and resilience while maintaining competitiveness. In particular, local governments need to find industrial agglomerations with related variety and work on regional industrial policies. Since the industries that form agglomerations with related varieties are assumed to cross over multiple industries, it is able to find multiple poles by analyzing by level of minor groups of manufacturing industry. Thus, this paper defines the "multi-polarization of industrial agglomeration" as attempting to develop the multiple poles and exploring the coexistence of competitiveness and durability. Nakamura (2008) and Machida (2009) also drew attention to the possibility of both specialized industries and diversities.

In addition, it is necessary to clarify what kind of regional distribution the poles of these industrial clusters have and what kind of characteristics they have in actual business transactions. It is important to pay attention not only to industries that appear as bundles of business activities, but also to the trends of individual companies (Schlunze et al. 2012). The management of individual companies differs, including companies with business relationships that play a role in global production network (GPN) and companies with local production networks even within a small region in Japan. In order to link these viewpoints, a local research perspective is also important in international management.

1.2 Purpose of This Research

The purpose of this study is to clarify the spatial nature of the industrial agglomeration that forms the basis of the manufacturing industry in Utsunomiya as a case study. I also consider the possibility of "multi-polarization of industrial agglomeration" from the perspective of area-wide industrial accumulation and inter-firm transaction networks. I then examine the promotion of sustainable manufacturing through "multi-polarization of industrial agglomeration."

2 Current Status of the Manufacturing Industry in the City of Utsunomiya

Here, I would like to take a look first at Tochigi Prefecture and the city of Utsunomiya. Tochigi Prefecture is located about 100 km north of Japan's capital, Tokyo, and has an area of 6408 km^2 with a population of 1,942,000 (as of Oct 1, 2019).[1] The prefectural capital, the city of Utsunomiya (approximately 417 km^2), is home to 519,000 people. The city of Oyama, the second largest in Tochigi Prefecture, has a population of 168,000. Therefore, the Utsunomiya has a high concentration of the population. The number of employees in Tochigi Prefecture is 845,605 (as of 2016), and the percentage of manufacturing employees is very high in Tochigi Prefecture, 25.7% compared to 16.5% in whole Japan according to the 2016 Economic Census.

Added value of manufacturing in Tochigi Prefecture is similar to employees, 35.6% compared to 20.3% in Japan. Various industries are clustered in a well-balanced mix in the region; in particular, this is the core region in Japan for transportation equipment industries including automotive, aviation, industrial equipment, pharmaceutical, and medical treatment-related industries.[2] Several studies have reported in detail the location of companies in Tochigi Prefecture (e.g., Kondo 2004; Ogawa 1995).

A number of manufacturing companies are located in the city of Utsunomiya because Utsunomiya has taken measures to make it easier for manufacturing companies from outside the city to locate in concentrated industrial areas by developing industrial parks and providing grants for them. The city of Utsunomiya has been promoting the next generation of mobility-related industries, environment and energy, and medical and health welfare industries in order to ensure competitiveness by taking advantage of its agglomeration.

The location quotient (LQ)[3] is a widely used measure to confirm the presence of industrial agglomeration. The city of Utsunomiya reported industrial agglomeration by using LQ in "Survey on the Promotion of Industrial Agglomeration in Utsunomiya." According to the survey results,[4] the five industries in the middle division of industrial categories[5] in manufacturing were found to be agglomerated in Utsunomiya: (1) Manufacturing of Beverages, Tobacco and Feed; (2) Precision Device/Instrument Manufacturers; (3) Plastics; (4) Manufacture of Information and Communication Electronics Equipment; and (5) Manufacture of general machinery. Nevertheless, only in the Precision Device/Instrument Manufacturers industry (LQ = 3.79) did the LQ exceed 2.

First, I summarize the relationship between LQ and the competitiveness of manufacturing industries from the Economic Census for Business Activity in 2016. I obtain the LQ of the number of business establishments in 181 minor groups of manufacturing industry by municipality,[6] and then define the number of specialized industries as those with three or more business establishments and in which the LQ exceeds 4. Large numbers of specialized industries are interpreted as the degree of "multi-polarization of industrial agglomeration." Next, I extract the top 100 municipalities in terms of the value of manufactured goods shipped (the M Value).[7] Compared to other cities, Utsunomiya has a lesser degree of "multi-polarization of industrial agglomeration" (Table 1). This is because only three industries[8] are found there, while the average and median of the top 100 municipalities are 4.94 and 4, respectively. This indicates that the manufacturing industry in Utsunomiya may have a weaker structure during economic recession than that in other industrial cities.

Table 1 Comparison between Utsunomiya and top 100 cities regarding economic indicators

	Number of Industries (LQ > = 4)	Change in Number of Business Establishments	Change in Number of Employees	Change in the real M Value	Rate of Change in Number of Business Establishments	Rate of Change in Number of Employees	Rate of Change in the real M Value
Utsunomiya	3.00	−28	−3,788	36,392,180	−0.05	−0.11	0.21
Average	4.94	−129	−1,428	8,670,813	−0.10	0.00	0.14
Median	4.00	−48	−335	6,756,627	−0.11	−0.01	0.07

Note The changes in the number of business establishments, employees, and the M Value from the Census of Manufacture in 2006 are summarized as economic indicators. Utsunomiya ranked 19th

Sources Created from Economic Census for Business Activity in 2016 and Census of Manufacture in 2006

3 GIS Analysis of Industrial Agglomeration

3.1 *Spatial Autocorrelation Using Moran's* I *Statistics*

As mentioned previously, I have used only LQ to summarize the conditions of "multi-polarization of industrial agglomeration." In this section, I analyze spatial autocorrelation using Moran's *I* statistic in order to discuss the spatiality of aggregation. The local Moran's *I* statistic is a measure of spatial autocorrelation developed by Anselin (1995), and is recognized as a counterpart analysis method to the global Moran's *I* statistic (Moran 1948), which measures the spatial autocorrelation of the entire region. In recent years, many studies have been conducted on spatial accumulation by researchers such as Ida (2006), Fukumoto (2010), Wakabayashi and Koizumi (2014), and Guillain (2010).

This paper tests the local Moran's *I* statistic with the False Discovery Rate (FDR) Correction method in order to solve multiple testing and spatial dependence issues. The multiple testing issue refers to the increase in the probability of rejecting the null hypothesis in the overall test due to repetition of the test.[9] Therefore, the significance probability *p*-value must be set lower than usual when testing multiple times. On the other hand, the spatial dependence issue refers to the fact that when the distance among neighboring features is short, each feature shares the same feature when calculating the local Moran's *I* statistic. As a result, it is easy to reach statistical significance. This is a problem caused by the misaligned independence of the features. The analysis has to use data divided by municipalities. This is because that the Economic Census for Business Activity in 2016 does not provide mesh statistics on the number of business establishments by level of minor groups of manufacturing industry.

In the Bonferroni correction method, the number of test districts *n* and the *p*-value for the whole subject are tested at the level of *p/n* for each test district (Yaginuma et al. 2013; Miyazawa 2003; Yamada and Kawakami 2012). However, this correction method makes the *p*-value lower than necessary to prevent false judgments.[10] As a result, false judgments may occur, which may cause oversights. Therefore, this paper uses the FDR correction method, which estimates the number of false judgments at a particular confidence level and adjusts the *p*-value accordingly (Benjamini and Hochberg 1995; Caldas de Castro and Singer 2006; Goovaerts 2010; Grekousis 2018).

Here, I calculate the local Moran's *I* statistic using the LQ based on the number of business establishments in 2016 for 181 minor groups of manufacturing industry by municipality, as discussed in the previous section.[11] If the Local Moran's *I* statistic is significant, then the municipality is classified into one of four types of agglomeration, as shown in Table 2.

Table 2 Classifications of the result of Local Moran's

Type	Z-Score of Local Moran's I in the feature	Z-Score of Local Moran's I in the surrounding feature	Character of industrial agglomeration
HH	High	High	widespread industrial agglomeration
HL	High	Low	industrial specialization
LH	Low	High	outside the area of widespread industrial agglomeration
LL	Low	Low	poor industrial agglomeration

Source The author

3.2 National Trends in Spatial Distribution of Industrial Agglomeration

First, the overall characteristics: out of 343,176 combinations of 181 minor groups of manufacturing industry and 1,896 municipalities, a total of 6,274 sets were found to have HH (High-High: widespread industrial agglomeration). HL (High–Low: industrial specialization) was found in 618 cases, LH (Low–High: outside the area of widespread industrial agglomeration) in 229 cases, and LL (Low–Low: poor industrial agglomeration) in 0 cases. The reason why the LL type was zero was that in the case of small industries such as the minor groups, there were often zero companies in many municipalities, and in such cases.

Next, I check the characteristics of each municipality, among which 1806 were found to have widespread industrial agglomeration of at least one industry. The most widespread industrial agglomeration was found in 27 industries in Chiyoda Ward, Tokyo. In addition, the top 20 municipalities with widespread industrial agglomeration are located in Tokyo or in a government-ordinance-designated city. Twelve of these are located in Tokyo. In terms of reflecting the concentration of companies in Tokyo, this point suggests that the spatial dependence issue has not been fully resolved. It seems unavoidable, because the GIS analysis is based on the boundaries of municipalities with different spatial sizes.

In addition, I compare the characteristics among the middle division of manufacturing industries (Fig. 1). The largest number of municipalities with HH (widespread industrial agglomeration) were classified as Manufacturing of Production Machinery, followed by Printing and Allied Industries, Manufacturing of Transportation Equipment, and Manufacturing of Business-Oriented Machinery. On the other hand, the industries with the widespread industrial agglomeration in a few municipalities were Manufacture of Petroleum and Coal Products, Manufacture of Leather Tanning, Leather Products and Fur Skins, and Manufacture of Chemical and Allied Products. This indicates that the location of petrochemical companies is concentrated in certain coastal areas, such as Ichihara and Sodegaura in Chiba Prefecture.

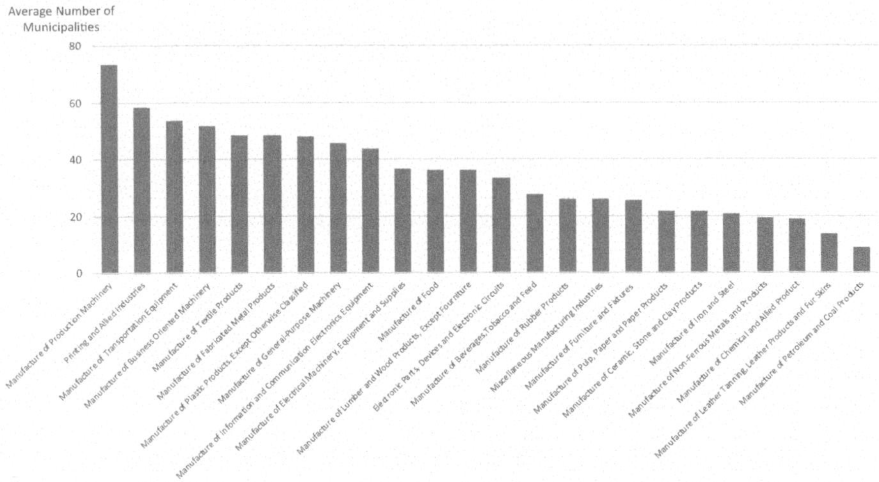

Fig. 1 Average number of municipalities with HH in the middle divisions of industries (*Note* The number of municipalities of the HH type in the minor groups were averaged by the middle divisions; *Source* Created from the Economic Census for Business Activity in 2016)

Turning to the level of the minor groups, the most common cat (Fig. 2a). For the industry, 132 municipalities were identified as HH, 5 as HL and 3 as LH. The widespread industrial agglomerations of this industry were recognized in municipalities in Aichi, Shizuoka, Nagano, Niigata, and Toyama Prefectures. Next, Motor Vehicles, Parts and Accessories were found in 125 municipalities (Fig. 2b). These municipalities are known as areas where automobile manufacturers and their suppliers are agglomerated. It also can be judged by the spatial autocorrelation result based on the LQ. Other industries with many municipalities categorized as HH included Measuring Instruments, Analytical Instruments, Testing Machines, Surveying Instruments and Physical and Chemical Instruments (116 municipalities), Printing (110 municipalities), and Sawing, Planning Mills and Wood Products (102 municipalities). In particular, Sawing, Planning Mills and Wood Products has widespread industrial agglomeration in central Hokkaido, Wakayama, Nara, Tokushima, Kochi and Miyazaki Prefectures, which are all surrounded by rich mountain forests (Fig. 2c). The specific local conditions of the natural environment contribute to unique industrial agglomerations.

4 Spatiality of Industrial Agglomeration in Utsunomiya

In this section, I use Utsunomiya as a case study, present the results of GIS analysis of local Moran's *I* statistics, and discuss how the government should implement industrial promotion policies.

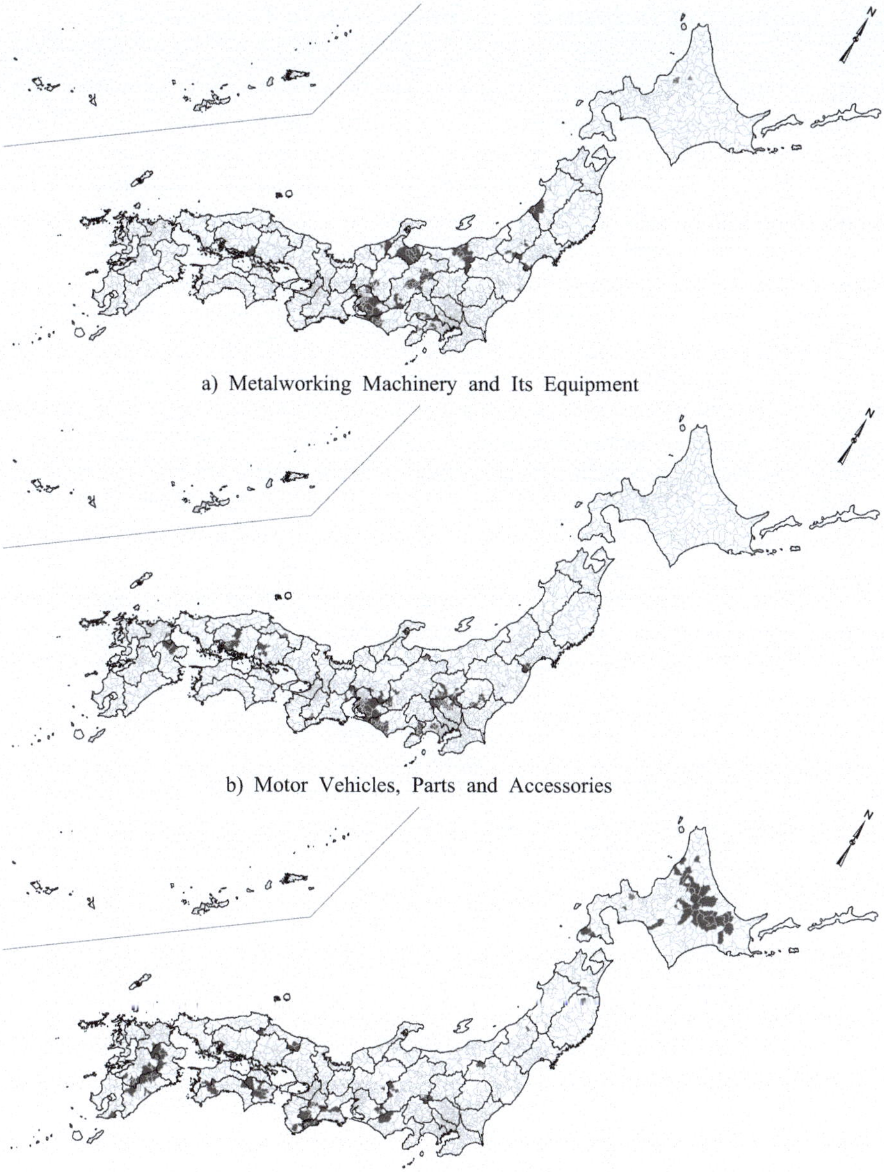

a) Metalworking Machinery and Its Equipment

b) Motor Vehicles, Parts and Accessories

c) Sawing, Planning Mills and Wood Products

Fig. 2 Location of local Moran's*I* significance for specific industries
(*Source* Created from the Economic Census for Business Activity in 2016)

4.1 Spatiality of Industrial Agglomeration in Utsunomiya

Results of the GIS analysis revealed that Utsunomiya has two industries with widespread industrial agglomeration: Establishment Engaged in Administrative or Ancillary Economic Activities (Manufacture of Transportation Equipment) and Aircraft and Parts. It was confirmed that only the aircraft industry is agglomerated in Utsunomiya (Fig. 3, top left). The background of the aircraft industry concentration in Utsunomiya originates in the evacuation of Nakajima Aircraft (now Aerospace Company, SUBARU Corporation) and its suppliers during the Second World War; the industry did not originate in Utsunomiya. Although the industry has high technology, it is a closed industry where strict quality standards and long-term business relationships are maintained, making it difficult for newcomers to enter.[12] Many manufacturing companies already engaged in the aircraft industry are making efforts to gain the trust of their business partners, such as acquiring JISQ9100 and Nadcap[13] certification. The aircraft industry is expected to develop based on two factors.

The first is the rise of low-cost carriers and economic growth in developing and emerging countries, which has led to increased demand for aircraft. This is expected to lead to increasing trading. The Boeing Company said it had a record 806 deliveries for commercial jets in 2018.[14] However, the aircraft industry has strict quality standards and a long track record of traceability, so it is not easy to change trading partners. For example, Boeing's Japanese corporate suppliers include Mitsubishi Heavy Industries Ltd., Kawasaki Heavy Industries Ltd., ShinMaywa Industries Ltd., NIPPI Corporation, and SUBARU Corporation as primary suppliers (Tier 1). Subaru is closely associated with the aircraft industry in Utsunomiya and has SMEs located there as secondary (Tier 2) and tertiary (Tier 3) suppliers. The process is so complex that Boeing must approve even a change of tertiary supplier. Such contracting practices are one of the hallmarks of the aircraft industry, which values quality and safety over price.

The second is the development of the next generation of passenger aircraft. Currently, Boeing is developing the 777X, Mitsubishi Aircraft Corporation is developing the Mitsubishi SpaceJet, and Honda Aircraft Company is developing the HondaJet. Production orders for these aircraft have already begun, and it is expected that their development will lead to new business opportunities and increased orders. As for the 777X, Subaru participates in manufacturing the center wing and the joint between the center wing and the main landing gear. As a result, there are likely to be transactions with aircraft companies in Utsunomiya. However, since Subaru is not a participant in the SpaceJet or HondaJet, there seems to be little involvement for aircraft companies in Utsunomiya.

The city of Utsunomiya also needs support to ensure its competitiveness. Many local governments currently promote the aircraft industry. Moreover, Utsunomiya should pay attention to the fact that other municipalities are leading in terms of widespread industrial agglomeration, such as Special Zone to Create Asia No.1 Aerospace Industrial Cluster promoted by the central government.

a) Aircraft and Part

b) Medical Instruments and Apparatus, and Medical Supplies

c) Motor Vehicles, Parts and Accessories

d) Optical Instruments and Apparatus, and Lenses

Fig. 3 Location of local Moran's *I* significance for specific industries around Tochigi Prefecture (*Source* Created from the Economic Census for Business Activity in 2016)

4.2 Spatiality of Industrial Agglomeration in Neighboring Municipalities of Utsunomiya

On the other hand, there are several industries that have been confirmed to have widespread industrial agglomeration in neighboring municipalities other than Utsunomiya. Support for these industries from the city of Utsunomiya will be important for the region to become more competitive and durable in the future. Three industries that are recognized as having the widespread industrial agglomeration in several neighboring municipalities: Medical Instruments and Apparatus, and Medical Supplies (7 municipalities), Motor Vehicles, Parts and Accessories (7 municipalities), and Optical Instruments and Apparatus, and Lenses (6 municipalities).

Figure 3 shows the distribution of each. In Medical Instruments and Apparatus, and Medical Supplies, for example, MANI Inc., a leading manufacturer of medical devices, and has their headquarters in Utsunomiya. However, Utsunomiya is not included in the widespread industrial agglomeration. This is thought to be due to the stronger concentration in neighboring areas. Canon Medical Systems Corporation, located in the city of Ohtawara, is famous in the medical industry world. The head office of Nakanishi Inc. is in the city of Kanuma.[15] Similarly, in Optical Instruments and Apparatus, and Lenses, while Canon, Inc. has their lens factory in Utsunomiya, Tochigi Nikon Corporation is also located in the northern part of the prefecture. On the other hand, Honda Motor Co., Ltd., which has plants and laboratories in Takanezawa Town and Haga Town, and Nissan Motor Co., Ltd., which has a plant in Kaminokawa Town, belong to the Motor Vehicles, Parts and Accessories category.

Although these industries do not have the widespread industrial agglomeration in Utsunomiya, they have formed in neighboring municipalities. It is, in other words, relatively easy for companies in Utsunomiya to find new transactions and recruit skilled workers. It is thus better for the Utsunomiya to provide intensive support to companies related to these industries when aiming at "multi-polarization of industrial agglomeration" (e.g., Optical Instruments and Apparatus, and Lenses, concentrated widely in the northern part of the prefecture). Nevertheless, Utsunomiya has Canon in the Kiyohara Industrial Complex, which was not included in this agglomeration. This is presumably due to the fact that there are almost no local companies that have business relationships with Canon. No vertical network has been formed. No horizontal network has been built, either, because there are no powerful SMEs in the industry. However, note that due to industry-academia collaborations, Utsunomiya can provide specialized technical labor, due to the establishment of the Center for Optical Research and Education at Utsunomiya University in 2007. Canon approached Utsunomiya University to restructure education around optical technology in Japan, and Utsunomiya University accepted the idea and decided to establish an educational and research organization for optical technology in cooperation with Canon.[16] Furthermore, in April 2015, a Department of Optical Engineering was newly established in the Graduate School of Engineering at the University.

There are several industries that have the potential to develop industrial agglomeration in Utsunomiya. As the Japanese central government promotes policies for regional revitalization, local governments must promote more attractive development plans through their own strategic management. For this reason, it is important to achieve financial independence, which is a fundamental goal, not only to maintain competitiveness of existing industries, but also to promote other industries that contribute to future development.

5 Corporate Promotion as a Local Industrial Promotion

5.1 Perspectives on Individual Companies

In recent years, it has been pointed out that it is important to focus more on innovative companies in the promotion of industry. Studies have focused on inter-firm networks involved in innovative R&D activities (Yamamoto and Matsuhashi 1999; Yokura 2014; Mizuno 2004; Rutten and Boekema 2007) and on inter-firm transaction networks themselves (Fujii et al. 2017; Goto et al. 2015; Kawamoto et al. 2015; Yokura 2016; Zuo and Kajikawa 2017). These research perspectives help identify the transactional characteristics of companies that connect to the region and beyond. In this section, we therefore examine the characteristics of transactions in manufacturing using network analysis. However, it is difficult to analyze only Utsunomiya because of the data limitations described later. The analysis is therefore mainly at the Tochigi Prefecture level.

5.2 Data and Methods

First, I introduce the data and methods to be analyzed. Here, I use data related to business-to-business transactions from a private company database, Teikoku Databank, Ltd.

Companies headquartered in Tochigi Prefecture that have at least seven transactions with other companies are eligible for the analysis, which covers approximately three years of business-to-business data from 2013 to January 2017. It should be noted, however, that the data based on companies is different from that used previously.[17] The size of the dataset is about 30,000 companies and 65,000 transactions in all industries.[18]

Characteristics of transactions can be quite different across industries. I therefore check the differences between the industries based on the indicator of Fukuda et al. (2015). This indicator calculates LQ, which is the ratio of inner-regional transactions of buy (Bx) and sell (Sx) to total transactions in company *x*, and classifies them according to whether the value exceeds 1. $Bx \geq 1$ and $Sx \geq 1$ are classified as a local service company, $Bx \geq 1$ and $Sx < 1$ are classified as a connected company, $Bx < 1$ and $Sx \geq 1$ are classified as a receptor company, and $Bx < 1$ and $Sx < 1$ are classified as a globally linked company. Figure 4 presents an overall picture of inter-firm transactions in the major divisions of industrial categories. We can see that the major divisions characterized by local service companies are mining and specific service industries, while the industries characterized by connected companies or globally linked companies are health and welfare, education, and manufacturing. In addition, Fig. 5 and Table 3 indicate whether transactions are within the same industry or between different industries in the major divisions. We can find that the connected companies have more transactions with different industries than the

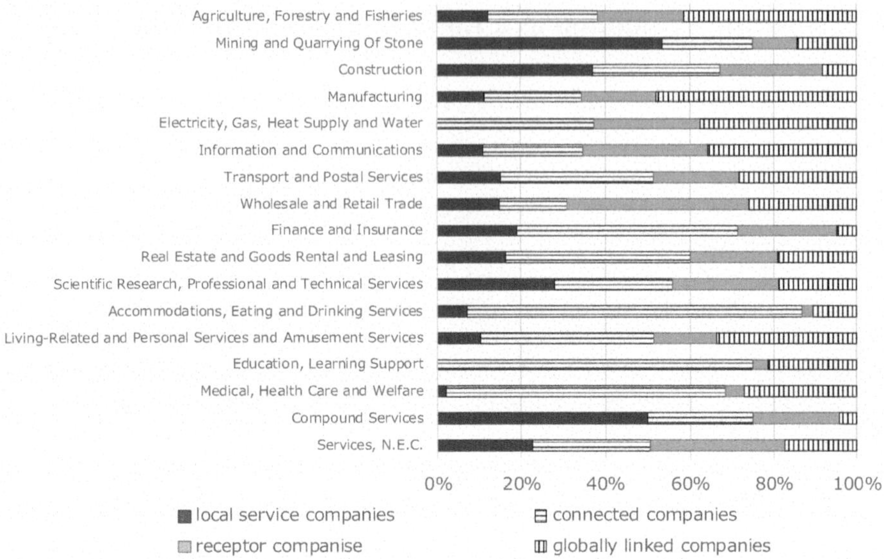

Fig. 4 Ratio of four types of companies by the major divisions of industry (*Source* Created from the database provided by Teikoku Databank, Ltd.)

other types of transactions. In other words, connected companies have become very important to the regional economy. Furthermore, I will discuss the Frontier Company Certification,[19] a technology brand, in Tochigi Prefecture.

The characteristics of the four trade types are analyzed by network theory. In particular, this paper uses two representative measures of centrality, one of which is closeness centrality.[20] This is an indicator that evaluates companies with small hypothetical transactional distances for each firm as having a high degree of centrality. The other is betweenness centrality. This is an indicator that evaluates companies that maintain network connectivity as having a high degree of centrality. Betweenness centrality can be used, for example, to find companies with characteristics that would negatively affect many trading partners if one company were lost.

5.3 Analysis Results

Figure 6 compares the centrality indicators for whether a company is on the frontier by transaction type. The closeness centrality index is higher for frontier companies in the globally linked, connected, and receptor companies. In other words, these types of companies have a central position in the transaction networks of the manufacturing industry in Tochigi Prefecture, and are involved in a large number of transactions. However, in the comparison of whether or not a company is a frontier company, the difference of value in the closeness centrality index is small, albeit statistically

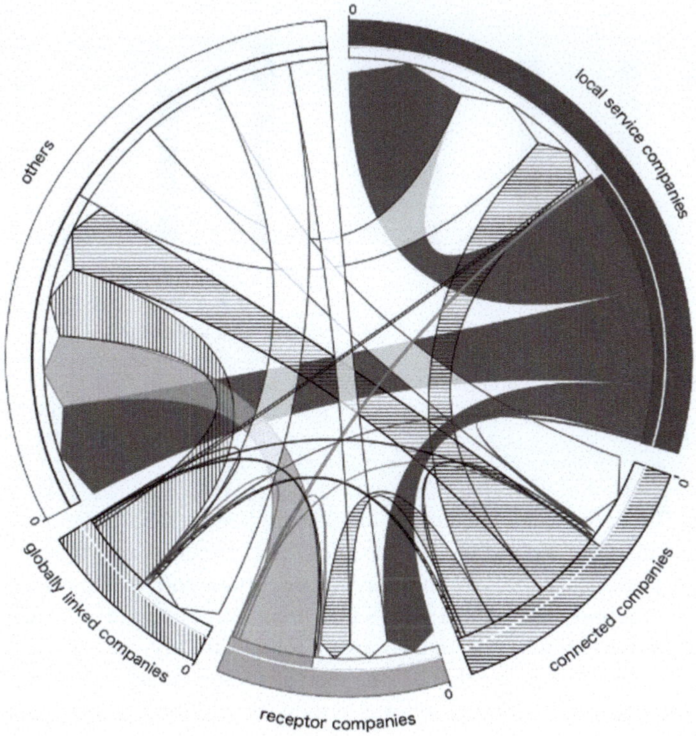

Fig. 5 Transaction flows among four types and others
(*Note* Others means companies located outside of Tochigi Prefecture. Generated by R with circlize package [Gu et al. 2014])

Table 3 Number of transactions among industries by four types

	Inter transaction among different industries	Inner transactions in same industries	Total
The global linked companies	2596	3315	5911
	(43.9)	(56.1)	(100)
The receptor companies	2853	3176	6029
	(47.3)	(52.7)	(100)
The connected companies	4333	7807	12,140
	(35.7)	(64.3)	(100)
The local service companies	8,299	11,712	20,011
	(41.5)	(58.5)	(100)
Total	18,081	26,010	44,091
	(41.0)	(59.0)	(100)

Source Created from the database provided by Teikoku Databank, Ltd

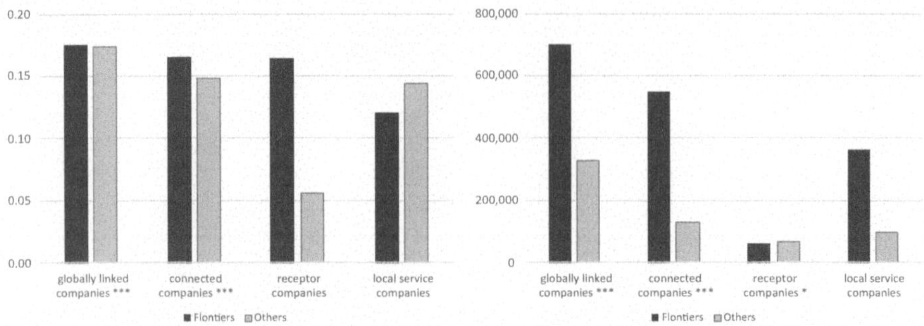

Left: closeness centrality Right: betweenness centrality

Fig. 6 Average value of the centrality indexes among transaction types
(*Note* *** $p < 0.01$, ** $p < 0.05$, *$p < 0.1$; *Source* Created from the database provided by Teikoku Databank, Ltd)

significant. The betweenness centrality index is higher for the frontier companies in the globally linked and connected companies. This suggests that these companies have high technical capabilities and play an important role in the connectivity of inter-firm transaction networks. It shows that it can have an indirect effect not only on the companies with which such a company trades directly, but also on a group of companies that are vertically related to it, such as its secondary suppliers.

Finally, I discuss the centrality indexes associated with the discussion in Sect. 4. I compare differences in the betweenness centrality in Utsunomiya and other cities in Tochigi Prefecture in certain industries (the four industries discussed previously).[21] There is not much difference between the companies in Utsunomiya and outside of the city in Medical Instruments and Apparatus, and Medical Supplies (Table 4). This is considered to reflect the fact that the industry is so precise that the companies have advanced technology and many customers. In other words, even though no widespread industrial agglomeration has been identified in Utsunomiya, it is still considered to play an important role as a center of the transaction networks in the manufacturing industry in Tochigi Prefecture. Next, both Optical Instruments and Apparatus, and Lenses and Motor Vehicles, Parts and Accessories show a higher degree of closeness centrality in out-of-town companies, and the difference is large. This means that these industries have business-to-business transaction networks mainly with out-of-town companies, and the companies in Utsunomiya are not growing sufficiently. Especially in Optical Instruments and Apparatus, and Lenses, there are no companies that have transactions with major lens manufacturers or other companies in a wide range of fields. As a result, it appears that widespread industrial agglomeration has not appeared in Utsunomiya. In Aircraft and Parts, the value of betweenness centrality index was higher for companies outside Utsunomiya. Compared to the other three industries, however, the value of the betweenness centrality index is much lower. This can be attributed to the relative closeness of the industry and its reliance on principal-subcontractor relationships.

Table 4 Average value of the betweenness centrality by municipality-specific industries

	Municipalities		
	Utsunomiya	Others	Total
Medical Instruments and Apparatus, and Medical Supplies	827,099	761,662	767,611
	(1)	(10)	(11)
Optical Instruments and Apparatus, and Lenses	53,930	564,546	479,444
	(2)	(10)	(12)
Motor Vehicles, Parts and Accessories	247,901	575,649	561,082
	(2)	(43)	(45)
Aircraft and Parts	86,993	137,209	123,514
	(3)	(8)	(11)

Source Created from the database provided by Teikoku Databank, Ltd

In this section, data from firm-level transaction networks are used to analyze the characteristics of the industries in Tochigi Prefecture and Utsunomiya. The results show that the value of the centrality index of frontier companies with high technical capabilities is high, and that these companies play an important role in the manufacturing industry in Tochigi Prefecture. Although the discussion at the level of 181 minor groups is inadequate, the centrality index of companies in Utsunomiya is low in the industries with widespread industrial agglomeration. Therefore, it is considered that there is still no agglomeration in these industries in Utsunomiya.

Promotional measures to help companies belonging to these industries expand their transaction networks will be important. In 2015, the Japanese central government developed the web-based analysis tool RESAS to enable local governments to use the results of analysis in their policy planning for industrial promotion.[22] The economic and industrial policy division of local governments has been able to understand the structure of the regional economy and the industrial agglomeration based on the analysis of business-to-business transaction networks. It will be important to analyze this kind of data to understand the actual state of the regional economy and link it to policy planning.

6 Case Studies

Finally, I discuss the characteristics of three manufacturing firms that are operating in the city of Utsunomiya. By discussing the characteristics of these firms, it is possible to link the industrial agglomeration and business management that have been previously analyzed. Firm A and Firm B are small and medium-sized firms that do business with MNEs in the city of Utsunomiya. Firm C, on the other hand, is an example of a medium-sized firm that does not do business with large firms, but has established an inter-firm network outside of its business activities.

Firm A is a general machinery and equipment manufacturing firm established in the city of Utsunomiya in 1964. Although it has a small number of employees, Firm A has an advantage in manufacturing a wide variety of products in small quantities using a variety of materials. At the time of its establishment, Firm A did 100% of its business with a large MNE (Firm X) in the city. Firm X has manufacturing plants on a global scale, however, it emphasizes domestic plants in order to keep its core technology in Japan. Firm A is currently managed by the second-generation president, who takes on work not only for Firm X but also for other companies. The president assumes that the business relationships with large companies as in the past will not continue in the future, and is taking actions to reduce the business risk. In addition, Firm A is beginning to focus on R&D, applying for grants from the government and Tochigi Prefecture.

Firm B is a medium-sized manufacturer of transport machinery and equipment, which moved from another prefecture in 1958 and is now headquartered in the city of Utsunomiya. Firm B is a supplier to a large MNE (Firm Y) in the city. Firm Y is both a manufacturer and a supplier of foreign firms. This industry is not an easy one to enter because of the demand for high-precision quality in GVCs. Firm B, as a subcontractor of Firm Y, participates in the design and prototyping stages, thereby achieving a high value-added business. Firm B focuses on development by utilizing government grants, and also conducts joint research with universities. Firm B has a strategy to increase its market share, and in fact, has been winning new transactions from inside and outside of Tochigi Prefecture. In addition, Firm B has started to develop new products and is aiming to expand into other industries.

Firm C is a medium-sized metal product manufacturing firm founded in 1984 in the city of Utsunomiya. Firm C does not do business with large firms, instead doing business with several firms in Tochigi Prefecture. Firm C's core technology is precision sheet metal and welding, and it engages in production to meet a wide range of needs from prototype to mass production. Firm C has been growing through business-to-business transactions, however, it has begun to expand into business-to-consumer business. Firm C has been able to expand and improve its business under the leadership of the president. The president himself has built up a personal network with other firms, which has led to the development of new businesses. This network has developed into a horizontal network of small and medium-sized companies outside of Tochigi Prefecture. This network is aimed at technical cooperation and joint orders, which is expected to improve their technology.

This section discusses two types of cases from the point of firm's management and strategy: one is cases in which the technological level is enhanced through ties with large firms, the other is a case in which the firm is trying to accumulate technology by using its own network. In the former cases, the firms continue to do business within the region, however, they function as part of GPNs. At that time, they are trying to improve their technical level by not only from their own resources but also by receiving technical support from the MNEs with which they have business relationships. Such technical support from the MNEs is also an opportunity for local SMEs to learn about the changes in the production environment under the global economy. In other words, SMEs are learning about current situation of global economy through the pipeline with the MNEs. These inter-firm linkages are thought to strengthen ties within the same industry and enhance the industrial concentration of the non-related variety. In the latter case, they do not have any connections with the GPNs. On the other hand, they do not bind themselves to business relationships within the region. They are seeking production linkages and technological communication with other firms in order to improve their own technological level, and are building networks with SMEs outside the region. This active networking with other companies is thought to strengthen ties among other industries and to enhance the industrial concentration of the related variety.

7 Conclusion

In regard to the future of Utsunomiya's economy, the weakness of its manufacturing industry could be overcome by multi-polarization of industrial agglomeration in relation to industries that are expected to expand their market size in the future. In other words, it will need to form a sustainable industrial structure that can cope with both economic growth and recession related to the global economy.

Evidence-based policymaking is becoming more important for regional economic policymaking. This represents a shift from decisions based on the intuition, experiences, and in some cases, assumptions of policymakers to more evidence-based analysis. It is necessary to search for new industrial promotion measures with an understanding of the industrial structure and trading structure of companies by data analysis. The city of Utsunomiya initiated the Utsunomiya Leading Company Support Project[23] in April 2019. This project supports companies that have a certain scale of sales and employment, which contribute to the regional economy through business transactions with other companies and have high growth potential as "leading companies in Utsunomiya" among companies headquartered in the city.[24] As of March 2020, six companies have been certified as leading companies.[25] It is not possible at this time to assess whether this policy has been successful. However, it is true that they have already developed evidence-based local industrial promotion measures. It is therefore possible to expect these innovative companies with the strategic management policy to have a positive impact on the regional economy in Utsunomiya.

Acknowledgements This paper is based on the contents of Niwa (2015, 2019), with modifications and data updates.

Notes

1. There are 25 municipalities in Tochigi Prefecture, including Utsunomiya.
2. Tochigi Prefecture, Industries in Tochigi ~ Advanced Fields of Industries are clustered ~ . Available online: http://www.pref.tochigi.lg.jp/kogyo/english/location/industry.html (accessed on April 1, 2020).
3. LQij is the ratio of the size of j industry in i region (the ratio of j industry to all industries in i region) to the size of the same j industry in the whole country (the ratio of j industry in the country to all industries in the country). If LQij exceeds 1, j industry in i region can be interpreted as specialization.
4. An industry with an LQ of more than 1 for the number of employees is interpreted as Industrial Agglomeration.
5. Ministry of Internal Affairs and Communications provided the "Japan Standard Industry Classification," which classifies businesses into the major divisions, the middle divisions, and the minor groups.
6. In the case of a government-ordinance-designated city, a ward unit was included in the analysis. However, since the city of Hamamatsu was not designated as of 2006, it is included in the analysis.
7. The M Value was replaced with a real value to compare in different time series, using the output price index of the manufacturing industry (2011 base) provided by the Bank of Japan.
8. These are Aircraft and Parts; Agricultural Machinery and Equipment, Except Agricultural Tools; and Establishments Engaged in Administrative or Ancillary Economic Activities (Miscellaneous Manufacturing Industries). It should be noted that the last one is not a factory mainly engaged in production.
9. For example, if the test with significance level $\alpha = 0.05$ is repeated 20 times, the likelihood of rejecting the null hypothesis even once is 0.642, and if it is repeated 100 times, it is 0.994. Available online: http://www.med.osaka-u.ac.jp/pub/kid/clinicaljournalclub1.html (in Japanese, accessed on April 1, 2020).
10. Assuming that the number of test districts is $n = 1000$, an accuracy of $\alpha = 0.00005$ is required for each test district to ensure an overall significance level of $\alpha = 0.05$.
11. The test was performed using the Cluster and Outlier Analysis of ArcGIS ver. 10.3.1. For the Spatial Relationships between features, the K-nearest neighbors was used and set to select the five neighboring municipalities from every feature. This was to reduce the impact of area size of the municipality. GeoDa ver.1.14.0 was used for this treatment (Anselin et al. 2006).
12. For example, Yamamoto (2011) and Research Institute, Japan Finance Corporation (2011).
13. It is an international certification for special process operations in the aerospace industry. Some companies have also obtained certification in Utsunomiya.
14. Boeing, Boeing Sets New Airplane Delivery Records, Expands Order Backlog, retrieved March 1, 2020, https://boeing.mediaroom.com/2019-01-08-Boeing-Sets-New-Airplane-Delivery-Records-Expands-Order-Backlog.
15. To make matters worse, Mani announced they will move their headquarter to Takanezawa Town. Shimotsuke Shinbun newspaper, "Mani to relocate head office functions by 2024, acquire former site of Kirin Brewery in Takanezawa." Available online: https://www.shimotsuke.co.jp/articles/-/297357 (in Japanese, accessed on April 4, 2020).
16. Utsunomiya University, "Roadmap of Utsunomiya University Center for Optical Research and Education." Available online: http://www.opt.utsunomiya-u.ac.jp/center/roadmap.html (in Japanese, accessed on April 1, 2020).
17. The physical distance of transactions through latitude and longitude is not useful for the analysis because it would have to be discussed at the headquarters level.
18. All of companies has been anonymized. As described in Niwa (2018), this data does not encompass all companies. Coverage in the manufacturing sector is expected to be about 40 percent.

19. Tochigi Prefecture started the certification of frontier companies in 2003. As of 2018, 246 companies had been certified, and this paper analyzes companies up to those certified as of 2017. Companies that are certified as a frontier must obtain technical certification every three years or lose their certification.
20. Both forms of centrality were calculated by Gephi ver.0.9.2 (Bastian et al. 2009).
21. Additionally, there remains the question of whether the figures are reliable or not due to the number of companies involved being extremely small.
22. The data on business-to-business networks in RESAS is available only to municipalities.
23. The city of Utsunomiya, "Utsunomiya Leading Company Support Project." Available online: https://www.city.utsunomiya.tochigi.jp/sangyo/sangyo/1018916.html (in Japanese, accessed on April 1, 2020).
24. The most recent sales must be 500 million yen or more and the number of regular employees must be 30 or more.
25. Nihon Keizai Shinbun newspaper, "Utsunomiya awarded six companies in the city with leading company certificates." Available online: https://www.nikkei.com/article/DGXMZO52451250R21C19A1L60000/ (in Japanese, accessed on April 1, 2020).

References

Anselin L (1995) Local indicators of spatial association: LISA. Geogr Anal 27:93–115

Anselin L, Syabri I, Kho Y (2006) GeoDa: An introduction to spatial data analysis. Geogr Anal 38:5–22

Arrow KJ (1962) The economic implications of learning by doing. Rev Econ Stud 29:155–173

Bastian M, Heymann S, Jacomy M (2009) Gephi: An open source software for exploring and manipulating networks. In: Proceedings of Third International AAAI Conference on Weblogs and Social Media, pp 361–362.

Beaudry C, Schiffauerova A (2009) Who's right, Marshall or Jacobs? The localization versus urbanization debate. Res Policy 38:318–337

Benjamini Y, Hochberg Y (1995) Controlling the false discovery rate: A practical and powerful approach to multiple testing. J Roy Stat Soc: Ser B (methodol) 57:289–300

Boschma RA, Frenken K (2006) Why is economic geography not an evolutionary science? Towards an evolutionary economic geography. J Econ Geogr 6:273–302

Boschma RA, Frenken K (2011) The emerging empirics of evolutionary economic geography. J Econ Geogr 11:295–307

Boschma RA, Martin R (2010) The aims and scope of evolutionary economic geography. In: Boschma RA, Martin R (eds) Handbook on evolutionary economic geography. Edward Elgar, Cheltenham, pp 3–39

Caldas de Castro M, Singer BH (2006) Controlling the false discovery rate: A new application to account for multiple and dependent tests in local statistics of spatial association. Geogr Anal 38:180–208

Economic and Enterprise Committee (2012) Corporate Location Strategy. Report on a specific theme of Economic and Enterprise Committee, Tochigi Prefecture. (J)

Frenken K, van Oort F, Verburg T (2007) Related variety, unrelated variety and regional economic growth. Reg Stud 41:685–697

Fujii D, Saito YU, Senga T (2017) The dynamics of inter-firm networks and firm growth. RIETI Discussion Paper Series 17-E-110.

Fujii S (2013) Economic resilience. Nippon Hyoron Sha, Tokyo.

Fukuda R, Kidokoro T, Sato R (2015) Peculiarity on structure of metropolitan areas based on networks of inter-firm deals: comprehensive demonstration all over Japan using Big Data. J City Plan Inst Japan 50:560–567. (J)

Fukumoto T (2010) Changes in spatial segregation of foreigners in Tokyo and Osaka: Differences between "Oldtimers" and "Newcomers." Geograph Rev Japan 83A:288–313. (J)
Glaeser EL, Kallal HD, Scheinkman JA et al (1992) Growth in cities. J Polit Econ 100:1126–1152
Goovaerts P (2010) How do multiple testing correction and spatial autocorrelation affect areal boundary analysis? Spatial and Spatio-Temporal Epidemiology 1:219–229
Goto H, Takayasu H, Takayasu M (2015) Empirical analysis of firm-dynamics on Japanese interfirm trade network. Proceedings of the International Conference on Social Modeling and Simulation, plus Econophysics Colloquium 2014. https://doi.org/10.1007/978-3-319-20591-5_18.
Grekousis G (2018) Further widening or bridging the gap? A cross-regional study of unemployment across the EU Amid Economic Crisis. Sustainability 10:1–18
de Groot HLF, Poot J, Smit MJ (2016) Which agglomeration externalities matter most and why? J Econ Surv 30:756–782
Gu Z, Gu L, Eils R, Schlesner M, Brors B (2014) Circlize implements and enhances circular visualization in R. Bioinformatics 30:2811–2812
Guillain R, Gallo JL (2010) Agglomeration and dispersion of economic activities in and around Paris: An exploratory spatial data analysis. Environment and Planning B: Urban Analytics and City Science 37:961–981
Hassink R, Hu X, Shin DH, Yamamura S, Gong H (2018) The restructuring of old industrial areas in East Asia. Area Development and Policy 3:185–202
Henderson V, Kuncoro A, Turner M (1995) Industrial development in cities. J Polit Econ 103:1067–1090
Ida N (2006) A Spatial Econometric Analysis of Manufacturing Agglomeration in Osaka. The Doshisha University Economic Review 57: 531–554. (J)
Ito M (2011). Shin chiiki sangyo ron (New theory of regional industries: Seeking to industrial localization). Gakubunsha, Tokyo. (J)
Ito M (2008) Chiiki koyo kaihatsu to jinzai ikusei (Local job creation and human resource development: Focusing on manufacturing and industrial agglomeration). Business Labor Trend 11:2–6. (J)
Jacobs J (1969) The economy of cities. Random House, New York
Kagami M, Tsuji M (2003) Industrial agglomeration: facts and lessons for developing countries. Institute of Developing Economies (IDE), JETRO, Chiba.
Kawamoto H, Takayasu H, Takayasu M (2015) Analysis of network robustness for a japanese business relation network by percolation simulation. In: Takayasu H, Ito N, Noda I, Takayasu M (eds), Proceedings of the international conference on social modeling and simulation, plus econophysics colloquium 2014. https://doi.org/10.1007/978-3-319-20591-5_11
Kondo A (2004) Restructuring interplant divisions of labor and local subcontracting linkages: A case study of a Japanese TV Manufacturer. Geographical Review of Japan 77:649–674. (J)
Machida M (2009) Industrial diversity, localized competition and agglomeration economies. Econ Business Rev 21:9–20. (J)
Malizia EE, Ke S (1993) The influence of economic diversity on unemployment and stability. J Reg Sci 33:221–235
Marshall A (1890) Principles of economics. Macmillan, London
Matsuhashi K, Mizuno M, Kashima H, Oda H (2013) A Review of geographical studies on manufacturing industries in Japan. Geographical Review of Japan 86B:82–91
Miyazawa H (2003) Uneven nursing care service opportunity and the behavior of service providers under the long-term care insurance system: a statistical analysis in the Kanto District. Geograph Rev Japan 76:59–80. (J)
Mizuno M (2004) Technological innovations and geographic proximity in interfirm networks: A case study of small and medium-sized enterprises in Osaka Prefecture. Geograph Rev Japan 77:940–953. (J)
Moran PAP (1948) The interpretation of statistical maps. J Roy Stat Soc B 10:243–251
Nakamura R (2008) Measurement of economic agglomeration in urban/regional area (1). Okayama Econ Rev 39(4):99–121. (J)

Niwa T (2015) GIS analysis for industrial agglomeration: Case study of Utsunomiya City. Hyogo Geograph J 60:57–66. (J)
Niwa T (2018) Outline of structures of transactions among companies in Tochigi prefecture, Japan. Annual Report of Research Center for Regional Revitalization Teikyo University 2:94–100. (J)
Niwa T (2019) Network Analysis of Manufacturing Companies in Tochigi Prefecture. Ann Japan Assoc Econ Geograph 65:213–216. (J)
Ogawa Y (1995) The spatial organization of Nissan's parts suppliers in Japan. Japanese J Human Geogr 47:313–334. (J)
Research Institute, Japan Finance Corporation (2011) The actual conditions of the parts supply structure and the entrance into the aircraft industry: the real image of suppliers of aircraft components including airframe, engine and individual parts. Report of Research Institute, Japan Finance Corporation No. 2010–3. (J)
Romer PM (1986) Increasing returns and long-run growth. J Polit Econ 94:1002–1037
Rutten R, Boekema F (2007) Regional social capital: embeddedness, innovation networks and regional economic development. Technol Forecast Soc Chang 74:1834–1846
Schlunze RD, Agola NO, Baber WW (eds) (2012) Spaces of international economy and management: launching new perspectives on management and geography. Palgrave MacMillan, Basingstoke, Hampshire
Tsujita M (2005) Wagakuni seizo gyo ni okeru sangyo shuseki kozo no henyo to sono genin (Transformation and Causes of the Industrial Agglomeration Structure in the Japanese Manufacturing Industry). The 21st Century Public Policy Institute Report 1–23. (J)
Ukai S (1990) Yuchi dai kojo gun to chusho kigyo (Attracting large factories and small and medium-sized enterprises: factory bases in north Kanto region and Utsunomiya technopolis). In: Seki M, Kashiwagi T (eds) Chiiki sangyo no shinko senryaku (Promotion strategies for regional industry). Shinhyoron, Tokyo: 86–114. (J)
Ukai S (2006) Utsunomiya chiiki ni okeru sangyo shinko no kadai (Issues for Industrial Promotion in Utsunomiya Region). Utsunomiya Machizukuri Ronshu (Essay on Utsunomiya City Planning) 2:1–6. (J)
Van der Panne G (2004) Agglomeration externalities: Marshall versus Jacobs. J Evol Econ 14:593–604
Wakabayashi Y, Koizumi R (2014) Spatial patterns of population change in the 23 Special Wards of Tokyo after the Period of the Bubble Economy. J Geogr (Chigaku Zasshi) 123:249–268. (J)
Yaginuma Y, Goto H, Yamamura S, Yamazaki Y (2013) Accumulation process of small knowledge service enterprises in the suburb of Tokyo metropolitan area: the relationship between location preference of the manager and the regionality of Kamakura & Zushi seaside accumulation area. J Arch Plan 78:1311–1320. (J)
Yamada E, Kawakami T (2012) Distribution of industrial growth in the Nagoya Metropolitan Area, Japan: Focusing on geographical and technological proximity. Working Paper Series No. E-24, Kinki University.
Yamamoto K, Matsuhashi K (1999) Networking in an industrial area characterized by agglomeration of SMEs. The Hosei Univ Econ Rev 66:85–182. (J)
Yamamoto M (2011) A study of new turn for entrance into the market based on the trend of aerospace industry in Japan: A case study of local level. Bull Econ Res Inst, Japan Society for the Promotion of Machine Industry 42:43–57. (J)
Yokura Y (2014) Performances and roles of local trade fairs in Japan: case study on the Suwa Area Industrial Messe, Nagano Prefecture. Komaba Studies in Human Geography 21:85–100
Yokura Y (2016) Temporary space and business-matching networks of the semiconductor industry in Kyushu, Japan. J Int Econ Stud 30:3–12

Zuo Y, Kajikawa Y (2017) Toward a theory of industrial supply networks: a multi-level perspective via network analysis. Entropy 19:382. https://doi.org/10.3390/e19080382
(J) denotes literature in Japanese.

Unique Functions of a Co-Working Space in a Metropolis: A Case Study in Tokyo, Japan

Kenta Yamamoto

Abstract As a new kind of workspace, a co-working space is distinguished from spaces for traditional telecommuters and nomad workers and from community third places. This paper examines co-working spaces and their functions on two spatial scales. First we will examine the co-working space on a micro scale, examining the function of each worker's space within the co-working space. Then we will explore its function on a macro scale, i.e., the role of the co-working space within the larger urban setting. Along with these discussions, the effects of such spaces on creativity in the metropolis are also mentioned. A questionnaire survey administered to the operators of Tokyo co-working spaces found that. Co-working spaces in Tokyo have developed in unique ways in accordance with Japanese corporate culture and working environment. In addition, co-working spaces serve as "creative nexuses," affecting the identity formation of users and offering them easy opportunities to encounter other users in different occupations. The co-working spaces of Tokyo provide space and basic services for professionals and allow them access to a variety of ways of working and expressing creativity in the metropolis.

Keywords Co-working space · Professionals · Start-ups · Freelances · Urban space · Tokyo

1 Introduction

1.1 Co-Working Spaces as Workplaces

In recent years, long-term employment trends such as increases in contract employment and freelance work and advances in communication and mobile technologies are driving changes to work environments. Such changes include work outside office spaces and collaboration in other kinds of spaces (Spinuzzi 2012). The growth of the knowledge economy and the service sector led to a range of changes in working style

K. Yamamoto (✉)
Faculty of Economics, Kokugakuin University, Tokyo 150-8440, Japan
e-mail: kenta@kokugakuin.ac.jp

A. Taira and R. D. Schlunze (eds.), *Management Geography*, International Perspectives in Geography 19, https://doi.org/10.1007/978-981-19-4403-1_7

and enhanced the mobility of workers. As a result, it has become difficult to assess the state of workers inside cities through analysis of census data or establishment registries (Pajević and Shearmur 2017). In Japan, a so-called "nomad" work style has been generally recognized since the 2000s. The working style of these nomads is also not traditional and is difficult to catch using these data. In relation to this background, a new type of workspace called a "co-working space" has attracted attention in mainly urban areas, especially after 2010.

In a co-working space, workers with different areas of expertise engaged in various different jobs work in the same space. Not only are the various amenities that support work provided, but so is the casual communication with other workers during break time, as are seminars for users, knowledge exchange meetings and so on. Therefore, a co-working space is expected to construct new collaborative relationships among users and to facilitate new ideas and innovations. There are different users in a co-working space from those in conventional teleworking spaces. The co-working space is a place to express the creativity of the metropolis.

On the other hand, as Capdevila (2015) and Merkel (2015) have noted, although co-working spaces are becoming ever more common in recent years, the phenomenon has not developed into more than a buzzword and has not yet been clearly defined in relation to its effects on urban space and working environments. As Tremblay and Scaillerez (2020) point out, there have been few studies that focus on co-working spaces, and the main targets of those studies are the self-employed. Not many studies focus on entrepreneurs and salaried workers, although there are no fewer of them. In addition, they note that some studies have provided focused investigations of certain professional fields, such as the information industries and creative industries. Overall, however, co-working spaces in Japan remain largely unstudied. To address this knowledge gap, one of the main aims of this study is to provide a picture of such spaces as one of the first steps in studying them in Japan. To date, the scarcity of such studies has prevented any comparison of the functions of co-working spaces in different cities and countries. This study compares Tokyo's co-working spaces with those of other countries as described in published works, so far as this is possible using available data.

1.2 Third Places and Co-Working Spaces

The study of co-working spaces has just begun and has not yet reached the systematic discussion stage. The accumulation of case studies therefore remains an urgent issue in this field of study. In this subsection, previous studies on co-working spaces are reviewed while related fields of study, especially third place theory, are considered.

There are discussions about "third places" and "co-working spaces" as spaces where workers gather beyond the boundaries of their industries. A third space, as described by Oldenburg (1989), refers to "the core setting of informal public life" other than home (first space) and work (second space) (Oldenburg 1989: 16). In other words, the third space is "a generic designation for a great variety of public places that host the regular, voluntary, informal, and happily anticipated gatherings of individuals beyond the realms of home and work" (Oldenburg 1989: 16). These spaces include the nineteenth century German-American beer gardens, the main streets of pre-war American small towns, English pubs, French cafés, American Taverns, and classic coffeehouses. These are spaces where regular people can talk freely beyond their own status and position. In these spaces, people are able to discover new things, influence others' views on life, and relieve work stress through conversation. The latter is a third space's major purpose, as friends gather there with similar intents.

Originally, the third place was considered a "third" space separate from one's home and workplace, with relationships at the third place separated from one's status and position at work. The concept of a third place was later expanded into the field of economic geography, where scholars pointed out its importance for regional competitiveness, whether directly or metaphorically. For example, in comparing industrial clusters that show two contrasting developments, Silicon Valley and Route 128, Saxenian (1996) discusses "the informal socializing that grew out of these quasi-familial relationships" (Saxenian 1996: 32) as one of the characteristics of Silicon Valley. There, managers and workers who are rivals at work go to bars and parties together informally, exchange information on their interesting technologies, and share helpful experiences. Managers and workers are also friendly with each other's families and the relationships they build are occasionally used when they change jobs. Such open relationships have become a source of innovation and synergy, and are becoming an advantage in Silicon Valley as an area with a concentration of start-up companies.

Merkel (2015) regards co-working as different from shared work and flexible work such as that of the traditional satellite office, the business incubator, and the coffee shop. Co-working is distinct because it is characterized by a "collaborative approach" which promotes the five values of community, collaboration, openness, diversity, and sustainability, and has a background bred by collaborative consumption, the sharing economy, and the open source movement. Fuzi (2015) notes that users of co-working spaces expect to not merely rent workplaces, but also a social environment with entrepreneurial networks and the existence of mentors. Fuzi points out further that the role played by hosts and facilitators in co-working spaces are important factors for facilitating these social aspects. From these studies, it can be concluded that the co-working space has different spatial features from the third place, where there are no defined leaders or managers, but implicit rules in the community, in the general meaning described above.

These social spaces, created by co-working space operators, affect their users' creative activities. Moriset (2013) describes co-working spaces as social spaces that promote meeting and collaboration among creative people and entrepreneurs who often work alone and calls for proper positioning of this new phenomenon, whose role boundaries are fuzzy, in the urban economy. Morrison (2018) also notes the importance of this new boundary in ambiguous places in the present urban space. The paper expands third place theory and finds new social spaces that combine the first, second, and third places, such as the first and second place, in co-living; the second and third place, co-working; the first and third place, comingling; and ones that combine all elements of the three, called the fourth. In addition, the paper notes that an understanding of the nature of these new places should be founded on knowledge of urban areas, where the knowledge industry is agglomerated, which can help scholars understand the spatial structure of urban economies under globalization and post-industrialization.

What role does the co-working space play in urban space? One possible answer is as a "middleground." Grandadam et al. (2013) suggest that traditional (urban economic) policies have focused on the existence of anchor companies and creative classes to attract other companies as a measure of policy effectiveness. However, Grandadam et al. also note, "these creative companies / institutions ('upperground') and individuals ('underground') do not intercommunicate with each other" because they exhibit different modes, or behavioral principles. Grandadam et al. mention also that policies, which only focus on static influences, cannot grasp the dynamics of the whole picture of the process of transferring creative ideas between the two layers of "underground" and "upperground," a process that creates a creative city atmosphere. The concept of "middleground," suggested in Cohendet et al. (2010), is installed between upperground and underground as a connector, and can be examined to understand the dynamics of creativity influenced by the interaction between companies and individuals. This middleground is a concept that includes not only specific spaces such as bars, clubs, concert halls, and galleries, but also so-called third places and some organizations. Workers belonging to the underground tend to have a more exploratory orientation and companies placed on the upperground tend to a have exploitative (profitable) orientation. Actors on this middle layer play the role of finding and stocking prior knowledge, skills, and members from the lower layer and providing these to the upper layer.

Capdevila (2015) examines the location of co-working spaces in Barcelona by utilizing the concept of middleground, by conducting a qualitative survey about 21 of the 118 co-working spaces in Barcelona. This study reveals the functions of co-working spaces at different spatial levels. At the individual level, co-working spaces promote collaboration among workers. At the community level, co-working spaces connect individuals' exploratory work and companies' profitable work. At the company level, the space provides inspiration, ideas, and talents to companies as an outsource. At the local city level, co-working spaces are a platform to integrate knowledge. At the global level, co-working spaces provide temporary clusters by hosting events that external actors can join and sharing external knowledge and local buzz with other participants.

These studies provide an interesting perspective that, on a micro level, explains the dynamics of creativity through concretely connecting actors' activities in inner urban space, and on a macro level, viewing urban activities as an aggregate space of micro activities by positioning the co-working space as an intermediate layer.

Thus, the study of co-working spaces has just begun. To date, there are insufficient reports on the interactions between the interior spaces of buildings and their exterior spaces, i.e., their surrounding urban settings, from conventional academic perspectives such as sociology, urban geography and architectural engineering. This study is expected to suggest a new way of looking at the interactions between these micro spaces and the macro space that is the metropolis.

1.3 Methodology and Outline of This Study

This study examines the spatial characteristics of creativity in Tokyo through the location of co-working spaces and their users. This examination was conducted using a questionnaire survey conducted with co-working spaces in Tokyo. Using the three major co-working space portals, we could find 189 spaces in Tokyo in February 2017.[1] In April 2017, questionnaires were mailed to all 189 studios. 41 spaces, with 38 operators (respondent rate: 22.9%) provided responses. Due to data constraints, it is important to note that these research findings do not indicate the overall industry trends. Although the number of responses is not statistically significant, this type of survey provides some accumulation of data and, as noted above, any data on this topic is currently highly scarce. Therefore, this tries to analyze the data obtained to the extent possible.

Including this section, this study consists of four parts. Section 2 provides an outline of responses. The relationships between the services provided by co-working spaces and the size of these spaces are also examined in this section. In general, space rental fees gradually increase as their size increases. It is necessary for the operators to cover rental costs by increasing the number of users and increasing the unit price for users. From the relationship between a co-working space's size and the service it provides, inferences are made about how spaces are responding to increasing costs.

Section 3 examines location characteristics through the categories of reasons for choosing a location, the users of co-working spaces. Reasons for choosing a location differ depending on the target users for each space. In the downtown area, each district has different functions and visitor characteristics. These factors are considered consciously or unconsciously when operators decide upon the locations of their spaces. After establishing the co-working space, differences in location influence how the space is operated. Such regional differences are also discussed in this section.

Finally, Sect. 4 summarizes the results of the analysis and considers the significance of the existence of co-working spaces for its users and the city.

2 Services in Co-Working Spaces

This section presents the characteristics of our survey respondents and reports on the functions of the interior spaces of co-working spaces in terms of the services that co-working spaces offer their users. As mentioned in Sect. 1, previous studies have pointed out that the community function of such spaces is one of the most appealing aspects of co-working spaces which enables them to attract creative and innovative users. One focus of this section is how co-working spaces serve these community functions as revealed through our survey.

2.1 Location Trends of Co-Working Spaces

Before analyzing the results of the questionnaire survey, the location trends of co-working space are discussed. As mentioned above, the co-working space industry is still considered to be in its takeoff period because of the novelty and scale of the market. In general, industries in this period are gradually expanding in scale due to the entry of entities from neighboring fields. In addition, structural changes within the industry are fast, social recognition and statistical improvement are insufficient, and the industry is defined in various ways by actors inside and outside the industry. It is difficult to grasp the industry's overall picture. Therefore, the spaces described as co-working spaces by the portal sites used for selecting respondents for the questionnaire survey are considered as co-working spaces in this paper and are shown in the location trends for co-working spaces.

The locations of co-working spaces on a nationwide scale are concentrated in urban areas, and mainly in Tokyo. Table 1 shows the number of registered co-working spaces in the portal sites by prefecture. The number of co-working spaces located in Tokyo is 3.4–4.8 times that compared with the next largest concentration, in Osaka.[2] Figure 1 shows the locations of co-working spaces in Tokyo. In the center of Tokyo, spaces are distributed in the area from Shimbashi to Nihonbashi, and even Akihabara, centering on Tokyo Station. On the west side of the JR Yamanote line, co-working spaces are concentrated around Shibuya Station and a 1 km radius around it, near places such as Omotesando Station and Meiji Jingumae Station. The locations of co-working spaces are also concentrated around major transfer stations such as Gotanda Station which connects to the JR Yamanote line, the Tokyu Ikegami line, and the Toei Asakusa line, and near the JR Chuo line connecting the western suburbs and the center of Tokyo, especially Kichijoji Station which connects with the Keio Inokashira line.

2.2 Outline of Responses

All 40 co-working spaces, excluding one established in 2007, opened after 2010. The number of co-working spaces hovers from 2 to 7 until 2015, but increases rapidly to 13 cases in 2016. Such a rapid increase in the number of establishments is generally seen when the industry arrives at the takeoff period from the run-up period. However, the possibility that this rapid increase is an example of a transient boom cannot be denied; thus, it will be necessary to carefully observe industry trends.

Thirty-four stations are listed as nearest station to the co-working spaces, in the 23 wards. Shibuya (3 cases), Ochanomizu, Gotanda, Jinbocho, Tameike-Sanno, and Hachioji (2 cases of each) were listed as their nearest station by multiple co-working spaces. The distribution of the respondents in Tokyo is consistent with the characteristics shown in Fig. 1.

The minimum area of a co-working space is 23 square meters and its maximum area is 991.7 square meters. The average is 232.0 square meters, and the median and

Table 1 The number of registered co-working spaces in the major portal sites

Region	Prefecture	Coworking coop	Co-working.com	Cocopo	Region	Prefecture	Coworking coop	Co-working.com	Cocopo
Hokkaido	Hokkaido	14	11	14	Kinki	Mie	1	4	4
Tohoku	Aomori	1	1	3		Shiga	2	6	6
	Iwate	5	4	5		Kyoto	9	16	19
	Miyagi	6	16	20		Osaka	25	47	52
	Akita	0	1	1		Hyogo	16	24	25
	Yamagata	2	9	8		Nara	1	5	6
	Fukushima	1	6	7		Wakayama	1	1	2
Kanto	Ibaraki	3	4	8	Chugoku	Tottori	0	1	2
	Tochigi	2	4	4		Shimane	0	3	3
	Gunma	4	4	5		Okayama	4	2	3
	Saitama	4	10	11		Hiroshima	3	7	8
	Chiba	8	11	11		Yamaguchi	1	5	5
	Tokyo	120	160	196	Shikoku	Tokushima	2	3	4
	Kanagawa	11	18	27		Kagawa	1	2	3
Chubu	Niigata	1	7	7		Ehime	3	1	2
	Toyama	3	2	3		Kochi	1	1	1
	Ishikawa	2	4	6	Kyushu	Fukuoka	6	10	15
	Fukui	1	3	4		Saga	1	2	2

(continued)

Table 1 (continued)

Region	Prefecture	Coworking coop	Co-working.com	Cocopo	Region	Prefecture	Coworking coop	Co-working.com	Cocopo
	Yamanashi	2	2	7		Nagasaki	4	2	3
	Nagano	9	11	16		Kumamoto	2	4	4
	Gifu	6	4	6		Oita	0	2	2
	Shizuoka	7	6	8		Miyazaki	1	2	3
	Aichi	20	23	24		Kagoshima	2	4	6
						Okinawa	9	4	8
					Total		327	479	589

Sources Coworking coop (http://coworking.coop/), co-working.com (http://co-work-ing.com/), cocopo (http://co-co-po.com/), accessed 20 February 2017

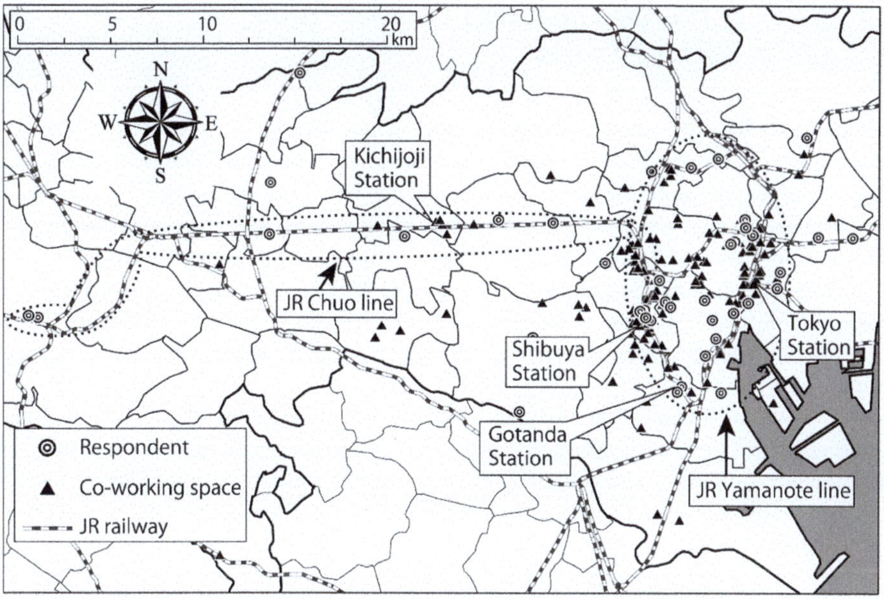

Fig. 1 Distribution of co-working spaces in Tokyo
(*Sources* Coworking coop [http://coworking.coop/], co-working.com [http://co-work-ing.com/], cocopo [http://co-co-po.com/], accessed 20 February 2017 and Questionnaire survey, surveyed April 2017)

the mode are 150 and 100 square meters, respectively. Many of the spaces which have a smaller than average size, occupy multiple-tenant buildings in the center of Tokyo or they are in multiple-tenant buildings or apartment complexes in suburban parts of the city. The spaces where area size is greater than the median are located in the center of Tokyo (3 in Shibuya Ward, 4 in Minato Ward, 1 in Shinagawa Ward), except for 1 case (Setagaya Ward).[3]

Eighteen respondents answered that their days off are every Sunday and holidays Fourteen co-working spaces are also closed on Saturdays. In addition, four spaces close during the Bon Festival and during the year-end and new-year holidays. Twenty-six of forty-one co-working spaces can be used 24 h a day (including "24 hours available for registered members"). Spaces that can be used throughout the day are located alongside the Tokyo Metro or the Toei metropolitan subway, with the exception of one store. One aspect of the various ways of working in the center of Tokyo can be noted from the presence of these spaces.

2.3 *Services Provided and Area Characteristics of Co-Working Spaces*

Services provided by each co-working space is shown in Fig. 2. Thirty-nine of 41 spaces provide "free access" in the lounge ("sharing lounge").[4] The average value, median value, and mode value of provided sheets on a "sharing lounge," as provided by 39 cases are 25.4 sheets, 24 sheets, and 20 sheets, respectively. According to information provided on co-working space websites, in one of the two cases that do not provide a "sharing lounge," many chairs and desks are arranged in a vast lounge space. In another case, a co-working space rents a room based on a charge by time. The first of these cases can be said to providing its space to users as a de facto sharing lounge.

Although it is thought that the types of services provided depend on the difference in the target users of each space, the provision of lounge space, lockers in which to keep business supplies, addresses for business cards, and mail reception are provided by more than 80% of respondents and can, thus, be regarded as the basic services of co-working spaces.

Baby-sitting is a signature response. The two respondents providing this service are located in suburban areas. One occupies a vacant storefront on a shopping street and the other is located in a room of an apartment house. These spaces are less than 100 square meters in size, the average value. These co-working spaces also

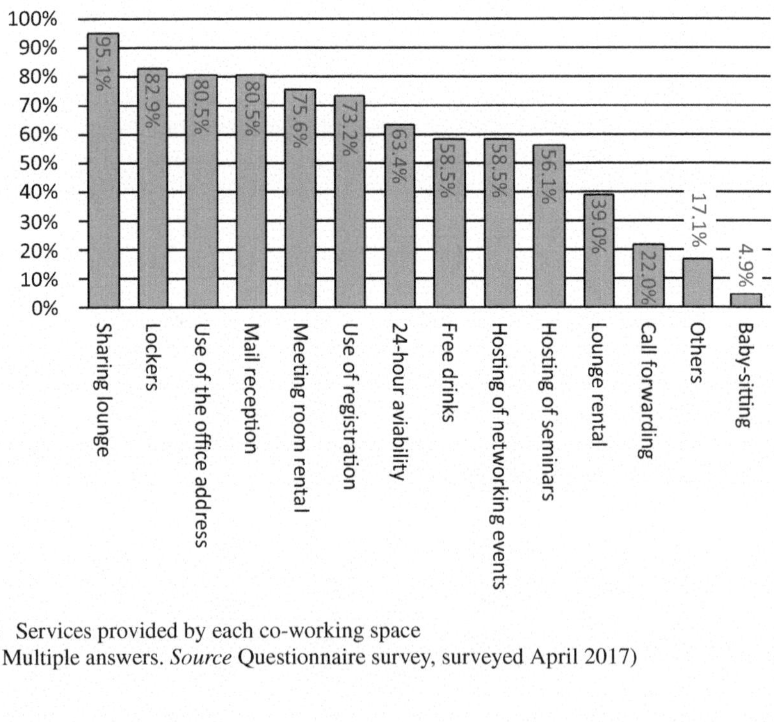

Fig. 2 Services provided by each co-working space
(*Note* Multiple answers. *Source* Questionnaire survey, surveyed April 2017)

provide hosting seminars and kitchen rentals. Their websites describe these spaces as providing services for "women wishing to work."[5] It is inferred that these spaces are also used as salons for information exchange between users.

With the exception of one respondent, all of the co-working spaces set the same price plans for individuals and corporations. In the exceptional case, the difference between individual plans and corporate plans is in the ability to use registration. Factually, this difference can be simply regarded as one of the plan's options. The lowest price range among the 34 co-working spaces that responded to the question of the cost of the monthly plan is 0–25,000 yen. The average monthly fee is 8,964 yen, and the median and mode values are each 5,000 yen. Spaces that answered that their lowest price is 0 yen do not allow drop-ins[6] and can only be used by registrants. In this case, the registration fee is free but use of the space costs 300 yen per hour. The ranges of the highest prices given by respondents, including adding all options, is from 5,000 to 570,000 yen. The average is 68,131 yen, with a median value of 30,000 yen, and a mode value of 15,000 yen. This indicates that a small number of shops set expensive prices and a large number of shops set inexpensive prices, because the average value exceeds the median value and the mode value is lower than the median value for both the lowest price and the highest price.

The average total membership number of individual and corporate members is 54.04, with a median value of 28. According to deskmag (2018), the mean number of members is 159, and the median is 45. The breakdown of the number of members in that survey shows that 33% of spaces have less than 25 members, and 17% are more than 200 members. As result of our survey, 48% of spaces, excepting those answering 0, responded less than 25 members, and 4% responded more than 200 members. The tendency of the number of members of the co-working space in this survey is smaller than the tendency worldwide.

As the size of the space increases, the facility management cost also increases. In order to secure the necessary operating expenses, large spaces are required to secure more users or set higher user unit prices than small spaces.

However, even some large co-working spaces set a relatively inexpensive highest membership price. Case A is situated in a suburban area, where land prices are lower than in the center of Tokyo. In addition, the number of users is secured by installing many lounge seats instead of booths[7] or private rooms with high unit prices. Case B is located in the center of the city, but the operating company's main business is investment in start-up companies and the provision of the lounge in the co-working space is viewed as part of that investment in start-up companies.

Two respondents are assumed to be co-working spaces for drop-in use only. On average, the number of users of these two co-working spaces is around 35 people on weekdays, and around 50 people on weekends and public holidays, indicating that these spaces are used on weekends and holidays rather than on weekdays. In all the respondents except these two cases, the number of drop-in users per day is less than 10 people. Thus, it is hard to say that drop-in is a general usage of a co-working space.

In Fuzi's (2015) report on the services provided by two typical co-working spaces in South Wales, each of the co-working spaces examined was used by 150–200 people, the workplace layout consists of open offices, private offices, meeting rooms, a coffee corner, and other common workplace features, and each space provides its users with a business address, an office, broadband internet, and holding professional events. Equivalent facilities and services are provided by co-working spaces in Tokyo. More than half of our respondents reported that they host social events at the co-working spaces and that they have opportunities to actively pursue interaction with their fellow users and with external actors. On the other hand, our survey found that relatively few drop-in users use the Tokyo co-working spaces. This suggests that a half-opened community has been formed, in which most users who use the space are registered users and have a clear sense of ownership or belonging in the co-working space. Some co-working spaces located in the city center tend to require high usage fees in exchange for high-quality services and large office spaces; in these spaces, users tend to avoid exchanging offices with others. Some of these spaces provide private offices and meeting rooms only without open lounges. This suggests that the operators and users of these spaces understand them not as spaces for building social networks but rather as new forms of rental offices and rental meeting rooms. In addition, some spaces offer workspace for women only and even provide onsite baby-sitting. These characteristics can be regarded as unique responses to the unique Japanese working environment.

3 Location Characteristics and User Characteristics of Co-Working Spaces

The relationships between the interior space of a co-working space and the services provided there were discussed in the previous section. In this section, the interactions between the interior space of a co-working space and the surrounding external space are examined with attention to the operators' choices regarding locations for co-working spaces and the characteristics of their users.

3.1 Reasons for Choosing a Location

There are positive and negative factors for operators to consider in choosing a location for such a space. Operators choose locations strategically to ensure their business success; in advertising the spaces, they often provide images of the surrounding locations, and emphasize the accessibility of the town and the proximity of the nearest station as positive reasons to work there.

Table 2 was created from the responses to three important reasons for choosing the district where the co-working space is located. The respondents who said that they could not rank reasons are viewed as having selected all of the reasons as the most important. Figure 3 shows the distribution of major responses. "Owning

Table 2 Three reasons for choosing location, ranked by importance

Reasons	First	Second	Third
Owning property	8	0	0
Positive images of the nearest station	6	4	1
Positive images of the district	6	3	3
Good accessibility to the terminal station	5	7	4
Good accessibility to the center of Tokyo	5	7	2
Others	5	0	2
Few other spaces located	2	4	3
Inexpensiveness of rents in the district	2	2	5
Quiet environment	2	0	2
Residential district	1	2	1
Support from administration	1	2	0
Shopping district	1	0	0
Business district	0	1	2
Much other spaces located	0	1	0
Bustling environment	0	0	2
Much commercial facilities located	0	0	1

Source Questionnaire survey, surveyed April 2017

property" and "positive images" related to the location are emphasized not only in the center of Tokyo, but also in suburban areas. By contrast, accessibility related items are emphasized by the spaces located around and inside the JR Yamanote line and shown as a spatially unevenly distributed tendency.

"Owning property" is distinct in being selected only as the most important reason. Considering the answer "a vacant room in the office" in "others," operators might, first, judge whether they have a property for that could serve as a co-working space when they choose a district. Because a co-working space business is highly novel and the business model is immature, investment in this business probably includes speculative possibilities, and it seems that business owners emphasize keeping the initial costs and the subsequent operation expenses low as a means of reducing risk.

Accessibility and the images of place garnered responses from all ranks. These are important factors for operators to consider when choosing the location of their space. The images of the district and the nearest station are formed as part of the entire landscape, including the people and stores in the area. This image is not separable from the intentions of the co-working space operator, which include questions about how to set a co-working space's atmosphere, and what kinds of users the space should target.

Yet, operators they do not emphasize the types of spaces around the location, such as offices, housing, the concentration of cultural facilities and commercial facilities. That is, while emphasizing the image of the place, when they choose a location,

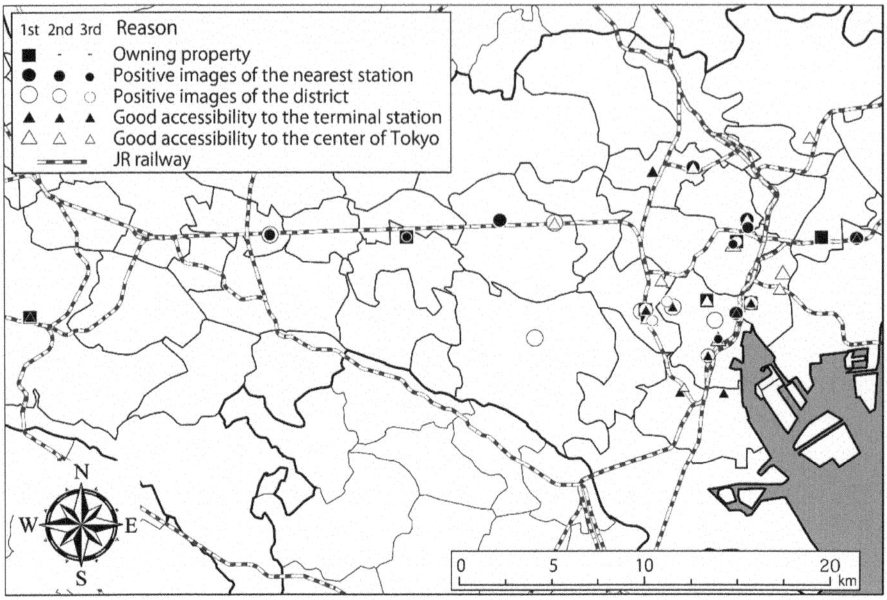

Fig. 3 Distribution of major reasons for choosing a location (*Source* Questionnaire survey, surveyed April 2017)

co-working space operators are not fully conscious of the interaction between the co-working space and its surrounding real environment. Nonetheless, some respondents are conscious of the connection with the surrounding environment. For example, in a space that is evaluated as a "residential area," points out "a quiet environment" and "a large number of waiting children" in the area as "others" without specifying a ranking. In another example, a space located in the center of Tokyo describes "a location similar to Silicon Valley," suggesting an accumulation of emerging companies or IT related companies.[8]

Three respondents emphasize support from the administration. These are located in suburban areas where the nearest stations are Kinshi-cho, Mitaka, and Hachioji. These co-working spaces are distinct in the particularity of their form of business, such as occupying a room in a public facility or holding a seminar for employment support as a space dedicated to women. There are also respondents that pointed out the existence of other spaces and inexpensive rents. However, these reasons are ranked second or lower, and are considered additional reasons for choosing a location.

Thus some co-working space operators location report that they chose their spaces based on relatively negative factors such as wishing to make use of vacant real estate that they had already owned. Others, however, chose their locations for positive reasons such as the locations' attractiveness to a specific user type, i.e., its proximity to a town where their target users prefer to gather. What kind of people actually use co-working spaces? Some answers are given in the next subsection.

3.2 User Characteristics

To shed light on the characteristics of the users of co-working spaces, our operator questionnaire asked about users' age distribution, employment status, occupational fields, and other facts. The uneven distribution of these attributes in specific areas of the city confirmed that different locations attract different types of users.

The employment status of registered individual users confirms that small business owners are users at 16 (80%) of the 20 spaces at which responses were obtained. The proportion of small business owners is more than 50% of users in 12 of these 16 respondents. Thus, it can be seen that small business owners are major users of these co-working spaces. Similarly, in terms of the proportion of corporate users by size, it is possible to confirm the use of small businesses in all 15 spaces that responded to this question. The proportion of corporate users in these 12 spaces exceeds 90%. The proportions of corporate users in the other three spaces are also 50% or more.

Twenty-six spaces responded to the questions about users' main age range. Sixteen co-working spaces (61.5%) answered "30s" while seven spaces (26.9%) answered "40s." According to "the Survey on State of Business Startups 2016" (Japan Finance Corporation Research Institute 2016), the average age at start-up in Japan is 35.3% in the 30s and 34.5% in the 40s. Thus, it can be inferred that the "small businesses" frequently referred to in this survey are start-up companies.

Freelancers are registered individual users at 17 (85%) of the 20 spaces from which responses were obtained. The proportion of freelancers to users in each space ranged from 3 to 93%. The average proportion is 31.4 which is the second highest after small business owners. Freelancers are under contract for each project, and a desk and chair are not always available to them at the company for which they are contracted to work. Although some freelancers do not have a corporate personality, they are actually treated as individual business owners.

The co-working space is an "office" which is a dedicated place for work, and, for teleworking or for nomads, the co-working space is different not only from home but also from libraries, cafés, and so on. As Tremblay and Scaillerez (2020) also point out, the space plays an important role for its owners, for start-up companies with poor capital, and for freelancers who change work place depending on the project.

The distribution of co-working spaces for each occupation type among individual registrants and business type among corporate registrants shows that individual users are distributed not only in the center of Tokyo, but also in Tokyo's western suburbs (for instance, alongside the JR Chuo line), while corporate users are mainly distributed along the Yamanote line and its inner side. As mentioned above, individual registrants are mainly composed of small business owners and freelancers. This constitution and the fact that individual registrants are also found at the spaces in the west suburbs of Tokyo might indicate that freelancers work close to their homes in the Tokyo suburbs. One of the reasons why corporate users are frequently found in the co-working spaces located in urban areas is that a suppression of transaction costs can be expected for companies with many business transactions, which emphasize proximity to business partners due to the necessity of face-to-face contact. At the same time, this finding suggests the possibility that the co-working space is an incubator for small businesses in the start-up phase as the spaces located in the center of Tokyo provide services such as registration and office rental to start-up companies.

The most popular occupational fields of individual users among respondents are "creative" (9), "consulting/finance/real-estate" (6), and "web/internet/video game" (5) (Table 3). The most popular business fields of corporate users are "IT/communication/Internet" (8), "consulting" (5), "service and leisure" (5) (Table 4).[9] There are also differences in the distribution of the occupational fields of individual users and business fields of corporate users (Fig. 4 and 5). For example, the distribution of individual registrants engaged in consulting and corporate registrants in the consulting industry are distributed on the east side of the JR Yamanote line, in areas like Shimbashi and Ginza. Individual users engaged in creative fields and corporate users in mass communication/advertisement/design industry are distributed mainly in the Shibuya and Shinagawa areas. Since the importance of the image of the district and the nearest station are emphasized as the reasons for choosing the location of these co-working spaces, it is suggested that the location preferences of these industries and their related industries are also concentrated in specific districts.

Table 3 Popular fields of work of individual users

Occupation fields	First	Second	Third
Creative	9	5	5
Consulting/finance/real-estate	6	5	4
Web/internet/video games	5	6	7
Childcare/education/translation	4	0	1
IT engineering	3	4	3
Corporate planning	2	3	5
Beauty care/bridal/lodging/traffic	1	0	0
Electric machine related	1	0	0
Sales/restaurant/amusement	0	1	1
Management	0	1	0
Medical/welfare	0	1	0
Architecture/engineering	0	1	0
Medicine/foods/chemical/materials	0	0	1

Source Questionnaire survey, surveyed April 2017

Table 4 Popular business fields of corporate users

Business fields	First	Second	Third
IT/communication/internet	8	7	7
Consulting	5	9	9
Service/leisure	5	3	3
Mass communication/advertising/design	4	1	1
Manufacturer	1	1	1
Public agency/others	1	0	0
Real estate/construction/equipment	0	2	2
Environment/energy	0	1	1

Source Questionnaire survey, surveyed April 2017

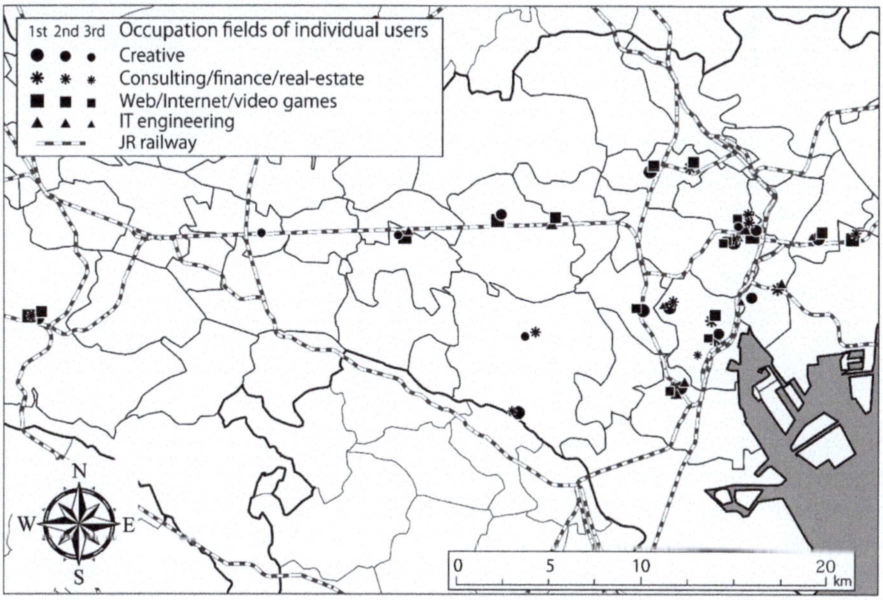

Fig. 4 Distribution of individual users engaged in major fields of work (*Source* Questionnaire survey, surveyed April 2017)

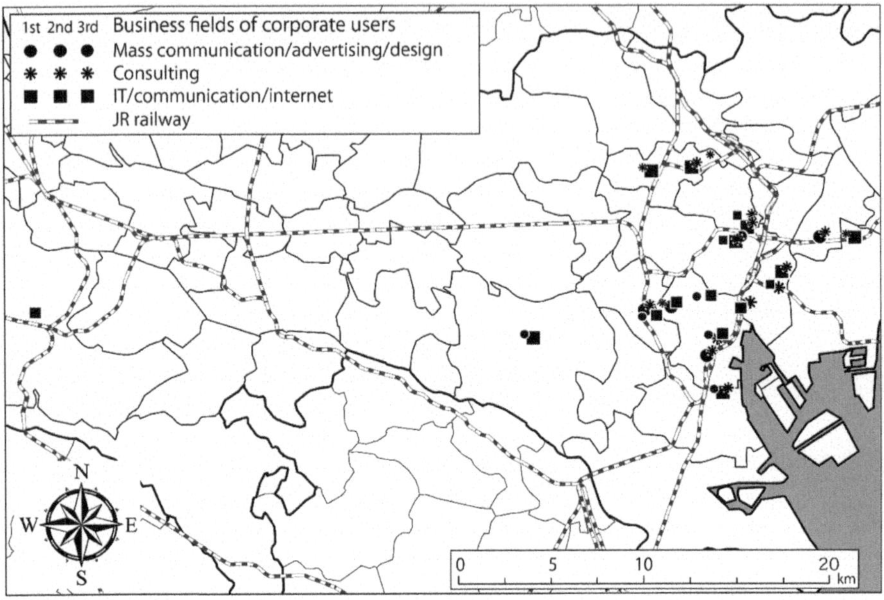

Fig. 5 Distribution of corporate users in major business fields (*Source* Questionnaire survey, surveyed April 2017)

4 Discussion

4.1 Findings of This Study

This chapter aims to discuss the spatial features of creativity in the metropolis. This chapter has found that the nationwide location trend for co-working spaces shows a concentration in Tokyo. Even within the broader Tokyo metropolitan area, Tokyo is preferred, and the number of co-working spaces located in the major cities of neighboring prefectures, such as Yokohama, Saitama, Chiba, are small in comparison with the size of the cities. In Tokyo, there is a concentration of co-working spaces on the east side of the JR Yamanote line centering around Tokyo Station and a concentration from Shibuya to Omotesando area. There are also co-working spaces scattered around Gotanda and around the terminal station along the JR Chuo Line.

The distribution of year co-working spaces was established begins from 2007, with the largest number established in 2016. It is suggested that the industry is expanding rapidly. Many of the spaces 100–150 square meters in size, and a small number of large spaces drive up the average value. It is rare that real estate is dedicated to a co-working space, and many of the co-working spaces occupy office buildings, multi-tenant buildings, apartment complexes, and so on.

Most co-working spaces are available 24 h a day, and more are located in the city center than in the suburbs. Lounge space, lockers, an address description on business cards, and mail receipt are the basic services provided by co-working spaces. The user cost varies depending on the location of the space, the space's size and the type of services offered, but it is suggested that a polarized structure exists where a small number of spaces make all options available at high prices and a large number of spaces make all options available at low prices.

As Capdevila (2015) and Moriset (2013) points out, the co-working space has functions that differ from traditional telework and nomad work. It functions as a platform for knowledge formed by users working and exchanging ideas with others in diverse positions and various jobs both inside and outside the space. These values were also reported by Nadant et al. (2018). Geographical proximity alone is not very effective in promoting collaborations among workers. Proximity of opportunity, such as casual encounters and social events, are also important for promoting collaboration. Agglomeration of the same or neighboring industries makes it easy to find common topics among users in these industries. Yet, only less than 60% of the respondents to this study provide seminars and networking events. Some of the respondents do provide lounge and meeting room rentals. These facts can be interpreted as indicating that a not insignificant number of co-working spaces do not sufficiently assume interactions between users. It is suggested that the current purpose of co-working spaces in Tokyo is different from that in Western countries, as developed based on the collaborative approach described by Merkel (2015).

Owning property, positive images of the district and the nearest station are emphasized as reasons for choosing a location. Location near the center of the city, good accessibility to the center and terminal stations are additional reasons for choosing a location for a co-working space.

These reasons show that working in the city itself, affects the identity formation for users of the co-working space. Co-working spaces have benefits for start-up companies with poor transaction results and freelancers without capital strength who can build business client by using the co-working spaces as a contact for business cards. Tremblay and Scaillerez (2020) point out that co-working space is an option for small-scale business and entrepreneurs to obtain new knowledge with low costs through collaboration with other users on the space. In fact, co-working spaces in Tokyo are not without such aspects but are not necessarily organized for social events, which tends to be preferred by entrepreneurs, partly because of their social reputation in where the space is located.

User characteristics depend on the location of the co-working space. It is suggested that creatives, IT engineers, programmers, professionals, and others prefer particular districts in the metropolis and loosely agglomerate in those districts. Many of these users are small start-ups and freelancers. Co-working spaces provide the basic functions necessary for their work. At the same time, co-working spaces functions as a guarantee for workers of diverse work styles in various categories within the metropolis of Tokyo.

As mentioned above, some co-working spaces are nothing more than rental offices. This is related to the fact that this industry is still at the starting line in Japan such that the definition of a co-working space remains ambiguous. Therefore, operators from various industries such as real estate agents have entered the market and are advertising their rental spaces as co-working spaces without truly understanding what a co-working space is. At the same time, the nature of the labor culture in Japan is also influential. Some operators have a sound knowledge of Western co-working spaces and how they work. These operators tend to manage their spaces through hosting social events and aggressively pursuing an open atmosphere. In fact, one co-working space operator who completed our survey mentioned that he had visited Santa Monica in California, one of the hottest spots for co-working spaces in the USA, and incorporated his experience there into the way he operated his co-working space in Tokyo. The most special aspect of a true co-working space is the idea that a new project could be born from any of the daily casual conversations that occur between the users or from an encounter between a company and a user at one of the space's social events. This underscores the co-working space's role as the ideal setting for a meeting of the minds, as Cohendet et al. (2010) have pointed out.

4.2 Co-Working Spaces and Creativity in the Metropolis

Finally, we would like to examine the functions of co-working spaces as they pertain to the cultural creativity of the metropolis.

The cultural creativity of metropolises had been discussed in the industrial cluster theory (such as Saxenian 1996), learning region theory (such as Florida 1995), creative class theory (such as Florida 2002), and so on. Several studies focus not only on inter-company transactions, but also on individual networks and the functions of the studio in particular industries, particularly in cultural and creative industries (such as Yamamoto 2014). This is because workers in these industries are often also artists, and thus the expression and development of creativity has a direct influence on the quality of the finished products of their work. However, there is not enough research on how the characteristics of concrete spaces are linked to creativity.

As the representative studies of the 2000s, both Bain (2004) and Vinodrai (2006) describe the relationships between artists (understood here as analogous to workers) and the studios they belong to in the Toronto visual arts industry. Bain (2004) points out that both belonging to a studio and the presence of fellow workers there has a great influence on workers' own identity formation and side job discovery. Furthermore, the studio space plays an important role for female artists to feel deeply involved or fit in as artists, a position often believed to be dominated by men. Owning or belonging to a studio is an important factor in the establishment of women's identity as artists. Using detailed interview surveys and work history surveys, Vinodrai (2006) examines how creative workers who work on projects move across companies or industries within the local labor market. The study also shows that introductions and reputations from colleagues who have worked in the same studio at the same time are important for securing creative workers' liquidity. That is, in order for a worker to gain a future skilled position, the reputation formed by working with others many times is important.

Yamamoto (2014) discusses agglomeration and the production systems of the animation industry in the metropolises of East Asia. This studies animation studios as "the creative nexus" where workers with different kinds of specialized knowledge and skills gather and collaborate on a project basis. The infrastructure and various amenities that support workers' production activities are prepared inside and outside the creative nexus, and workers engage in production activities by using this infrastructure and its amenities. In Tokyo, Seoul, and Shanghai, networks connecting such nodes form and support workers' creative production activities.

These studies show how workers in the cultural and creative industries, such as designers, avoid the instability of employment and express their creativity to build careers by using networks created among workers. At the same time, the studio plays an important role as a place to form such networks or as a place to express creativity. In other words, for freelancers and individual business owners in the cultural and creative industries facing unstable employment opportunities, the studio is a base for getting jobs and making full use of their skills both within and outside the industry. This shows that the agglomeration of studios ensures creativity in urban spaces.

A co-working space is a space where workers from various industries can gather. Thus, it is different from a studio providing space for workers from the same industry. Yet the attractiveness of the surrounding urban setting and the association of a space's location with particular industries are known reasons for choosing the location for a co-working space. This suggests that the location and address of the space contributes to the formation of the users' identities through its function as their official business address. In addition, co-working spaces provide many of the same creative nexus functions that studios offer, such as enabling users in different occupations to easily chat and talk about business and supporting various ways of working by providing the necessary infrastructure. Users of co-working spaces come from their homes to co-working spaces to work, and return home from co-working spaces. This time between presence as work and leaving work is so to speak, a time to switch between working and living. These workers do not simply move back and forth between "home" and "workplace," but, during that switch time, they use the various amenities provided by urban economics, such as restaurants, shopping spaces, and possibilities for cultural consumption at "third places." The positive images of the district that are emphasized as a reason for choosing the location of a co-working space are formed as an aggregate of the behavior of specific facilities and their users.

In order to understand the creativity of the metropolis and the role of co-working space in this creativity, it is important to examine this relationship by not only focusing on the suppliers of co-working spaces but also on how users behave in the city and in co-working spaces. Empirical analyses of the indirect influence of the surrounding environment, through actions by users, on co-working spaces are needed. In other words, it is important to study the interaction between the external economic effects of the city and co-working spaces. These issues will serve as future themes for this research.

Finally, due in part to the pandemic of COVID-19, some companies are shifting its working environment from in traditional office working to teleworking and working in distributed offices that utilize information technology. In relation to this, some companies are also paying more attention to co-working spaces. In addition, an increasing number of workers are starting dual residence to use telework, and demand for co-working spaces in provincial areas would be rising in Japan. It will be necessary to keep a close eye on the location trends of co-working spaces in the future.

Acknowledgements I would like to express my gratitude to each of the co-working space managers who cooperated in the research in this research with the aid of this opportunity. The outline of this paper was presented at the 12th Korea–China–Japan Joint Conference on Geography.

Notes

1. The name and URLs of the portal sites are: coworking coop (http://coworking.coop/); co-working.com (http://co-work-ing.com/); cocopo (http://co-co-po.com/).
2. There is a difference in location trends within these two urban regions. In the case of Kinki (consisting of Osaka, Kyoto, Hyogo, Nara, Mie, Shiga, and Wakayama), a small number of spaces are located not only in Osaka City, as the central city in the region, but also in neighboring cities such as Kyoto City and Kobe City. In contrast, in the Tokyo metropolitan area (Tokyo, Saitama, Chiba, and Kanagawa), the number of co-working spaces located in Saitama, Chiba, and Kanagawa is relatively small in proportion to the scale of the cities in those prefectures. Co-working spaces in this region tend to prefer locations in Tokyo. This difference in the location trends for the co-working space in these two urban regions can be regarded as due to the influence of the power relationships among the cities within the region.
3. According to deskmag (2018), the median size of such spaces is 459 square meters in 2018. Co-working spaces in this survey were not found to have large space available, compared with the results of that statistical survey.
4. The lounge is an open space with desks and chairs in a co-working space. Drinks are provided for a fee or free of charge in some cases. Users of free access share desks and chairs in the lounge with other users. Thus, seating differs depending on the use date and time, and some users cannot use the space when there is no vacancy in the lounge.
5. In Japan, there are women who have left their jobs due to marriage and childbirth, and engage in domestic work. The national system and society have developed to correspond to this situation. Although government support is being prepared under the Basic Law on Equal Participation Society since 1999, it is continuously difficult to reemploy all women who had left jobs and wish to work after the life events of marriage and childbirth.
6. The drop-in plan is often limited in services, such as one-drink order system and only free address use in the lounge.
7. A semi-private room using partitions etc.
8. Show also Subsects. 2.3 and 3.1.
9. Occupation fields and business fields are in accordance with "Mainabi tenshoku," a career matching site by Recruits (https://tenshoku.mynavi.jp/index.cfm) accessed 18 January 2017.

References

Bain A (2004) Female artistic identity in place: the studio. Soc Cult Geogr 5(2):171–193. https://doi.org/10.1080/14649360410001690204

Capdevila I (2015) Co-working spaces and the localised dynamics of innovation in Barcelona. Int J Innov Manag 19(3):1540004. https://doi.org/10.1142/S1363919615400046

Cohendet P, Grandadam D, Simon L (2010) The anatomy of the creative city. Ind Innov 17(1):91–111. https://doi.org/10.1080/13662710903573869

deskmag (2018) The 2018 global coworking survey. http://www.deskmag.com/en/coworking-statistics-all-results-of-the-global-coworking-survey-research-studies-948. Accessed 2 Nov 2020

Florida R (1995) Toward the learning region. Futures 27:527–536

Florida R (2002) The rise of the creative class: and how it's transforming work, leisure, community and everyday life. Basic Books, New York

Fuzi A (2015) Co-working spaces for promoting entrepreneurship in sparse regions: the case of South Wales. Reg Stud Reg Sci 2(1):462–469. https://doi.org/10.1080/21681376.2015.1072053

Grandadam D, Cohendet P, Simon L (2013) Places, spaces and the dynamics of creativity: the video game industry in Montreal. Reg Stud 47(10):1701–1714. https://doi.org/10.1080/00343404.2012.699191

Japan Finance Corporation Research Institute (2016) The survey on state of business startups 2016. https://www.jfc.go.jp/n/findings/pdf/topics_161222_1.pdf

Merkel J (2015) Coworking in the city. Ephemera Theory Politics Organ 15(1):121–139

Moriset B (2013) Building new places of the creative economy: the rise of coworking spaces. Territoire en Mouvement. https://doi.org/10.4000/tem.3868

Morrison A (2018) A typology of places in the knowledge economy: towards the fourth place: new metropolitan perspectives. ISHIT 2018 Smart Innov Syst Technol 100:444–451. https://doi.org/10.2139/ssrn.3056754

Nadant A-LL, Marinos C, Krauss G (2018) Les espaces de coworking: Le rôle des proximités dans les dynamiques collaborative. Rev Fr Gest 272:121–137

Oldenburg R (1989) The great good place: café, coffee shops, community centers, beauty parlors, general stores, bars, hangouts, and how they get you through the day. Paragon House Publishers, New York

Pajević F, Shearmur RG (2017) Catch me if you can: workplace mobility and big data. J Urban Technol 24(3):99–115. https://doi.org/10.1080/10630732.2017.1334855

Saxenian A (1996) Regional advantage. Harvard University Press, Cambridge

Spinuzzi C (2012) Working alone, together: coworking as emergent collaborative activity. J Bus Tech Commun 26(4):399–441. https://doi.org/10.1177/1050651912444070

Tremblay D-G, Scaillerez A (2020) Coworking spaces: new places for business initiatives? J Innov Econ Manage 31:39–67. https://doi.org/10.3917/jie.pr1.0063

Vinodrai T (2006) Reproducing Toronto's design ecology: career paths, intermediaries, and local labor markets. Econ Geogr 82(3):237–263

Yamamoto K (2014) The agglomeration of the animation industry in East Asia. Springer, London

How Customer Service Centers in Foreign Cities Serving Japan Changed Their Business?: A Case Study of the City of Dalian, China

Yasuhisa Abe

Abstract The author chose Dalian to illustrate an outsourced Japanese customer service center (CC) established in China, and how it adapted to locational environment changes. With the infrastructural improvements that the opening of Software Park had brought in 1998, it was found that CCs serving Japan soon followed, especially between 2000 and 2005, ignoring the merits of provincial cities in Japan. The CC service was for end-users, and required that employees had (1) native-level Japanese; (2) developed customer service skills; and (3) an in-depth knowledge of the company's products. There was consequently a regressive presence of Japanese companies or the Japanese operations of global companies. To make matters worse, prices and labor costs rose in China from 2006 and companies were facing difficulty in acquiring operators who satisfied the job criteria. As of 2010, when this survey was conducted, it was said that only 20–30% of Chinese alumni from Japanese universities were capable of working as CC operators. In response, some companies moved their CCs or relocated back to provincial cities in Japan, while continuing to maintain offices in Dalian for other offshore business. In recent years, utilizing ICT in business processes has also expanded new business opportunities.

Keywords Customer service center · Offshoring · Human resources skilled in Japanese · Wage level · Locational condition · Dalian

1 Introduction

Simultaneously with the rapid popularization of information and communication technologies, the configuration of the information service industry was also gradually changing. From the end of the 1990s in Japan, benefiting from liberalization of the communication industry and increasing availability of inexpensive communication technologies like the Internet, the cost of communication dropped dramatically (Hayashi 2005: 145–153). From a global scale perspective, enterprises in developed

Y. Abe (✉)
Graduate School of Social and Cultural Studies, Kyushu University, Fukuoka 819-0395, Japan
e-mail: snc11960@nifty.com

A. Taira and R. D. Schlunze (eds.), *Management Geography*, International Perspectives in Geography 19, https://doi.org/10.1007/978-981-19-4403-1_8

countries noticeably transferred their software development and logistical operations to countries with lower costs, of which the best-known examples were from English-speaking countries, led by the UK and USA's relocation (offshoring)[1] of their service industries to emerging countries like India (Dicken 1998; Arai 2005; Friedman 2007).

Indirect businesses like commissioned software development, salary accounting, employee welfare and customer and sales data entry were all treated as offshoring services. The customer service center (hereinafter referred to as CC) sector studied in this paper was generally regarded as direct customer access,[2] not the remote, often suburban experience it was in reality, for which it was also sometimes referred to as a 'back office' (Hayashi 2005: 192). Specifically speaking, CCs sold commodities and services, and received inquiries and complaints by telephone, fax and over the internet (Hayashi 2005: 147–148).

Kuwatsuka (2004) studied offshoring in Delhi, while Arai and Sugizaki's work (2003) on Japanese CCs in Hokkaido and Okinawa influenced Sunakawa (2005), Kuwatsuka again (2008), et al. Their studies concluded CCs had been inclined to locate in Japanese provincial or prefectural cities with relatively large populations since the mid-1990s.

In Japan, service businesses like CCs had been largely located in peripheral areas, where the Japanese language was a barrier for overseas suitors. After 2000 however, many Japanese enterprises transferred their operations to business process outsourcing (BPO) in other Asian countries.[3] This appeared to encourage an acceleration in BPO start-ups, with the service and indirect business (Friedman 2007; Oomae 2008), in particular, prospering, after China—which had the highest number of Japanese language students outside Japan—opened its labor market. There were also growing numbers of roles reversed, with examples of foreign enterprises offshoring in Japan growing faster than domestic operations such as accounting, general affairs or personnel management.

After 2006, the conditions became even more complicated. With significant development of the Chinese economy and implementation of job security policies by the Chinese government, labor costs and office rents also increased. Coinciding with that, competition for skilled staff between enterprises that had moved to China intensified. One reason given by Japanese markets for offshoring business overseas was the relatively low labor costs, which was still applicable at the time of the survey in 2010, but in addition to with office rents, rethinking was required as they rose.

The study direction appertaining to changes in the regional migration of the above enterprises was also highlighted in the book edited by Matsubara (2009), in which he explored the reconfiguration of Japanese enterprises. The book indicated the necessity of "establishing and reorganizing facilities and functions for not only establishment, closure and transfer of production sites and facilities, but also including when the enterprises are changing product or conducting function transformation, and increases or decreases in functions" (Matsubara 2009: 3).

Moreover, because the service industry was generic customer oriented, foreign staff in the offshoring service industry not only mastered the customer specific language of the outsourcing company, but also the business etiquette of their market.

It was necessary to create a system that could overcome culture barriers, but with a high threshold in Japan and attaining the standard proving both elusive and expensive, CCs were usually located in Japanese provincial cities, where they provided much-needed employment opportunities (Arai and Sugizaki 2003).

As an example of this kind of offshoring business, the author selected CCs, since publicly available data showed Japanese speaking services were generally responsible for the increase in offshoring to places like Dalian, even at the time of the study. However, many CCs had downsized or even closed. Therefore, it was necessary to contextualize differences in contemporaneous conditions vis-a-vis different business operations.

CCs were different from other offshoring businesses. In communicating with customers directly, labor forces conversant in Japanese were a pre-requisite. Furthermore, telephone operators needed to know commodities thoroughly, with a commensurate ability to describe them and be even more culturally sensitive, e.g. with business etiquette on the phone. Guaranteeing a supply line of appropriately skilled staff was therefore difficult. Consequently, it was envisaged the CC vulnerability to the susceptibility of local conditions to change would limit capacity. According to Satoh and Arai (2003), an analysis of departmental features and differentials was important for understanding service industry offshoring, and was why CCs were of interest to the writer.

As it was a well-known offshoring hub for many Japanese enterprises, with the above central tenet, a study of CCs in Dalian was conducted. In differentiating businesses, we asked: (1) How would rising labor costs, rising commodity prices, and acclimatizing to Japanese business etiquette affect business development? (2) If the answer to Question 1 would prompt departments to transfer and/or merge.

Moreover, in this paper, on the basis of the contents of the survey conducted in 2010, trends concerning Japanese-language call centers up to the same period are examined. The year 2010, when the survey was conducted, was a time when wage levels in China's major cities were clearly rising. In response to this situation, almost no new expansion of Japanese-language call centers was seen; in fact, many of the companies that had entered the market began to downsize their call-center operations or switch to other businesses. Therefore, it is considered that by examining the situation of Japanese-language call-center operations up to the same period, it is possible to understand the situation from their entry into the market to their closure.

On the contrary, if the information-services industry is looked at as a whole, it becomes clear that Dalian, the target region, has become a powerful base for BPO operations for Japanese companies since 2010 (Yamamoto 2016), As for the BPO business other than call-center operations that provide such voice support, we supplemented the situation after 2010 with some additional surveys and examined its position. According to Del Prado (2015), since 2010, due to the consolidating primacy of IT, the BPO business had been shifting from low-end contact center services to back-office operations and high-value-added services. As a result, it was becoming ever more dependent on an educated workforce and good communication infrastructure for the success. While the voice-support business via call centers has been shrinking, in recent years, new business opportunities have emerged in the form of the introduction and spread of IT systems in business processes (Yamamoto 2016), and we reported to some extent on the transformation of the BPO business under these circumstances.

2 Study Method and Objective

It was not just as an offshore base for the Japanese service industry, Dalian's symbolization of an internationalized, flattening world economy resounded as far afield as Europe and America (Friedman 2007).

There were 14 colleges and universities in Dalian offering Japanese themed major courses, making it the richest academic environment for Japanese studies outside of Japan. Dalian was consequently the best-placed non-Japanese city to supply a workforce with the requisite Japanese language skills (Oomae 2008; Unno 2008). For example, since regional statistical data had become available in 1998, fluctuations in the number of candidates taking Level 1 of the Japanese-Language Proficiency Test (JLPT) in China indicated Dalian had been in the top three in absolute terms, and, from 2005, was first relatively, second only to Shanghai (Fig. 1) absolutely. Low office rents and other favorable operating costs in comparison to Beijing, Shanghai and other major Chinese cities added to the appeal.

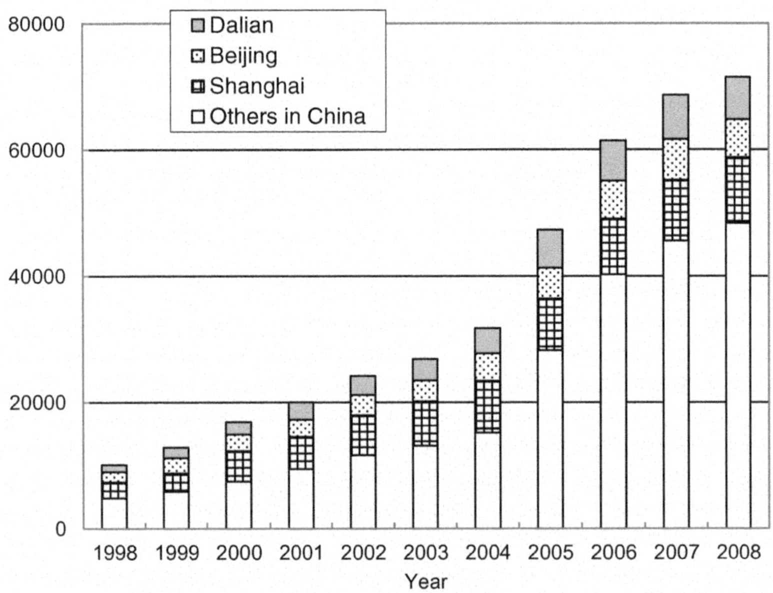

Fig. 1 Numbers of Level 1 of JLPT examinees, by regions
(*Source* Based on data provided by Japan Foundation)

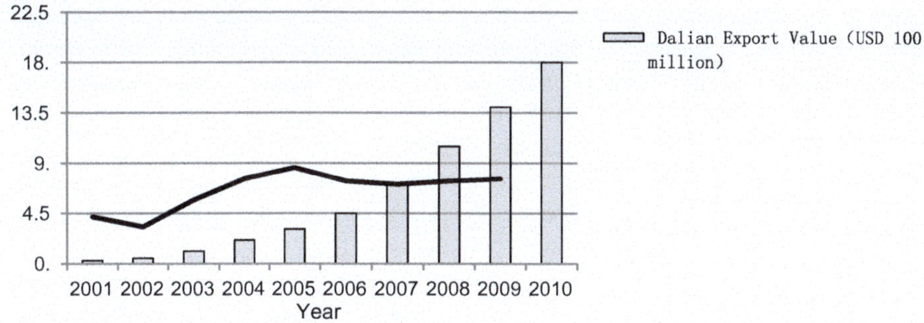

Fig. 2 Export value of the Dalian software information service industry and its percentage of China's exports
(*Source* Collated by JETRO Dalian Office from *White Paper for Software Information Service Industry of Dalian* [version 2007 and 2009], which was edited by Dalian Municipal Bureau of Information Industry and Dalian Software Industry Association, and translated by JETRO Dalian Office [2008 and 2010])

Export volume trends of information services (software development, technical services for software and system integration, etc.) (Fig. 2) clearly demonstrated increased offshoring activity in Dalian from 2000, numbering, according to the Dalian Foreign Trade and Economic Cooperation Bureau, 941 enterprises by the end of 2010. With offshored foreign exports accounting for USD 1.8bn, the combined sales volume was USD 53.5bn. Services in Dalian were mainly oriented to the Japanese market, for example, representing 80% of all exports in 2010.[4] Although since 2004 only accounting for 7–8% of China's total exports to its eastern neighbor across the sea, Dalian had still proportionally been the world's biggest conduit to Japan.[5]

Even if Japanese enterprises generally continued to locate in Dalian for the purpose of providing Japan-oriented services, the business units had discernibly little in common. Neither statistics nor data supported any integral trends, among Japanese language CCs for example, many of which were established nevertheless.[6] In recent years, the city had ceased to be a cheap source of labor as liabilities gradually increased. With changing location conditions, it was to be expected some enterprises would reassess their circumstances in China and adapt accordingly.

Next, we explained survey methods and means that were used to acquire information about the enterprises that had arrived in Dalian, which we found the locations and total number of very hard to ascertain. Even in Dalian, neither contemporaneous data nor statistics for Japanese language CCs existed. Although "*White Paper on CCs*" referenced CCs in Japan, only major enterprises had been investigated, which was insufficient to realistically portray the overall situation in the industry,[7] with uncertainty regarding the circumstances and motives for the arrivals and departures of businesses.

Moreover, as the competition for telephone operators among CCs in Dalian became intense, many surveyed enterprises were strictly controlling the disclosure of telephone operator remuneration and other pertinent information. For instance, salary levels and contract details for telephone operators could only be obtained directly from HR departments, not from recruitment advertisements. Furthermore, labor contracts contained confidentiality clauses with regard to remuneration and other matters.[8] Visits to local subsidiaries, interviews with telephone operators and the collection of data were consequently subjected to many constraints.

Thus, in order to obtain information on major Japanese language CCs in Dalian from the time they arrived, this survey collected recruitment data for telephone operators published on Chinese recruitment networks and from reports on previous CCs.[9] Furthermore, the number of Japanese speaking CCs moving to the area was acquired through information provided by local peers and labor agencies. As visiting enterprises during start-ups in Dalian would have been inopportune, by phone or email, the author contacted the company headquarters (subsidiaries if located elsewhere) in Japan and appropriate personnel agencies, and collected supplementary material published by the surveyed enterprises.

As the establishment of Japanese speaking CCs outside Japan was newsworthy, we readily found that a total of 14 Japanese language CCs (including those subsequently closed) had existed in Dalian.

14 was fewer CCs than might have been expected if accolades such as "Dalian is the Ginza for CCs of Japanese enterprises" (*Aera*, July 19, 2004: 12) that typified press coverage were to be believed. However, the same newspapers actually only reported on 6 enterprises, including those that had not finalized decisions to move to Dalian. Because the novel establishment of Japanese speaking CCs outside Japan had made a big impact on readers, the mass media may have exaggerated the number. The author consequently believed that there were unlikely to have been more than the 14. Small in number the CCs may have been, but Dalian was a benchmark for research and discussion of the prevailing conditions and potential of Japanese offshore service development.

3 Background and Arrival of Japanese Speaking CCs in Dalian

Most of the 14 enterprises in the survey embedded in Dalian during the period from 2000 to 2005 (Table 1). In Japan, local city CCs had surfaced in the late 1990s (Arai and Sugizaki 2003), while Dalian's magnetism emerged later.

During this period, Dalian advertised its commitment to low-cost communications by developing a purpose-built infrastructure, with work starting on a software park for the ICT industry in 1998 (completed in 1999). Local governments also established and supported the information service sector to bolster the BPO business (Katoku 2005: 29–31). After the creation of the software park, Neusoft Group and the India branch of General Electric (hereinafter referred to as "GE," which was then renamed Genpact after a company restructure) expanded their BPO businesses in 1999 and

Table 1 Enterprises that set up CCs in Dalian, and their prevailing condition

Name of headquarters	Time of setting up subsidiary in Dalian	Business operations when stationing	Business type	Condition after stationing
Dalian Hi-Think Computer	Headquarters located in Dalian	All BPO businesses, Mainly CSD	O	Main business was developing software. Business lines of CCs were actually very few
Neusoft Group	1999	All BPO businesses, Mainly CSD	O	Main business was developing software. Business lines of CCs were actually very few
General Electric (GENPACT)	2000	All BPO businesses, Mainly CSD	I & O	Business of CCs was reduced and jointly operated with other enterprises. CC was also located in Changchun, Jilin
Dell Computer	2002	M & S of computer related equipment	I	While the CC in Dalian was still in service, a 500-people CC was located in Miyazaki
Master-piece	2003	BPO business (DE)	O	Transferred to Oita or Bangkok. Dalian was mainly engaged in DE
IBM	2003	M & S of computer devices and software IT service industry consultation	I & O	With expansion of other O industries in preceding years, the overall percentage was decreasing gradually
Livedoor (Swing-by 2020)	2003	BPO business (DE)	I & O	It was sold due to the operation difficulties of the head office, and its business was changed

(continued)

Table 1 (continued)

Name of headquarters	Time of setting up subsidiary in Dalian	Business operations when stationing	Business type	Condition after stationing
Recom	2003	S of information communication equipment	I	Cut businesses of the CC and changed it to be a DE center and ~~a~~ sales base facing China
Hewlett-Packard	2004	M & S of computer related equipment	I	Expanded to become one of the three biggest strongholds of the Company in the world
Hikari Tsushin	2006	BPO businesses	O	Businesses were jointly operated with GENPACT Company
JLL	2007	Provide real estate information	I	Mainly in China and business in Japan was less, relatively
CSK	2003	BPO businesses	O	Transferred to Japan. The CC in Dalian changed into a DE
NHST	2009	IT services like online games	I	Were mainly creating Japanese websites, etc.
Japan Invest	Unknown, headquarters were established in 2000	Sales of real estate	I	Abandoned due to insolvency of the head office

Note CSD referred to Commissioned software development and ED to data entry; O referred to outsourcing type and I to internal type; M referred to manufacture and S to sales
Source Combining interview survey on target enterprise and HR intermediary enterprises, and supplemented by other online information, such as reports in magazines and retrieval websites

2000 respectively, which facilitated the arrival of the information service industry in Dalian.

GE was considered a pioneer in the information service field, as it was the first to launch a Japanese speaking CC business for its subsidiaries. Other international enterprises such as Dell (2002), IBM Japan (2003) and Hewlett-Packard (hereinafter referred to as "HP," 2004) were not far behind and moved to Dalian too. On the other hand, the Japanese model was mainly BPO contractors operating the CC business on behalf of client enterprises. The distribution and number of Dalian based enterprises could not be stated with confidence due to changes in lines of business or the departures of many. However, through interviews and online sources, it could be concluded that most of these enterprises were located around the software park or in the development zone, with many manufacturing factories in the north of the city.

There were recurring features of the new arrivals in the area. US based global player Japanese speaking CC start-ups in Dalian received more publicity than ICT affiliated Japanese venture capital enterprises. Dell, IBM, HP, and GE, referred to above, were examples of the former, and CSK, Hikari Tsushin and Livedoor of the latter. Other categories included Chinese funded enterprises such as Neusoft Group and Dalian Hi-Think Computer Technology Corp whose headquarters were located in Dalian or elsewhere in Liaoning Province. At the same time, many Japanese enterprises manufacturing mechanical devices and fibers also set up operations in Dalian (Seki 2000; Abe and Fan 2010). Although, through software development and other businesses, those enterprises understood the Japanese milieu in Dalian well, we could not confirm whether they had established Japanese language CCs,[10] while it was determined large Japanese enterprises had not considered setting up Japanese speaking CCs in Dalian oriented to the Japanese market.

There were 2 forms of CCs: (1) internal, in-house operations; and (2) outsourced, operated by proxy (Sugiura 2009: 92–93). The survey studied both in roughly equal measure. Besides CCs, indirect businesses were also categorized as BPOs, such as in commissioned software development, salary accounting, employee welfare, and customer and sales data entry and storage. Added to that, the survey clarified the in-bound business, i.e. dealing with client inquiries and complaints, and the out-bound business, i.e. developing potential clients, with non-native Japanese speakers more adept at the latter than the former. It was found the enterprises dealing with out-bound matters (Recom, Hikari Tsusin, etc.) were outnumbered by larger enterprises investing heavily in telephone operators to handle in-bound business.

Reasons for locating in Dalian included low operation costs, such as for labor, communications and office rent, and the highest density quality Japanese speaking labor market in China, as mentioned in previous studies. However, not only the quantity, but also the qualifications of the Japanese speakers should be considered, as stated in Sect. 2, with the increase in Level 1 JLPT examinees giving Dalian a ranking in the top three from 1998 in regard to the absolute number of candidates, and a ranking of 1 for the relative numbers studying Japanese.

Nevertheless, the telephone operators in the Japanese speaking CCs were required to have at least achieved a high score in the Level 1 Test or studied in Japan. Contemporaneous Japan Census data showed most Chinese residents in Japan hailed from Liaoning Province, home to Dalian. Moreover, the next biggest reservoirs of Japanese speakers were fellow north-eastern Heilongjiang and Jilin Provinces. As that represented about 35% of all Chinese passport holders, it was assumed many of the telephone operators had studied in Japan[11] and chosen to work near to their roots in Dalian after returning to China (Abe and Xu 2011: 182–183).

On similar salaries to Chinese workers, many Japanese nationals were employed too, which supported their Chinese studies, and consolidated both Dalian's appeal to live in and as a breeding ground for Japanese speaking telephone operators. The reasons were: (1) Many Japanese nationals could survive without Chinese language skills. (2) It was only a short distance to Japan. (3) The cost of living was lower than in major cities such as Beijing and Shanghai.[12] Thereupon, with a compatible Japanese speaking labor supply, Dalian became the favored location of Japanese speaking CCs.

4 Survival Conditions and Operating Costs of Japanese Speaking CCs

4.1 Survival Conditions of Japanese Speaking CCs

While Dalian was attractive to Japanese speaking CCs in Chinese terms, the number of new arrivals was small in comparison to the number of Japan-based start-ups in Hokkaido, Kyushu and Okinawa, where telephone operators were required to have: (1) mother tongue level Japanese capability; (2) relatively advanced customer service skills; and (3) an in-depth knowledge of commodities. The majority of surveyed enterprises had arrived in Dalian before 2006, with just a few doing so thereafter.

Coincidentally, prices and salaries in China visibly increased after 2006 (Abe and Fan 2010: 273–274), making experienced telephone operators even more difficult to find. For example, although there was a large pool of Japanese language speakers in Dalian, only 20–30% of those who had studied in Japan had the required telephone skills. Especially when an enterprise wanted to expand, a guaranteed supply of telephone operators was a major consideration (based on a survey of Chinese employment agencies with Japanese language speakers on their books).

Due to the increased operating costs in China and consequent narrowing profit differentials between Chinese and Japanese based CCs, many in Dalian reduced their operation capacity or switched operations to data input and/or other such tasks.[13] For example, GE, a pioneer in the CC business, and the first company to establish a Japanese speaking CC in Dalian, saw the number of its telephone operators drop from an initial 110 to 50–60 by 2007. Nevertheless, from the perspective of the overall functions of the company in Dalian, 13 employees had snowballed into 2,500 by 2007 (2,660 employees took part in the 2010 survey), representing a noticeable scale increase. However, the GE experience was at variance to the overall scale of CC businesses. Reasons for the industry's struggles were: (1) the cost of training Chinese telephone operators to the language level of Japanese telephone operators was too high, (2) An increasing number of CC enterprises oriented to Japan, e.g. IBM, HP, DELL, which therefore pushed the cost of retaining quality Japanese speaking telephone operators upwards, and (3) the increasingly dominant hegemony of e-mail resulted in a correlative decline in oral communication.[14]

The CC Dell established in 2002 was often criticized by users for its "poor Japanese". Especially when electronic products like computers failed, telephone operators needed rigorously detailed and refined descriptive and explanatory skills to steer clients through and verify the success of restitutive operations, which proved difficult for Chinese telephone operators.[15] The company only employed by the dozen at the beginning, but customer satisfaction regressed exponentially as the scale of the CC in Dalian expanded,[16] so that, from being first in 2003 (Table 2),[17] by 2005, it was last of 10 in the quality of service standings.

Conversely, the company established a CC in Miyazaki in November 2005, where the number of operators had reached about 500 by the following year (2006). Both Miyazaki CC and the headquarters in Kawasaki mainly performed tasks for business-oriented users.[18] At the time of the survey, although the company had also set up a CC in Dalian, it was only responsible for private users with small sales volume.

Many other enterprises returned their CCs to Japan too, moved to a third country, and/or merged them. On the other hand, Master-piece, an outsourcing-type CC established in February 2003, paid newly-hired Japanese staff the same salaries as the Chinese workers, with Chinese language training proffered as a perk. Consequently, even in Dalian, native Japanese language and service levels were attained. The company had taken on 80 Japanese staff by October 2005.[19]

However, due to the low starting salary and strict working conditions, many Japanese telephone operators soon resigned. In addition, in prioritizing the employment of Chinese citizens, the Chinese government tightened the visa qualification criteria for Japanese telephone operators from 2008, which made their finding a guarantor more difficult. That is, in principle, a Bachelor's degree at least plus 2 or more years working experience[20] were required to qualify for work visas, making it more difficult to hire new graduates or first-jobbers, and therefore negatively impacted the cost of employing Japanese telephone operators.

The company subsequently divided its Dalian operation and relocated to, respectively, Bangkok, Thailand and Oita, Japan,[21] with the unreliability of an autonomous labor supply in foreign countries and the necessity of viable alternatives in the event of communication glitches cited as the reasons, which the 2 new CCs, in collaboration, proved better-placed to deal with (from the interview survey of the company).

Table 2 Annual ranking table for the after-sales services of Dell and HP

	2002	2003	2004	2005	2006	2007	2008	2009	2010
Dell	1	1	4	9	10	10	7	8	9
HP				9		8	10	9	8
Number of enterprises	12	12	10	10	11	12	11	11	12

Note The rankings of HP from 2002 to 2004 and in 2006 were empty

Source Nikkei PC (electronic version) of every year (http://pc.nikkeibp.co.jp/ [viewed on April 12, 2012])

4.2 *Wage Levels of Telephone Operators*

In line with substantial salary increases in urban areas across China from 2005, telephone operator salaries in Dalian had visibly been rising at the time of the survey (Abe and Fan 2010: 273–274), with the improvement on the "RMB 3,000–4,000 of Japanese speaking telephone operators a typical example (RMB 1 = JPY 12.4: September 02, 2010)" (Chinese Labor Agencies). According to survey data, the annual median income of a Japanese telephone operator in China with professional knowledge and/or ITC related skills had risen to RMB 93,447 (about JPY 1,159,000), rising to RMB 155,550 (about JPY 1,929,000), which was higher than similarly classified work in other businesses. In fact, telephone operators with business standard Japanese earned twice the salary of those without (Table 3).

The higher telephone operator pays rates in Dalian amounted to only just less than (Table 4) the JPY 800–899 per hour at the top end of the pay scale the same work paid in Okinawa and the Northeast of Japan, where the largely temporary, dispatched and contract workers received few bonuses and subsidies,[22] suggesting minimal salary differentials between Chinese and Japanese provincial cities.

Although only salaries at HP and Master-piece were analyzed in the survey, wage differentials between other enterprises were noted from previous interview surveys of several enterprises and recruitment agencies. At HP (a global enterprise), a Chinese telephone operator could get a basic salary of RMB 4,500 (net), housing subsidy (10% of the basic salary), special language subsidy (15% of the basic salary) and a bonus (equivalent to two months of salary),[23] as well as enjoy the security of the company's social insurance scheme. In addition to the same basic salary, housing and special language subsidies as Chinese telephone operators, Japanese colleagues also qualified for supplementary foreign subsidies (equivalent to 35% of the basic subsidy), totaling RMB 7200 (about JPY 100,000).[24] The cost of recruitment and employment, handling of visas and air tickets, moving, etc., involved in hiring Japanese people

Table 3 Salary level of telephone operators and other positions

	Those who **could** speak business Japanese		Those who **could not** speak any foreign languages	
	Median	Mean	Median	Mean
Customer service	93,447	106,700	65,000	76,579
Technical support	155,550	172,408	61,080	70,249
Secretary	88,000	99,083	33,916	37,009
General business	84,500	96,384	36,400	38,405
Business assistant	80,960	87,068	45,000	49,083
Business department	114,000	140,671	68,274	84,594

Note According to a national survey conducted between November and December 2010. The amounts represented annual income (including all the subsidies) in RMB (RMB 1 = about JPY 12.4)
Source PASONA (2011)

Table 4 Salary level of call reception and telephone operators in various Japanese locations (2010)

	Average salary (number of enterprises)	Top salary level (number of enterprises)	Highest	Lowest
Hokkaido	800 (96)	1,000–1,100 (24)	1,500	760
Tohoku	970 (38)	800–900 (11)	1,200	760
Kanto	1,350 (789)	1,500–1,600 (137)	2,500	750
Tokai	1,135 (55)	1,000–1,100 (17)	1,500	800
Kinki	1,185 (199)	1,200–1,300 (57)	2,000	800
	1,085 (27)	1,000–1,100 (9)	1,400	900
Kyushu	994 (81)	1,000–1,100 (26)	1,250	700
Okinawa	896 (60)	800–900 (21)	1,200	700
Other	1,041 (17)	1,100–1,200 (5)	1,300	750
Nationwide	1,233 (1,361)	1,200–1,300 (200)	2,500	700

Data White Paper on Call Reception (2009/2010: 21)
Source Survey Results from between February and April 2010. Unit: JPY. Salary level was the hourly rate for employment, excluding subsidies

in China was much higher than administration in Japan.[25] On the other hand, there was little difference between Chinese and standard Japanese labor costs overall, after the settlement of various social insurance obligations were taken into account (from Japanese service enterprises interview).

Since the above referred to Master-piece subsequently moved and no longer had a CC in Dalian or Beijing after collaboratively transferring the operation to Oita, Japan and Bangkok, Thailand, the salaries of Japanese staff engaged in data entry were shown in Table 5. Because of the relatively low job skills required, this sector paid less than telephone operator work, for which reason the study also looked at the CC in Bangkok. Table 5 shows Oita had the highest salaries of the 4 locations listed, 40–50% higher than Japanese workers at HP in Dalian received. Since HP and Master-piece had different configurations and economies of scale, the internal situation at Master-piece was used as a barometer. The company had offices in Beijing, Dalian and Bangkok, with the highest overseas salaries in Beijing (various subsidies included in weighting), followed by Bangkok, which by then had a CC. Salaries in Bangkok were only half those of Oita. However, the true nature of the pay gap was not as stark, as the stated salary in Bangkok was net of insurance and subsidies. For the same reasons, Dalian's salaries may be translated as half of Oita's, not one third.[26] Although relatively low compared to in metropolises such as Beijing and Bangkok, it was doubtful whether the cost of establishing a CC anywhere outside the capital in China was much lower than in Japan, given other costs of recruiting and hiring.

Table 5 Salary levels of Japanese staff HP and master-piece sites

Stronghold location		Business content	Number of Japanese	Monthly starting salary (JPY)	Other subsidies, etc. (JPY)
Dalian CC of HP		CC	100	55,800 (take-up salary)	Foreign staff subsidy 19,530 Special language subsidy 8,370 Housing subsidy 5,580 Bonus of two months (year) Including health insurance
Master-peace	Dalian	DE	30	43,400 (take-up salary)	Salary increase, Promotion (reviewed every three months) Housing subsidy (9,920/month) Commuting subsidy System of medical subsidy (maximum 49,600/month) Chinese support system—Subsidy for welcome (paid to Japanese staff after 1 year) Bonus (paid every 6 months after the completion of 1 year's work)
	Beijing	DE	10	49,600 (take-up salary)	Promotion (reviewed every three months) Housing subsidy (24,800/month) Commuting subsidy System of medical subsidy (maximum JPY 49,600/month) Subsidy for welcome (paid to Japanese staff after1 year paid) Bonus (paid every 6 months after the completion of 1 year's work)

(continued)

Table 5 (continued)

Stronghold location		Business content	Number of Japanese	Monthly starting salary (JPY)	Other subsidies, etc. (JPY)
	Bangkok	CC	120–130	67,834 (take-up salary)	40 working hours and two days- off every week Salary increase, Promotion (reviewed every three months) Commuting subsidy Thailand social insurance Subsidy for welcome (paid to Japanese staff after1 year) Bonus (paid every 6 months after the completion 1 year's work)
	Oita	CC	62 (including 46 female staff)	134,400 (tax included)	Employed as part-time staff (including employment, occupational injury, health insurance, pension benefits) Commuting subsidy: actual costs (maximum 20,000/month)

Note The salary amount was converted from the foreign exchange rate on September 2, 2010 (RMB 1 = about JPY 12.4 = about THB 4.57); CC referred to customer service center and ED to data entry
Source Official websites of the companies (retrieved on September 2, 2010) and interview survey

4.3 Change of Services

For those enterprises that had already withdrawn their CC services from Dalian, many of them kept their offices open in Dalian for other purposes. Most businesses converted those CC services that required a higher level of Japanese language ability into less demanding Japanese language dependent ones, such as customer, personnel, accounting and financial data entry, and commissioned software development for Japan.

Master-piece followed the same policy because it was difficult to hold onto valued Japanese speakers. In commissioning some technical colleges to educate Chinese students how to input Japanese data, the company hired about 300 graduates to engage in the work, for which they earned less than the telephone operators in the CC. Although there were not many qualified Japanese speaking telephone operators using Japanese in Dalian, there were many lower level Japanese speakers available for appealingly lower wages (e.g., than in Beijing or Japan). Even then, the company had about 30 Japanese staff, mainly responsible for confirming job descriptions with clients, determining the progress and distribution of work, final confirmation and management of the data entered, etc. In fact, all the data entry was performed by the Chinese staff.[27]

CSK and the former Livedoor (Swing-by 2020) similarly converted CCs into other kinds of back offices. CSK took orders from life insurance, credit card and labor service enterprises, public institutions, etc. to do accounting and customer data entry. The company "has a high level of technology at security domain, so there are more orders from financial-related clients in particular" (from interviews with the enterprise). As mentioned earlier, during the survey in 2010, Dalian was also promoting Japan-oriented software development and other services. Even though both prices and labor costs then rose there, it was still appealing to large enterprises as jobs not requiring a very high level of Japanese or the ability to handle clients was cheaper than in Japan.

The Chinese enterprises with CCs in Dalian the survey identified were Neusoft (headquartered in Shenyang, Liaoning Province) and DHC (Dalian Hi-Think Computer Technology, headquartered in Dalian), both known for commissioned software development for Japan (Oomae 2008). In reality, based on a survey of the Japanese branch offices of the two enterprises, the BPO divisions of both enterprises largely commissioned software development, whereas the CC operations were low-key. It might thus be inferred that Dalian had a high status as a destination for the offshore business of Japanese enterprises, but conditions for the CCs to operate there were difficult.

In other respects, there were also enterprises that used Dalian as a domestically oriented CC or China outlet. Recom, which sold office machines to the Japanese government and enterprises, had about 40 staff in Dalian, of who only 8 of the original 40 telephone operators in the CC from 2004 remained. The company had used to deal with external business, but at the time of the survey was only dealing with the company's internal work, with the head office delegating business management to it from 2006, e.g. debt management and settlement of sales accounts. In 2005 it had also started providing services in China, including sales and maintenance of communication and OA equipment, and image design and printing. Although the proportion of its business in China was still not high, it was actively responding to the expansion of the Chinese market (based on a survey of the enterprise).

There were also global enterprises that centralized their CC operations in Dalian to cut costs and standardize services by developing multi-language solutions. In the northeastern region of China where Dalian is located, it was easier to recruit qualified personnel who could speak Chinese, Korean and Japanese as many ethnic Korean-Chinese lived there. As a result, as well as Japanese, HP and DELL set up CCs providing Korean, Mandarin, Cantonese and other language services in Dalian, making them CC hubs for East Asia. Alongside offices in Bangalore, India (for the English-speaking regions) and Costa Rica, Central America (for the Spanish and Portuguese-speaking regions) HP's office in Dalian was one of the world's three leading CCs for the company's service sector. According to survey interviews, the company had about 700 telephone operators in Dalian, with 300 employed for the Japanese market.

However, one-third were Japanese, which, while theoretically good for resolving customer issues, it was questionable if it could compete financially with CCs based in Japan. And if CCs serving across different countries and territories were debased, they were prone to be oblivious to local cultural etiquette, with the risk of deteriorating service standards. In the case of DELL for example, even for the problems that arose with products during delivery, or for the faults that occurred during the warranty period, if a user was found to be negligent in the process of using their purchase, the company would not provide free repair and return services. If a client consulted the company's CC, not only were time and effort spent on explaining the fault location and circumstances, they also had to be verified. Therefore, in many cases, repair costs were incurred even for the problems that arose when the products had just been delivered or during the warranty period, which is why customers had disputes with the company,[28] which, to avoid, at the risk of further antagonism, customers had to pay a premium for after-sales service when they purchased the products (learned from the company's survey). The company did not have such disputes with its corporate clients in Japan however, which explained the lower rating for the CC in Dalian from private users.

With HP, which also established computer and other after-sales service centers, customer unrest was much less common due to the large number of Japanese staffs hired as telephone operators and managerial personnel. However, the user evaluation of HP's support system after 2005 was as low as that of DELL (Table 2) according to Computer Service Centers rankings compiled by the Nikkei PC editorial board (computer satisfaction ranking).

It was not possible to confirm whether there were other Japanese-based global enterprises that imitated HP and establish CCs outside of Japan. This suggested that the strategy advocated by the above enterprises to try and reduce the costs and improve the efficiency of services by concentrating multi-lingual support staff in the same place was uncommon. Even HP set up its sales and marketing department CCs in Japan instead of centralizing in Dalian. As far as the company was concerned from the management perspective, the sales and marketing departments were vitally important, and as different countries had their own idiosyncratic business practices, it was unreasonable to expect to be able to standardize such disparate operations on a world-wide scale. It was therefore more efficacious to separate the CCs serving markets with higher expectations, such as in Japan.

As of 2010, main survey of this paper was held, due to factors such as rising wage levels throughout China, it has been observed that the growth rate of BPOs that do no entail ICT systems, such as CCs and other business processing operations, has been declining (Yamamoto 2016).

In this regard, the author conducted an interview survey with the person who was in charge of outsourced back office work, such as expense settlement, and who had negotiated with a BPO company in Dalian in 2016. According to her, although the outsourcing companies in Dalian had higher overheads, e.g. wages, her company could still reduce costs by outsourcing their work, and there were other advantages to using an outsourcing company. She said "I don't think this situation has changed. It is not any different even now in 2020." However, if the tasks that are being outsourced are not made clear enough, they may need to be redone by the client. She said, "Especially in Japan, what is expected may seem like common sense, but, in fact, unless you explain so carefully, and specify exactly what it is that needs doing, the outsourcing company will not fulfill the task to satisfaction, so the client company also needs to be careful" (according to an interview survey conducted on July 6, 2020). In order to stem the duplication of labor and consequent budget leakage incurred, it could be said that it is necessary to consider a method that allows both the client and outsourcing company to synchronize their work more efficiently.

Another important change since 2010 is the increase in the number of companies seeking to improve work efficiency by introducing ICT systems in their BPO operations. To confirm this point, on June 20, 2020, the author conducted an interview with IBM Japan (Mr. Z, an IT management consultant), which is executing BPO operations by deploying ICT systems. The company said that its BPO business in Dalian has continued and is expanding, especially since 2020 due to the rise of telework as COVID-19 spread. As a result, the demand for improved business efficiency through the introduction of ICT systems has risen sharply, leading to increased orders for BPO services. Before 2019, BPO businesses in Dalian had been gradually experiencing increasingly more difficulty in securing profit due to rising costs such as the growth in wage levels. Nevertheless, businesses continued their presence in Dalian. One reason was that there were no other regions in which to establish BPO business centers, as a sufficient number of ICT engineers could be secured in Dalian. IBM Japan understood that relocating to another region would be difficult because it entailed securing and training staff and engineers from scratch. Besides work such as simple data entry and confirmations, IBM Japan is also gradually carrying out core work such as system development in Dalian. This is an effort to reduce costs by bringing work to the Dalian to meet the increase in costs there.

It can thus be said that even as of 2021, Dalian will continue to maintain its role as a base for Japanese companies' BPO operations, not including work that is difficult to perform in overseas centers, such as voice CCs. In particular, in addition to the growth in demand associated with ICT deployment, especially due to the spread of telework, examples of responses to rising costs by having engineers in Dalian take on core work, which has higher added value, could be observed.

Also, with regard to deciding on the location for a BPO center, one point of consideration is that ICT engineers often move to companies in big cities such as Shanghai and Shenzhen. Wage levels are thus rising in order to retain engineers. For BPO businesses that seek to improve work efficiency with ICT systems, non-metropolitan regions in China are especially facing fierce competition with major cities in China, compared to competition with cities in other countries. There is thus a possibility that BPO operations will transform to a metropolitan industry.

5 Conclusion

In this paper, the author used the CC business as an example to examine and analyze the Japan-oriented service industry in Dalian, and discussed operational conversions and relocations to other regions. Between 2000 and 2005 a few CCs moved to Dalian after realizing the potential that the establishment of Software Park in 1998 and supporting infrastructure presented. However, customer-oriented businesses like CCs serving the Japanese market required: (1) native-level Japanese language proficiency; (2) high level customer service competency; and (3) expert product knowledge; criteria which, because all except a few enterprises could satisfy, not many stationed themselves in Dalian, with the headquarters of what were mainly global enterprises or BPO contractors in the United States.

From 2006, because (1) prices and wage levels across China, including in Dalian, had been rising; (2) acquiring experienced telephone operators with Japanese proficiency had become very difficult—as their wage levels had risen relatively—and, significantly; and (3) due to the cultural differences between China and Japan—such as in business etiquette—Chinese operators had been struggling to cope with customers, necessitating training sessions for foreign replacements, and resulting in education and operating cost increases, thereby eroding its cost advantage over Japan from 2006, even before the cost of education and other overheads were considered.

In response to the above issues, first, some Japanese enterprises in Dalian tried to attract Japanese operators by extolling the merits of learning Chinese in Dalian. However, starting from around 2008, the Chinese government tightened the visa qualification criteria by stipulating "having academic qualifications and work experience", which made recruitment more costly.

Second, many global enterprises were in a position to take advantage of Dalian's multi-lingual services by merging CCs from Japan, Hong Kong and other parts of mainland China to reduce costs and standardize the services. These enterprises focused more on reducing operating costs than improving service quality. However, for those enterprises that still maintained Japanese-speaking CCs in Dalian, there was often no apparent cost reduction where Japanese staff accounted for as much as one-third of the workforce. Moreover, as a result of the compromise on the quality of service that bracketing mottled countries and regions together inevitably involved, meeting expectations in the Japanese market could not be maintained, with a consequent significant drop in Japanese customer satisfaction levels. Some enterprises subsequently set up simultaneous operations in Japan.

A number of enterprises both transferred operations to Japanese provincial cities and merged CCs while maintaining and redefining their offices in Dalian. Specifically, they transformed their CC operations requiring high level Japanese speaking ability into businesses with a lower threshold, e.g. customer information, personnel and financial management data input, or commissioned software development for Japan, which, because of the disparity between labor costs in China and Japan, returned high yields. As a conclusion to this article, the author advocated that in the analysis of office work offshore, businesses that could readily be transferred overseas and businesses burdened by transfer obstacles needed to be analyzed separately from the management perspective. Furthermore, appreciation was required of the business practices in the countries and regions in which the offshoring companies operated. Many of the Japanese-speaking CCs in Dalian were U.S. concerns expanding their business in Japan, whereas to serve English-speaking markets, a lot of their CCs were in emerging countries.

However, telephone operators serving the Japanese market not only required advanced Japanese language skills, they were also expected to be flexible and deferential in the spirit of Japanese business etiquette, an insight global headquarters far removed in the United States appeared detached from, but one of the key factors in determining whether enterprises should set up CCs outside of Japan and if they would survive.

Nevertheless, enterprises continued to offshore their commissioned software development, financial management and customer information and other data management information services to Dalian. In the case of Japanese-speaking CCs, some had no immediate plans to depart from Dalian, but there were also cases of Japanese-language CCs in Dalian returning to Japan. This reflected the regional characteristics of the Japanese market, too. This globalization and localization in juxtaposition is what we meant by "glocalization" (Miyamachi 2008: 1).

The author had focused on the stagnation of the Dalian CC business, which was the catalyst for the service industry to hasten its return to Japan in homage to the home market. However, from the perspective of the information service industry as a whole, it was envisaged the appetite for this business offshoring would continue. In particular, the rapid shift to ICT in business processes, triggered by the COVID-19 pandemic in 2020, may expand the role of Dalian as a base for BPO business for Japanese companies. On the contrary, competition among Chinese cities to secure human resources for the BPO business has become fierce, and from a geographical viewpoint, it can be pointed out that the BPO business may be transforming into a more metropolitan type.

These questions were predicted to be the subject of future research. As the direction of future research in the context of management geography, the following studies are deemed necessary: (1) on the method of improving the efficiency of both the client and offshored operation in the BPO business, (2) on reverting to the domestic or in-house model from the BPO model, research on the spatialization and theorization, and (3) on changes in the content of the BPO business due to the spread of ICT.

Acknowledgements This paper is based on (1) the contents of the Japanese paper "Chuugoku Dairenshi ni sinshutsu shita Nihongo kourucentaa no sonzoku joukyou," published in *Geographical Science* (Chiri-Kagaku) Vol. 67, No. 2 in 2012, and (2) a post-2012 addendum found in the final section.

Notes

1. This paper referred to definitions coined by Sugiura (2009: 92–94). Where an enterprise exports its main business was 'offshore,' while the business of offshoring 'offshoring business.' Similar terms such as 'outsourcing' and 'business process outsourcing (BPO)' mentioned hereunder embodied 'business execution of overseas subsidiaries,' but not 'entrustment on domestic external contractors.'
2. Dictionary of information management terms. http://www.stmarkit.co.jp/im/terminology/ (viewed on September 16, 2010).
3. Abbreviation of business process outsourcing. In general, when enterprises entrusted some of their businesses to external enterprises was called outsourcing. However, with the development of informatization, external entrustment gradually came to prevail in financial accounting, salary management and customer management, that were closely linked with enterprise information systems in the 1990s, from which the term "BPO" emerged (BPO Business Study Group 2011: 19–20).
4. According to j.people.com.cn (February 24, 2011): One Hundred Thousand Software Talents in Dalian. http://j.people.com.cn/94476/7298707.html (viewed on January 21, 2012).
5. According to Kitakyushu Foreign Trade Association (2010).
6. According to database findings, examples of CCs other than in Dalian include the GE CC in Changchun, Jilin and Master-Piece CC in Chengdu, Sichuan. Besides CCs in Japan, Transcosmos also had CCs in Shanghai, Beijing and Wuxi in China. And Master-Piece had CCs in Beijing. However, these were Chinese language CCs for the Chinese market. All their Japanese language CCs were set up in Japan. Transcosmos had a software development site in Dalian with no CC (according to an interview survey on the Company).
7. Edited by Computer and Telephony Editorial Department (2009/2010) White Paper on CC, Ric Telecom.
8. According to an interview survey on telephone operators and intermediary recruitment personnel of several local enterprises.
9. According to reports in old newspapers and magazines: "Business Nifty News Magazine Reports Cross Retrieval." http://business.nifty.com/gsh/RXCN/.
10. The representatives in this paper included Alpine Electronics and Toshiba, that contributed to Neusoft Group.
11. For example, Dalian is in Liaoning Province. According to survey data, Liaoning Province accounted for the largest Chinese representation in Japan during the period 2001–2009. In the same period, Heilongjiang Province ranked 2nd–3rd, and Jilin Province 4th (edited by Foundation Immigration Association, Counting of Foreign Residents, 2002–2010).
12. According to an interview survey of the Master-Piece Company.
13. Among enterprises investigated in this paper, only one company closed its CC due to bankruptcy and insolvency of the head office. When other enterprises were investigated, it was found major head office business operations were unaffected. Moreover, cases where the BPO business was independent of major head office business interests also existed, like with the former Livedoor Company and CSK. Therefore, examples of the number of CCs being reduced and abandoned due to poor head office operation conditions were rare.
14. Contents of Kin Kenbin (2007) were corroborated in an interview survey of several HR intermediary personnel. Kin Kenbin (2007): Successful Examples of BPO vender in China (3). http://jp.fujitsu.com/group/fri/report/china-research/topics/2007/no-74.html (viewed on September 3, 2010).
15. Website for users of the company's products. http://www.contact.co.jp/blog/index.php?/archives/258_DELL.html (viewed on September 4, 2010).
16. According to company data, the number of employees in businesses, excluding the Japanese CC of the Dalian Subsidiary of Dell in 2008, was about 1,300.
17. According to an explanation of Nikkei PC (electronic version), which conducted an annual survey, the reason why the assessments of Dell and HP Company were relatively low was that

the Japanese spoken in the after-sales system, especially in CC centers, was hard to understand and consequently tarred the entire after-sales service system.

18. This fact was confirmed in an interview survey of the company, which had a lot of CCs in emerging countries. Ookawara K (2006): Dell Opened Customer Service in Miyazaki. http://pc.watch.impress.co.jp/docs/2006/0619/gyokai165.htm (viewed on September 1, 2010).
19. In reference to Fuji Sankei Business Eye (October 7, 2005: 13) and reports based on the company. http://www.chainavi.jp/dalian/blog.html?sid=12999 (viewed on September 2, 2010).
20. When conducting both the main and supplementary surveys in November 2011, the review criteria in Dalian were relatively relaxed compared with those applied to other cities in China. Even though cases of being granted a visa without meeting the above requirements did exist, there were increasingly fewer people who acquired employment/work visas without meeting the requirements.
21. The company established a CC in Bangkok as, due to the salary and relative low price of commodities, it was the most popular emerging city with Japanese telephone operators, and employment/work visas were easily acquired. In 2007, the company also set up Japanese language CCs in Chengdu, China, and New Delhi, India, in 2007. However, they were all later closed due to the difficulty in recruiting Japanese telephone operators (according to an interview survey of the company).
22. Edited by Computer and Telephony Editorial Department, mentioned in Note 8 (2010: 26).
23. In China, the stated salary generally indicated the net amount. The gross salary was about 1.5 times that.
24. Other subsidies included a commuting subsidy for night work. Moreover, the enterprise had to provide health insurance.
25. According to an interview survey on intermediary employment agencies that supplied staff such as telephone operators, the company did not require the telephone operators to have professional knowledge in computer products at the time of recruitment.
26. The opinion on the prevailing salary level was the same as that of Oomae (2008).
27. According to the interview survey, many Japanese jobseekers also wished to work in Dalian, despite a higher salary level in Beijing, due to the low cost of commodities and high profile of the Japanese language in Dalian. Therefore, the Company was likely to concentrate its Chinese business sites in Dalian.
28. According to the user page referred to in Note 15.

References

Arai Y (2005) Geographies of information society and cyberspace: a research perspective. Jpn J Hum Geog 57:47–67 (J)

Abe Y, Fan J (2010) Changes in locational environment of Japanese machinery and instrument industry in China: a case study of Dalian economic and technological development area. Geog Sci 65:266–283 (J)

Abe Y, Xu Y (2011) Employment status and evaluation of study abroad experience after returning to Japan. In: Matsunaga N, Se T, Yoshioka H (eds) Beginning of ‘knowledge processing studies.’ Shinjuku Shobo, Tokyo, pp. 171–191 (J)

Arai Y, Sugizaki K (2003) Concentrations of call centers in peripheral areas: cases in Japan. Netcom 17:187–202

BPO Business Study Group (2011) BPO business from the limit. Diamond, Tokyo (J)

Computer and Telephony Editorial Department (ed) (2009/2010) White Paper on CC, Ric Telecom. Tokyo (J)

Del Prado FE (2015) The BPO challenge: leveraging capabilities, creating opportunities. PIDS Discussion Paper Series, 2015-36:1–26 (E). Institute for Development Studies (PIDS), Makati City

Dicken P (1998) Global shift: transforming the world economy, 3rd edn. Guilford Publishers, New York
Friedman TL (2007) The world is flat: a brief history of the twenty-first century, 3rd edn. Holtzbrinck Publishers, Stuttgart
Hayashi N (2005) Urban service area theory. Hara Shobo, Tokyo (J)
Katoku R (2005) Dalian is burning with passion. SCC Books, Tokyo (J)
Kenbin K (2007) Successful examples of BPO vender in China (3). http://jp.fujitsu.com/group/fri/report/china-research/topics/2007/no-74.html. Accessed 3 Sept 2010.
Kitakyushu Foreign Trade Association (2010) Scale of outsourcing service to Japan in Dalian ranked first in the world. http://www.kfta.or.jp/jyouhou003.html. Accessed 20 Mar 2012
Kuwatsuka K (2004) Expanding export of business process outsourcing services and the location of call centers in India: case study on Gurgaon, national capital region. Humanities Social Sci (University of the Ryukyus) 14:89–119 (J)
Kuwatsuka K (2008) Growth of ICT industry and knowledge acquisition at remote area: study on experiences of call centers in Okinawa. Geog Sci 63:205–219 (J)
Matsubara H (ed) (2009) Economic geography of location adjustment. Hara Shobo, Tokyo (J)
Miyamachi Y (2008) What is 'glocalization'? In: Oita University Faculty of Economics (eds) Glocalized economy and society. Minerva Shobo, Tokyo, pp. 1–20 (J)
Oomae K (2008) Study of Dalian, a strong Japanese outsourcing base (Part 1). http://www.nikkeibp.co.jp/sj/2/column/a/149. Accessed 12 July 2011 (J)
PASONA (2011) *2011 Salary information/welfare analysis report Chinese version*. Pasona, Tokyo (J)
Satoh H, Arai Y (2003) The suburbanization of the office location due to progress in information and communication technologies: case study of Makuhari Shintoshin. Hum Geog Soc Jpn 55:367–382 (J)
Seki M (2000) A new era of entering China on Japanese companies. Shinhyoron Publishing Inc., Tokyo (J)
Sugiura S (2009) Transnational world. Keio University Press, Tokyo (J)
Sunakawa T (2005) Verifications and issues relating to concentrating of call center in Okinawa. J Ind Inf Sci (Okinawa International University) 1–1:31–46 (J)
Unno K (2008) Head office and accounting move to China. Diamond, Tokyo (J)
Yamamoto M (2016) Japanese BPOs left behind by overseas trends Part 1: utilization of ineffective BPOs in Japan. LTS, Inc. https://lt-s.jp/lts-column/2016-4-22-1. Accessed 5 July 2020

Factors Influencing Enterprise Development in the Inland Regions of Fujian Province in China

Lin Chen and Guandong Su

Abstract This chapter aims to examine the characteristics of growing enterprises and their location factors in the inland regions of eastern coastal China by taking Fujian province as an example. The main research methods include a face-to-face interview with plant managers and town offices, and a questionnaire survey to workers. The main results are as follows: First, since the mid-1990s, the growth of enterprises which depend on agricultural and forestry products is remarkable in the inland regions of Fujian province. Second, analysis of a case study in the inland region of the province indicates that large-scale enterprises are now playing a leading role in the enterprise development and have successfully approached domestic and international markets with the help of partner enterprises in coastal urban areas or abroad. Third, such enterprises obtain their workforce from nearby rural areas and draw workers from relatively distant areas both inside and outside of the province. This is a key factor that supports the continuous development of enterprises in recent years. Finally, the space of the inland regions play different roles in different stages of enterprises development. Initial investment costs, income expansion and newly-added value are the three most striking factors affecting the development of enterprises in the inland regions of the province.

Keywords Enterprises Development · Large-scale Enterprises · Inland Regions · Eastern Costal China

---

L. Chen (✉)
School of Geograhy & Center for Asian Geographical Studies, South China Normal University, Guangzhou 510631, China
e-mail: chenlin.geo@m.scnu.edu.cn

G. Su
ZENRIN Co., Ltd., Fukuoka 804-0003, Japan
e-mail: guandongsue@gmail.com

A. Taira and R. D. Schlunze (eds.), *Management Geography*, International Perspectives in Geography 19, https://doi.org/10.1007/978-981-19-4403-1_9

1 Introduction

Since the implementation of the "Open Door" policy in 1978, China has experienced drastic economic environmental changes such as the transition from a planned economy to a market economy, and from a closed economy to an open economy. This development resulted in the transfer of decision-making authority, on the one hand, from the central government to local government at the macro level; and on the other hand, from the government to companies or households at the micro level. In the context of economic globalization, the participation in economic reform varies greatly by regions, and the industrial space in China has undergone major changes. Particularly, comparative advantages, economies of scale, and economic globalization have a significant impact on the formation of China's manufacturing industry space. This brought about that the labor-intensive industries and industries closely related to the international labor division were increasingly concentrated in eastern coastal China. However, with the adjustment of China's economic structure, the industrial upgrading speed in eastern coastal regions has accelerated, and the spatial expansion of labor-intensive industries has emerged. Especially, the inland regions in the eastern coastal China is crucial space for the industrial dispersion.

Regarding the development of enterprises in the inland regions of eastern coastal China, Township[1]and Village Enterprises (hereafter "TVEs")[2] have been drawing attention and playing a major role as a receiving station for rural labor (Liang et al. 2002). The development of China's TVEs was initially driven by "collectively-owned township and village enterprises" (hereafter "collective enterprises").[3] The development of collective enterprises has been driven primarily by the following four factors (Shen and Ma 2005). The first is that the entry costs of collective enterprises are very low because they can use rural land freely. Second, labor costs are low because a lot of surplus labor is pooled in rural areas with the transition from collective ownership to household contract responsibility system. Third, collective enterprises can use bank loans more easily with the involvement of local governments. Fourth, the availability of product markets that the state-owned enterprises were unable or unwilling to occupy in the 1980s and the early 1990s.

The above factors have driven the development of collective enterprises and other TVEs in China. However, since the early 1990s, collective enterprises began to lose their vitality and competitiveness (Shen and Ma 2005). This is due to the increased competition between collective enterprises as a result of the transition to a market economy and the entry of foreign enterprises. In addition, in order to reduce non-performing loans of banks, collective enterprises were restricted from using bank loans with the involvement of the local government. The lack of clarity in the ownership of the assets of the collective enterprises has led to frequent interferences in their management by the local governments. To address these issues, ownership reforms were carried out since the mid-1990s, and the privatization of TVEs was promoted (Rozelle et al. 2002).

The privatization of TVEs has promoted the development of rural industry and other industries (Li and Rozelle 2000, 2003), and had a significant impact on the overall rural economy and the growth of small towns (Shen and Ma 2005). However, this development has not necessarily led to a reduction in economic disparities between regions in China. For example, Yang and Fan (2005) analyzed the competitiveness of rural industries by province and reported that the disparity between eastern and western regions[4] is increasing. Besides, the development of TVEs has contributed to the reduction of intra-provincial disparities, especially in some provinces in eastern coastal China (Cheong and Wu 2014). This means that in recent years, the development of enterprises in the eastern coastal China has extended not only to the large cities but also to the inland regions within the province.

Therefore, this chapter aims to examine the characteristics of growing enterprises and their location factors in the inland regions of eastern coastal China. In order to elucidate the above issues, this chapter will be organized from two main perspectives. Specifically, which types of enterprises are prominent, and why this development is possible in the inland regions of eastern coastal China.

This chapter selects Fujian province (福建省) as a case study for the following two reasons. First, the development of TVEs has been remarkable since the mid-1990s; the growth rate of employees in Fujian's TVEs from 1996 to 2010 was 72.6%, which is much higher than the average of 59.7% for the provinces in the eastern coastal China. Second, in recent years, the development of TVEs in Fujian province (福建省) has not only been in the coastal areas, but also in the inland regions. Therefore, it is an appropriate region to consider the restructuring of enterprises in the inland region of eastern coastal China.

2 Methodology

2.1 Study Area

Fujian province is located in the southeastern China and can be divided into coastal and inland regions (Fig. 1). The coastal region includes Fuzhou (福州), Xiamen (厦门), Putian (莆田), Quanzhou (泉州) and Zhangzhou (漳州), and the inland region includes Ningde (宁德), Nanping (南平), Sanming (三明) and Longyan (龙岩) (Fig. 1). Recently the province has enjoyed dramatic development in its rural enterprises. The number of people employed by rural enterprises grew sharply from 4.93 million in 1996 to 8.51 million in 2010 with an increase of 72.6%, which is significantly higher than the 59.7% for the average in eastern coastal regions as a whole (China Township Enterprise Yearbook Editorial Committee 1996; China Rural Enterprise and Agro-processing Industry Yearbook Editorial Committee 2011).

Figure 2 shows the ratio and its growth rate in the number of people employed in rural industries since 2000. The speed of rural industry development in recent years has been higher in the inland region of Fujian province (福建省) than in coastal region. In the inland region, 25 counties exhibit a growth in the number of people employed in rural industries and that is above the province average level of 83%,

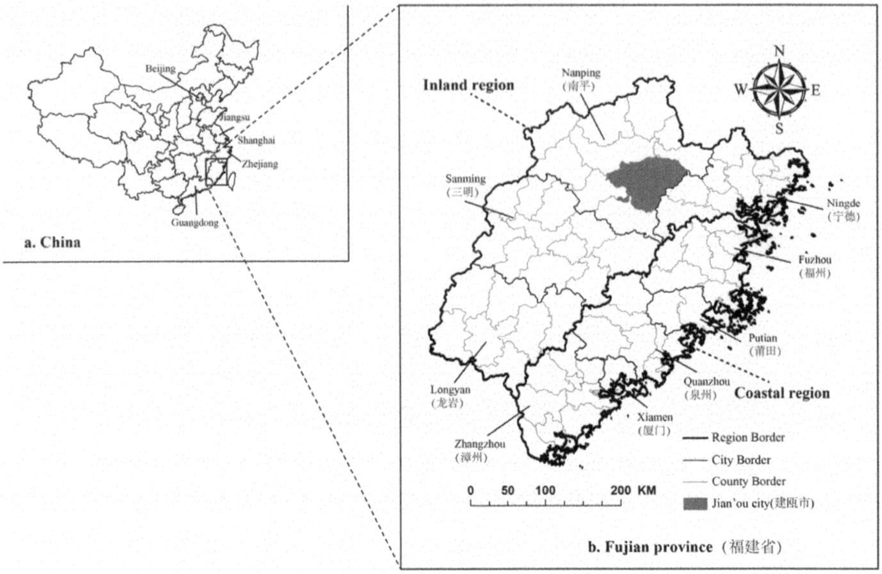

Fig. 1 Location of Fujian province (福建省)

and these districts account for around 70% of the whole inland region. In the coastal region, 16 counties (accounting for 50% of the whole coastal region) show a rate of increase in the number of people employed in rural industry and that is above the province average.

Among the inland region, the largest increase in rural industrial workers growth rate was in Nanping city (南平市),[5] where there are several counties with an increase rate of more than 200%. Nanping city (南平市) used to be a district of Fujian province (福建省) where economy was under-developed, but its rural industry has been developing due to the improvement of transportation infrastructure in recent years. Particularly, the growth of rural industries utilizing local agricultural and forestry resources has progressed due to the preferential industrial policies of the local government. Jian'ou city (建瓯市), where we conducted our filed work, is a county-level city under the jurisdiction of Nanping city (南平市), has achieved remarkable growth with a 210% of increase rate in the number of rural industrial workers.

Jian'ou city (建瓯市) has achieved a high annual economic growth rate of 18.2% since 2000. The regional gross production amount in 2000 was 3.6 billion yuan, and the composition ratio by primary industry, secondary industry and tertiary industry were 28, 30 and 42%, respectively. The regional gross product reached 10.3 billion yuan in 2010, and the composition ratio by industries changed to primary industries (28%), secondary industries (34%), and tertiary industries (38%). This change suggests that secondary industries played a more important role in Jian'ou city's (建瓯市) economic growth.

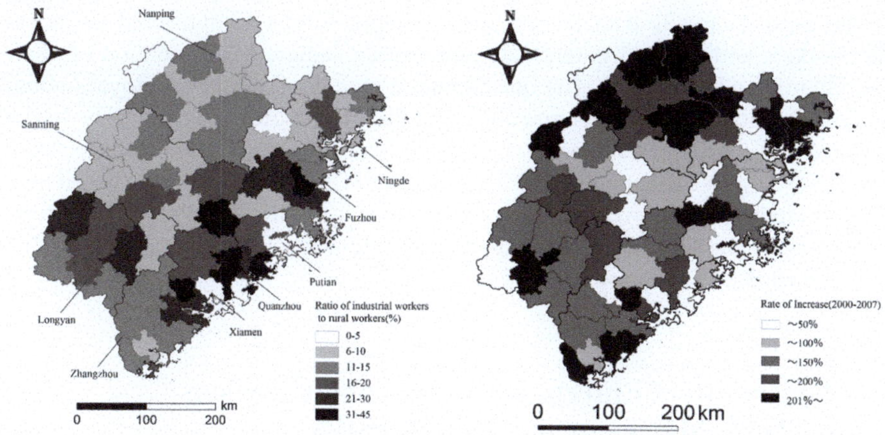

a) Ratio of industrial workers to rural workers (2007)

b) Rate of increase in rural industrial workers (2000-2007)

Fig. 2 Growth of rural enterprises in Fujian province (福建省) by county
(*Source* Fujian Rural Statistical Yearbook 1991 and Fujian Economic and Social Statistical Yearbook [rural economy section])

The rapid economic growth of Jian'ou city (建瓯市) has brought about significant changes in the employment structures in rural areas. In 1995, the number of primary industry workers was 117,350, accounting for 76% of rural workers. After that, the number of primary industry workers slightly increased to 129,602 in 2007, but the ratio of primary industry workers to rural workers decreased to 65%. In contrast, the number of secondary industry workers increased by 74% from 9,516 in 1995 to 26,140 in 2007, and the ratio of secondary industry workers to rural workers also increased from 6% in 1995 to 13% in 2007.

2.2 Data Resources

We mainly employed the following three datasets in the analysis. The first one is the Township and Villages Enterprise Annual Report in Xudun town (徐墩镇) of Jian'ou city (建瓯市). This report has been continuously collected, and includes basic information relating to rural enterprises such as types of enterprises, the number of enterprises and employees. As a result, it is crucial to capture the changes of enterprises in the study area over time.

The second dataset is data from face-to-face interviews to enterprises' managers and local government officials. In the survey of enterprises' managers, we mainly asked for basic information on their business and about the circumstances of employment and so on. The survey of town officials centered on the circumstances of enterprises in the survey area and preferential industrial strategies.

The third dataset is data from a questionnaire survey administered to industrial workers and a list of enterprises' employees, including information on their age, job title and birthplace. The questionnaire mainly asked the employees about employment condition, job history, and agricultural activities and so on. The list of employees is used to examine the characteristics of the employees' supply structure. From August to September 2012, a total of 300 questionnaires were distributed to the companies' employees through factory managers in 7 large-scale enterprises accounting for one-third of the total large-scale enterprises in the town, of which 271 were collected (response rate is 90.3%).

3 The Growth of Enterprises in the Inland Regions and Their Management Characteristics

3.1 Changes in the Number of Enterprises in Xudun Town (徐墩镇)

Xudun town (徐墩镇), adjacent to the built-up area of Jian'ou city (建瓯市), is selected as a specific case study site in this chapter. The ratio of industrial workers to the total number of workers in the town is 22.1% (2007), which greatly exceeds the average of 13% in the whole Jian'ou city (建瓯市). Thus, it is considered that Xudun town (徐墩镇) is one of the most advancing areas of industrial development in Jian'ou city (建瓯市).

The statistics of Xudun town (徐墩镇) on enterprises are different before 2003 and after. Before 2003, all enterprises in the town were included in the statistics, and after 2003, only enterprises with eight or more employees were included in the statistics. Figure 3 shows the trend in the number of enterprises from 1984 to 2003. The enterprises in Xudun town (徐墩镇) increased rapidly after 1984, and especially, the increase until 1987 is remarkable. The number of enterprises jumped from 118 in 1984 to 602 in 1988, which was a five times increase from 1984. The private enterprises were dominating for this increase, accounting for nearly 80% of the total in 1988.

The number of enterprises showed a slightly decrease from 1988 to 1991, and this is supposed to be temporary with the stagnation of domestic consumption market in the whole China in this period. After 1992, the transition to the market economy advanced in China, and the enterprises increased again. The number reached 740 in 1996. The self-employed business drastically increased from 480 in 1992 to 620 in 1996, and it greatly contributed to the increase of enterprises in this period.

From 1997, the reorganization of enterprises was advanced, and small enterprises were weeded out. The number of enterprises decreased to 549 in 2003. Especially, the self-employed business rapidly decreased from 620 in 1996 to 483 in 2003. In contrast, the number of private enterprises with relatively large scale increased from 31 in 1996 to 51. Simultaneously, the privatization of collective enterprises was

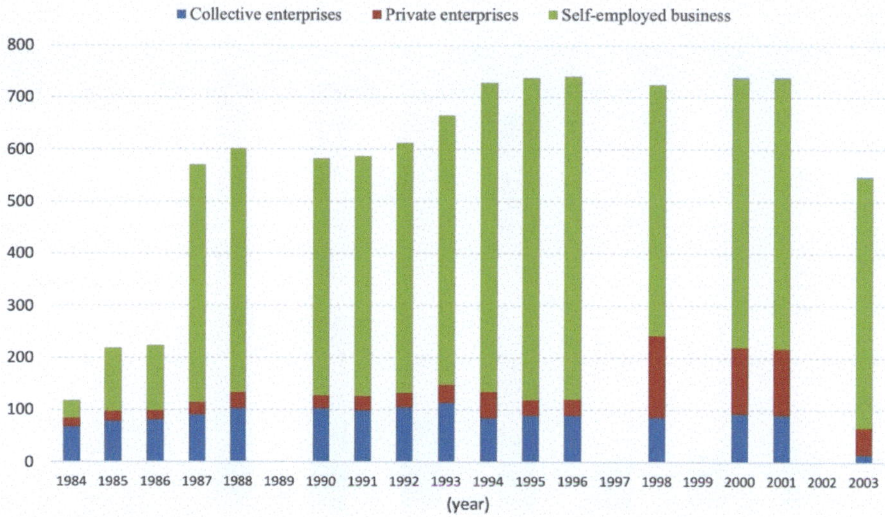

Fig. 3 Changes in the number of enterprises in the study area (1984–2003) (*Sources* Xudun Township and Village Enterprises Annual Report [various years])

promoted by the ownership reform in the end of 1990s, and the number of enterprises rapidly decreased from 89 in 1996 to 15 in 2003.

Figure 4 shows the trend of enterprises in Xudun town (徐墩镇) from 2004 to 2010. The enterprises are classified by their ownership system into Limited Liability Enterprises (hereafter "LLEs"), Private Enterprises (hereafter "PEs"), and Foreign Enterprises (hereafter "FEs"), of which the scale of LLEs and FEs is considered to be larger than that of PEs. The number of enterprises has been increasing since 2004. Concretely, the number of LLEs increased from 13 in 2004 to 23 in 2010, and the number of PEs also increased from 48 to 62 during the same period. In addition, there were 4 enterprises which were established by the investment of foreign capitals in 2004, but they disappeared because they merged with the local enterprises in 2008.

From the above, it can be concluded that the number of enterprises in the study area has been increasing since the mid-1980s, mainly by self-employed business. In the 2000s, the increase in the number of enterprises in the study area was mainly caused by the growth of LLEs and PEs.

3.2 *Job Creation of Large-Scale Enterprises and Their Characteristics*

Large-scale enterprises in China are normally defined as those with annual sales of 5 million yuan or more and doing their businesses as a corporation. However, in the Xudun town (徐墩镇), the enterprise with the capital over 3 million yuan is

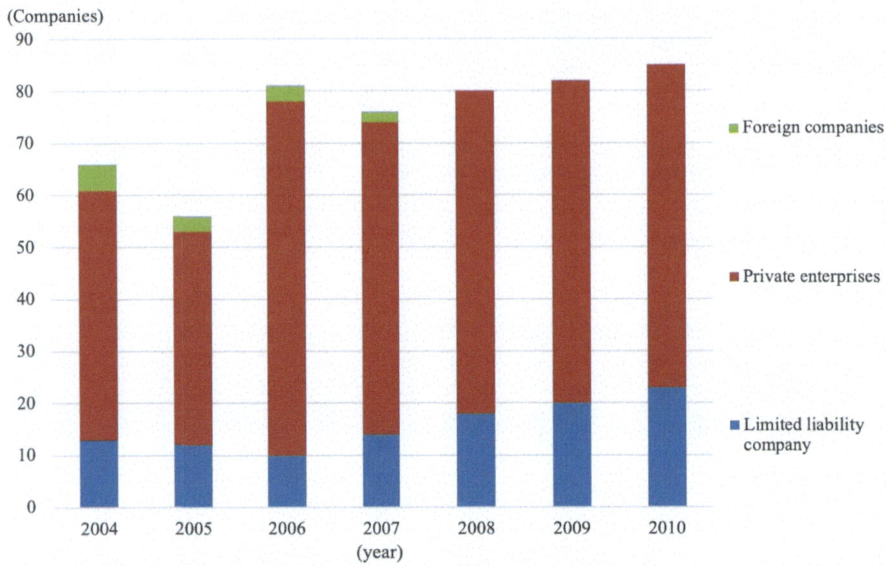

Fig. 4 Changes in the number of enterprises in the study area (2004–2010) (*Source* Xudun Township and Villages Enterprise Annual Report [various years])

also recognized as a large-scale enterprise. And, the ownership of the large-scale enterprise in the study area is mainly LLEs. The proportion of employees in the large-scale enterprises to the total enterprise employees was 28.4% in 2000, and it increased to 45.4% in 2005, and it has occupied 85.9% in 2010. Thus, it can be considered that the large-scale enterprises play an important role in the employment of the study area.

In Xudun town (徐墩镇), large-scale enterprises can be broadly categorized into the following four types: the first is the timber products manufacturing industry, which accounts for the largest number of enterprises (12 out of 25); and the second is the food products manufacturing industry (4 out 25); the third is craft manufacturing enterprises (3 out of 25); and the forth is other enterprises (6 out of 25).

Table 1 shows the overview and their features of the surveyed large-scale enterprises in Xudun town (徐墩镇). According to it, it is apparent that all enterprises were founded after 2000. Since the mid-1990s, the privatization and large-scale restructuring of TVEs across China has been promoted. Under such background, it seems that the enlargement of the enterprises progressed in the study area. The size of employment can be confirmed from the number of employees per enterprises. Many of them have more than 100 employees, and the largest enterprise has 600 employees.

In addition, in terms of capital the smallest enterprise S had 3 million yuan, while three other enterprises such as M, F and H had more than 10 million yuan. Such a large amount of capital mainly depends on urban capitals and foreign capitals. For example, enterprise F is a joint establishment between a company in Fuzhou city

Table 1 The overview of surveyed enterprises in Xudun town (徐墩镇)

Enterprise	Capital stock (million yuan)	Establishment year	Ownership	Level of leading enterprises	Main products	Number of employees
S	3	2001	Limited liability enterprises	Province	Plywood	120
WF	5	2009	Limited liability enterprises		Plywood	67
WML	8	2000	Limited liability enterprises	City	Plywood, wood toy	259
M	47	2002	Joint venture	Province	Frozen vegetables	600
F	46	2004	Limited liability enterprises	province	Plywood	236
H	50	2006	Limited liability enterprises	province	Bamboo plywood	500

Source Authors' survey

(福州市) (Capital city of Fujian province [福建省]) and a company in Jian'ou city (建瓯市), and company M is a joint venture company with Japanese capitals. Since the large-scale enterprises are recognized as leading enterprises at various levels, it is also favored in respect of tax payment unlike the relatively small-scale PEs.

3.3 Management Characteristics of Large-Scale Enterprises

3.3.1 Location Factors of Large-Scale Enterprises

Based on the interviews of local officials, large-scale enterprises in the study area prefer to make a large investment and hope to obtain land-use right for long-term and stable operation. Therefore, how to reduce the management risk and cost is an important factor to attract their initial location. Table 2 shows the location factors of large-scale enterprises in Xudun town (徐墩镇). According to it, it is evident that local government attraction is the most important factor for large-scale enterprises' location. Other factors mentioned are the hometown of the founders and the convenience of transportation. In addition, many of the enterprises have acquired a certain size of land in industrial parks, which tends to ensure the long-term stability for their operations.

Table 2 Location factors of large-scale enterprises in Xudun town (徐墩镇)

Enterprise	Head office	Reason for the advance	Land acquisition status	Acquisition price and tenure
S	Xudun town (徐墩镇)	Good transportation	Land purchase in industrial park	Purchase price: 20,000 yuan/mu, tenure: 50 years
WF	Downtown of Jian'ou (建瓯市)	Invitation by the town government	Land purchase (15 mu)	Purchase price: 60,000 yuan/mu, tenure: 50 years
WML	Downtown of Jian'ou	Founder's hometown is nearby	Land purchase in industrial park (70mu)	Purchase price: 30,000 yuan/mu, tenure: 50 years
M	Xudun town (徐墩镇)	Invitation by the town and city government	Land purchase (160 mu)	unknown
F	Fuzhou City (福州市)	Invitation by the town government	Land leasing and land purchase (222 mu)	Purchase price: 26,000 yuan/mu, rental price: 530 yuan/mu
H	Downtown of Jian'ou (建瓯市)	Invitation by the town government	Land purchase (200 mu)	Purchase price: 15,000 yuan/mu

Note 1 mu = 667 m^2
Source Authors' survey

Due to the contribution not only to employment but also to increase in tax revenue and gross regional product, the local government is actively inviting large-scale enterprises. Therefore, the location of large-scale enterprises is strongly influenced by the development strategy of the local government. According to Fig. 5 which shows the location of the large-scale enterprises in Xudun town (徐墩镇), it is apparent that they are mainly located along the National Highway 205. Since there are few industrial lands in rural areas of China, it is important for the local government to actively participate in the construction of industrial parks. This led to the concentration of large-scale enterprises in the industrial parks along the National Highway 205 in the study area.

3.3.2 Raw Material Procurement and Commodity Markets

Table 3 shows the current status of raw material procurement in the surveyed large-scale enterprises in Xudun town (徐墩镇). Most of the enterprises in the study area use bamboo, wood, vegetables, etc. as raw materials and can be classified as a raw material location industry. For this reason, raw materials are mainly procured within the same county, but in recent years, the enterprises have begun to procure raw materials from neighboring counties in the same city by increasing the scale of production. There are two main ways to procure raw materials within the county.

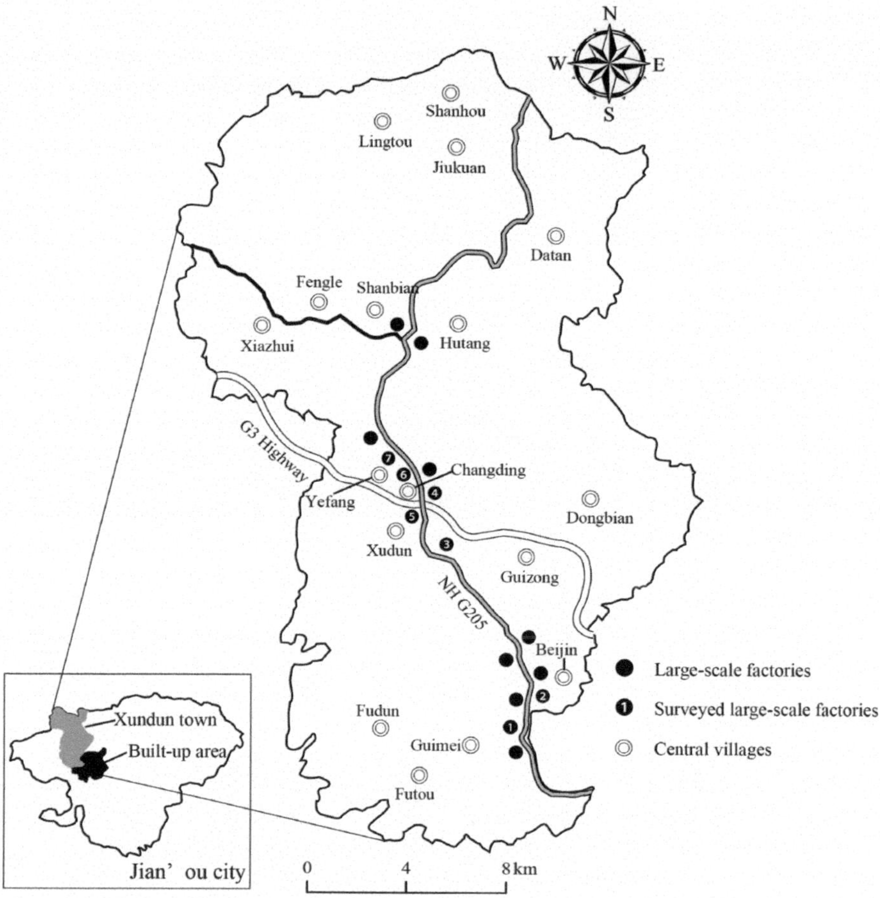

Fig. 5 Distribution of large-scale enterprises in Xudun town (徐墩镇) (*Source* A list of scale-industry enterprises provided by Xudun town office)

The first is for the enterprises to have its own production bases, where it can directly produce and control the quality of the raw materials. This type of enterprises mainly processes vegetables and bamboo shoots, etc. The other type is to deliver semi-processed products from subcontractors in the same county. This type of enterprises are mainly plywood production factories. The advantage of this method is that the subcontractor bears the transportation cost of the semi-processed goods, and thus it is easier for the enterprises to control the production cost. In addition, with the growth of enterprises in recent years, raw materials in the region tended to be scarce, and some enterprises tended to procure them from neighboring provinces and resource-rich inland provinces in China.

Table 4 shows the distribution of the main consumer markets for the products of large-scale enterprises. The consumer market for commodities is a major domestic

Table 3 Procurement of raw materials for large-scale enterprises in Xudun town (徐墩镇)

Enterprise	Raw material	Local procurement	Procurement in neighboring areas	Procurement within province	Procurement outside the province	Note
S	Bamboo	Yes	Within Nanping (南平市)			About 1/4 is procured from neighboring areas
WF	unknown	unknown	unknown	unknown	unknown	
WML	Cedar	Yes	Within Nanping (南平市)	Sha'xian (沙县)	Guizhou (贵州), Jiangxi (江西), Zhejiang (浙江), Hunan (湖南)	Raw material from resource-rich provinces
M	Bamboo shoot, vegetables	Yes	Within Nanping (南平市)		Jiangxi (江西)	The spring bamboo shoots are procured from outside the province
F	Wood, Wood chips	Yes	Within Nanping (南平市)			
H	Bamboo	Yes	Within Nanping (南平市)		Zhejiang (浙江)	

Source Authors' survey

and international consumption destination and differs from the source of raw materials. Consumers outside the country are mainly from the United States, Japan and European countries, but in recent years it has spread to Africa and the Middle East countries. The domestic market is mainly the building materials market in eastern coastal China, including Beijing (北京), Shanghai (上海) and Guangdong (广东). Most enterprises are not doing much to sell products within the province.

Since the early 1990s, competition among enterprises has been intense, and as a result, enterprises located in urban areas in the eastern coastal China have developed by focusing on exporting their products overseas. However, the enterprises in the inland regions of the eastern coastal China were restricted in exporting their products overseas due to their poor geographical location. Large-scale enterprises in the Xudun town (徐墩镇) overcame this constraint mainly by cooperating with companies in Fuzhou city (福州市) or with the help of oversea capital such as Japan, and were able to produce products using local agricultural products for the domestic and international markets.

4 Employment Structure of Large-Scale Enterprises

4.1 Age Structure

Table 5 shows the age structure and occupations of employees in large-scale enterprises in Xudun town (徐墩镇). Of the total 650 employees, 167 (26.7%) were in their 30s and 349 (53.7%) were in their 40s, which together accounted for 80% of the total number of employees.

The concentration of workers in their 30s and 40s can be attributed to the following two reasons. The first reason is because urban areas absorb a large number of young workers from rural areas, the labor supply in their 20s is low in the Xudun town (徐墩镇). The second reason is that large-scale enterprises in the study area prefer a relatively young age range of up to the 40s as production processing workers. However, we can also see a small number of workers over 50 years old were employed as production processing workers, because the shortage of young workers is becoming apparent in the surrounding rural areas.

The occupations of the employees are diversified such as managers, technical workers, clerical workers, salespersons, security, and production processing workers. The majority of the employees (510 persons) are engaged in production processing (78.5% of the total number of employees). The number of the production processing were 33 persons in their 20s (6.5%), 129 persons in their 30s (25.3%), 287 persons in their 40s (56.3%), and 53 persons in their 50s (10.4%). It is apparent that production processing workers are concentrated in their 40s and 30s, the same as the trend for the whole employees. In contrast, those in their 40s and 50s tend to be heavily weighted toward production processing workers, while those in their 20s and 30s tend to be relatively less likely to be employed in production processing workers.

Table 4 Buyers of large-scale enterprises in Xudun town (徐墩镇)

Enterprise	Products	Within province	Outside the province	Abroad	Note
S	Bamboo and plywood		Building Materials Market in Northern and Northeast China	Africa and Middle East	Certified products for the 2008 Beijing Olympics
WF	Plywood		Guangdong (广东), Shanghai (上海), Shandong (山东)		Focus on domestic market
WML	Plywood and toys			European countries, America and Middle East countries	In recent years, the company has been developing the domestic market
M	Frozen and boiled vegetables		Unknown	Japan, Europe and America	The percentages are 50 for Japan, 40 for domestic market and 10 for other markets
F	Plywood	No details	Eastern coastal region		
H	Bamboo and plywood			Japan, Korea and the United States	Exports make up 90% of the business

Source Authors' survey

Table 5 Age structure of employees in large-scale enterprises in Xudun town (徐墩镇)

Age group	Gender	Occupational categories								
		M	TW	CW	S	SP	PW	Others	Unknown	Total
10s	Male	0	0	0	0	0	2	0	0	2
	Female	0	0	0	0	0	0	0	0	0
20s	Male	2	2	4	6	0	22	1	0	37
	Female	0	0	3	1	0	11	1	0	16
30s	Male	4	5	3	4	1	70	0	0	87
	Female	0	4	5	10	0	59	2	0	80
40s	Male	15	3	5	7	4	115	0	0	149
	Female	5	4	9	9	0	172	1	0	200
50s	Male	8	0	0	0	1	33	1	1	44
	Female	0	1	3	2	0	20	1	0	27
60+	Male	1	0	0	0	0	5	0	0	6
	Female	0	0	0	0	1	1	0	0	2

Note M = managers, TW = technical workers, CW = clerical workers, S = salesperson, SP = security personnel, PW = production processing workers
Source Data provided by Xudun town (徐墩镇) Enterprise Association

Focusing on the occupations except for production processing workers, there are 35 managers, 19 technical workers, 32 clerical workers, 39 salespersons. The managers are mainly concentrated in their 40s and 50s, and both occupy 80% of this type of occupation. Among them, male tend to engage in more managerial occupations than female. The technical workers are mainly concentrated in the age group of 30s and 40s, and both occupy 84.2% of the total. Unlike managerial occupation, there is no difference between males and females, with five and four males in their 30s and three and four females in their 40s. Many of the clerical workers are young, and people in their 20s–40s account for 90.6% of the total. Salespersons are also concentrated mainly in their 20s–40s, accounting for 94.9% of the total.

4.2 *Educational Level*

The level of education of employees varies in its composition depending on the type of occupations (Table 6). The educational level of production processing workers is relatively low, with elementary and junior high school graduates accounting for 90.8% of the total number of employees. In addition, salespersons are also concentrated in elementary and junior high school graduates, which accounted for 92.3% of the total. The educational level of workers in managerial, technical and clerical occupations is higher than that of high school graduates. The number of high school graduates or higher education were 26 persons in managers, 12 persons in technical

Table 6 Educational level of employees in large-scale enterprises in Xudun town (徐墩镇)

Occupational categories	ES	MS	HS	SS	CG	UG	Unknown	Total
Managers	2	7	14	4	6	2	0	35
Technical workers	0	7	5	7	0	0	0	19
Clerical worker	1	6	9	6	10	0	0	32
Salesperson	14	22	0	0	0	0	3	39
Security personnel	1	6	0	0	0	0	0	7
Production process worker	166	297	35	10	1	0	1	510
Others	1	5	1	0	0	0	0	7
Unknown	0	1	0	0	0	0	0	1
Total	185	351	64	27	17	2	4	650

Note ES = elementary school graduate (6–11 years old), MS = middle school graduate (12–14 years old), HS = high school graduate (15–17 years old), SS = specialized secondary school graduate (15–17 years old), CG = college graduate (19–21 years old), UG = university graduate (19–22 years old)

Source Data provided by Xudun town (徐墩镇) Enterprise Association

workers and 25 persons in clerical workers, accounting for 74.3%, 63.2% and 81.3% of the total, respectively. Thus, it can be witnessed that the educational level is an important requirement for employment in the above three occupations. However, there are some differences among the age groups in the above occupations as well, as some of the workers in their 50s are employed in the above occupations even if their educational level is junior high school graduates. This is because there are few people in these generations who have graduated from high schools or higher. For those in their 20s and 30s, the educational background of a high school graduates or higher is a prerequisite to work in the above three occupations.

As mentioned above, although the large-scale enterprises in the Xudun town (徐墩镇) are predominantly production processing workers, they also provide employment in a variety of other occupations. In terms of age, it is a feature that the employees of the wide age group from 20 years-old to 50 years-old are attracted. It was also clarified that educational level and age group differed by occupations.

4.3 Supply Range of Employees

In this section, we examined the range and characteristics of labor supply based on the employee's place of origin and employment history. Table 7 shows the previous jobs of employees in the large-scale enterprises and their places of employment in Xudun town (徐墩镇).

The results show that the majority of the employees in large-scale enterprises are rural household registration (229 persons), and those who moved from agriculture are 122, which accounts for 53.3% of the total number of rural household registration

Table 7 Previous employment of employees and their place of employment in large-scale enterprises in Xudun town (徐墩镇)

Previous employment	Within Nanping city (南平市)							Within Fujian province (福建省)			Outside Fujian province		NA		Total		
	Within Xudun town (徐墩镇)		Within Jian'ou city (建瓯市)		Other counties												
	RH	UH	RH	UH	RH	UH	NA	RH	UH	NA	RH	UH	RH	UH	RH	UH	NA
Agriculture	102	0	7	1	7	0	0	0	0	0	1	0	5	0	122	1	0
Manufacturing	17	0	22	15	3	3	1	7	1	1	1	0	7	0	57	19	2
Service	1	0	2	2	0	0	0	3	1	0	0	0	1	0	7	3	0
Construction	0	0	0	1	0	0	0	1	0	0	1	0	0	0	2	1	0
Restaurant and lodging	1	0	0	0	0	0	0	3	0	0	0	0	0	0	4	0	0
Lodging and dining	0	0	0	1	0	0	0	0	0	0	0	0	0	0	0	1	0
Wholesale and retail	0	0	1	0	1	0	0	4	0	0	0	0	0	0	6	0	0
Finance and insurance	0	0	0	0	0	0	0	1	0	0	0	0	0	0	1	0	0
Domestic service	1	0	0	0	0	0	0	0	0	0	0	0	0	0	1	0	0
Unemployed	0	0	0	0	0	2	0	0	0	0	0	0	0	0	0	2	0
Self-employed	0	1	3	1	0	0	0	0	0	0	0	0	0	0	3	2	0
Students	0	0	0	0	0	0	0	0	0	0	0	0	4	1	4	1	0
Others	0	1	3	3	0	0	0	0	1	0	0	0	0	3	3	8	0
Unknown	0	0	4	2	2	0	0	1	0	0	6	0	6	0	19	2	0
Total	122	2	42	26	13	5	1	20	3	1	9	0	23	4	229	40	2

Note RH = rural household registration, UH = urban household registration, NA = unknown
Source Authors' questionnaire survey

employees. The next largest number of employees were from the manufacturing industry, which accounted for 24.9% of the total, or 57 employees. In addition, there were employees from the service industry, wholesale and retail trade, food service and lodging industry and students. In China, the household registration system severely restricts the movement of population from rural areas to urban areas. This resulted that the overwhelming majority of employees working in the large-scale enterprises in the study area are rural household holders. In contrast, there are 40 employees who have urban household registration in the large-scale enterprises. Among them, employees from the manufacturing industry are the largest with 19 persons, accounting for 47.5%.

In terms of their previous places of employment, Xudun town (徐墩镇) had the largest number of workers (124 persons), accounting for 45.8% of the total number of workers. 68 persons, or 25.1% of the total workers, were employed in other towns of Jian'ou city (建瓯市). In addition, there were 19 and 24 persons in other counties in Nanping city (南平市) and other cities in Fujian province (福建省), respectively.

According to the above previous jobs and places of employment, it was found that the employees of the large-scale enterprises in the study area mainly consisted the following four types. The first type is the labor force which is precipitated from the agriculture and has the rural household registration in the Xudun town (徐墩镇). The number is the largest with 102 persons and which occupies 37.6% of the whole. The second type consists of those who are former employees of manufacturing industry and have rural household registration in Jian'ou city (建瓯市). The third type is migrant workers with rural household registration in other counties in Nanping city (南平市) or within and outside Fujian province (福建省). The number is 25 persons, accounting for 9.2% of the total. The fourth is the number of former manufacturing employees with urban household registration in Jian'ou city (建瓯市), which is only 15 persons, or 5.5% of the total.

From the above, the labor supply and demand of workers in large-scale enterprises can be summarized as follows. The production processing workers are mainly supplied by the local agricultural labor force. There is also the participation of experienced employees of manufacturing and other industries in Jian'ou city (建瓯市). The managers and technical workers are mainly composed of those who have worked in manufacturing industries outside of the city, and their entry contributes to the development of large-scale enterprises.

5 Discussion and Conclusion

Thus far, China's enterprises had been concentrated in the urban areas of the eastern coastal regions. However, during the privatization process of TVEs since the mid-1990s, it became apparent that the development of enterprises has extended to the inland regions of the eastern coastal regions as well. The results of this chapter suggest that the development of enterprises in the inland region of Fujian province (福建省) can be attributed to the following factors.

The first is that there has traditionally been some development of collective enterprises. In the early 1980s, enterprises were established in the Xudun town (徐墩镇), mainly as collective enterprises. Since the mid-1990s, LLEs, which have shifted from collective enterprises, have played the most important role in economic growth and employment. Thus, it can be concluded that the collective enterprise has become an important foundation for the development of the enterprises in the inland region of the province.

The second is that the existence of large-scale enterprises which can raise funds from the outside of the region. Since the middle of 1990s, with the privatization of TVEs in China, collective enterprises in the study area transferred to the private sector have succeeded in attracting funds from outside the region, and have contributed greatly to the development of enterprises. In addition, large-scale enterprises have been certified as leading enterprises at various levels and are again expanding their scale with government's support. Large-scale enterprises have employed more workers and have become more important to the inland region of the province.

The third is that the approach to the domestic and international consumer market, mainly through large-scale enterprises. Since the early 1990s, competition among enterprises has been intense, and as a result, enterprises located in urban areas in the eastern coastal China have developed by focusing on exporting their products abroad. In contrast, the enterprises in the inland rural areas of the eastern coastal China were restricted in exporting their products overseas due to their poor geographical location. Large-scale enterprises in the study area overcame this constraint mainly by cooperating with companies in Fuzhou city (福州市) or abroad, and were able to produce products by using local agricultural products for the domestic and international markets.

The fourth is that labor supplied from within and outside the region. In the context of management strategy, managers and technical workers play an important role in the development of large-scale enterprises in the region, and they consist of well-educated workers in the age group of 30–50 years old. Many of them have experience in the manufacturing industry in Jian'ou city (建瓯市) or other counties in Fujian province (福建省), contributing to the management and technical development of large-scale enterprises. In contrast, many of the unskilled workers in the production processing position come from Jian'ou city (建瓯市). The participation of local agricultural workers in their 30s and 40s as production processing workers plays a large role in the development of enterprises. As a result of the above factors, the growth of enterprises, mainly large-scale enterprises, was observed in the inland region of the province.

Finally, we have identified that the space of the inland regions played different roles in different stages of enterprises development. In the first stage, when enterprises are considering expansion, they focus on how to reduce initial investment costs and risk. Thus, it is important for the inland regions to develop public infrastructure such as water, electricity, and land, and to take measures such as tax exemptions to reduce the initial investment cost and risk of companies. These policies are effective means of attracting companies to locate in the inland regions. In the second stage, the focus of the enterprise shifts to how to proceed with the expansion of production and management and improve profits. Accordingly, the inland region plays an important role in the supply of raw materials and labor for enterprises. The managers and technicians precipitated from state-owned and collective enterprises in the inland regions have also made a significant contribution to the management and technological improvement of enterprises. Currently, enterprises in the inland regions are in the third stage of development process. How enterprises in the inland regions increase their added value is more important for their survival and sustainable development. As part of these efforts, in recent years some enterprises organically integrating the flow from raw materials and product processing to sales, and by raising the quality level and adding value of products, successfully approached international markets such as Japan and other countries.

As mentioned above, initial investment costs, income expansion and newly-added value are the three most striking factors affecting the sustainable development of enterprises in the inland regions of the province. Therefore, how to recognize and utilize the "value" of the inland regions and how to adapt and create the "new value" within the space have become key challenges for enterprises to enhance their competitiveness. In the process of utilizing and creating the space value in the inland regions, we found that it is important for enterprises to produce goods based on local resources and knowledge for the domestic and international markets and whether they can succeed or not is closely related to their connections with cities and foreign companies. It further suggests that non-territorial inter-firm network formation and organizational proximity play a significant role in the development of enterprises in the inland regions. Such findings are meaningful for the understanding of enterprise development and management, and space value in the inland region of eastern coastal China and other countries.

Notes

1. China's administrative divisions are mainly divided into (1) provinces (省), municipalities directly under the central government (直辖市), (2) prefecture-level city (地级市), (3) county-level city (县级市), county (县), (4) town (镇), township (乡), and (5) village (村), and are organized hierarchically.
2. We follow Ueno's (1992) definition and define Township and Village Enterprises (TVEs) as not only collectively owned enterprises, but also individual owned enterprises and diversified federated and cooperative enterprises.
3. A collectively owned township and village enterprise is an enterprise established by an economic organization owned by a township or a village.
4. The eastern region of China includes Hebei, Beijing, Tianjin, Shandong, Jiangsu, Shanghai, Zhejiang, Fujian, Guangdong and Hainan provinces. The western region of China refers to Chongqing, Sichuan, Yunnan, Guizhou, Shaanxi, Qinghai, Gansu, Ningxia, Xinjiang, Tibet, Guangxi and Inner Mongolia provinces.
5. In China, cities are divided into municipalities (such as Beijing (北京) and Shanghai (上海)), prefecture-level cities and county-level cities. The municipality is on the same level as the province, designated by the State Council. A prefecture-level city is established as a branch organization of the province, and the province directly manages the prefecture-level city. A

county-level city is one of the county-level administrative districts, and many of them have changed their names from the previous counties. In this study, Nanping city (南平市) is a prefecture-level city, and Jianou city (建瓯市) is a county-level city.

References

Cheong T, Wu Y (2014) The impacts of structural transformation and industrial upgrading on regional inequality in China. China Econ Revi 31: 339–350. https://doi.org/10.1016/j.chieco.2014.09.007

China Township Enterprise Yearbook Editorial Committee (Zhong Guo Xiang Zhen Qi Ye Nian Jian Bian Ji Wei Yuan Hui) (ed) (1996) China township enterprise yearbook 1996 (Zhong Guo Xiang Zhen Qi Ye Nian Jian 1996). China Agricultural Press (Zhong Guo Nong Ye Chu Ban She), Beijing. (C)

China Rural Enterprise and Agro-processing Industry Yearbook Editorial Committee (Zhong Guo Xiang Zhen Qi Ye Ji Nong Chan Pin Jia Gong Ye Nian Jian Bian Ji Wei Yuan Hui) (ed) (2011) China rural enterprise and agro-processing industry yearbook 2011 (Zhong Guo Xiang Zhen Qi Ye Ji Nong Chan Pin Jia Gong Ye Nian Jian 2011). China Agricultural Press (Zhong Guo Nong Ye Chu Ban She), Beijing. (C)

Li H, Rozelle S (2000) Saving or stripping rural industry: an analysis of privatization and efficiency in China. Agricu Econ 23: 241–252. https://doi.org/10.1016/S0169-5150(00)00086-4

Li H, Rozelle S (2003) Privatizing rural China: insider privatization, innovative contracts and the performance of township enterprises. The China Q 176:981–1005. https://doi.org/10.1017/S0305741003000584

Liang Z, Chen YP, Gu Y (2002) Rural industrialization and internal migration in China. Urban Stud 39:2175–2187. https://doi.org/10.1080/0042098022000033926

Rozelle S, Huang J, Zhang L (2002) Emerging markets, evolving institutions, and the new opportunities for growth in China's rural economy. China Econ Rev 13:345–353. https://doi.org/10.1016/S1043-951X(02)00091-3

Shen X, Ma JC (2005) Privatization of rural industry and de facto urbanization from below in southern Jiangsu, China. Geoforum 36:761–777. https://doi.org/10.1016/j.geoforum.2005.01.005

Ueno K (1992) Development and regional inequalities of rural nonagricultural enterprises in China. Japanese J Hum Geogr 44(2):242–261. https://doi.org/10.4200/jjhg1948.44.242 (J)

Yang X, Fan J (2005) Analysis of regional rural industrial competitive power in China. Scientia Geographica Sinica 25(1):1–6. (C)

(C) denotes literature in Chinese

(J) denotes literature in Japanese

Transformation of Agricultural Management in Japan Under Globalization Pressure: A Focus on Product Differentiation Strategy

Atsushi Kawakubo

Abstract This chapter analyzes the unique characteristics of the management strategy of Japan's agricultural sector under globalization pressure since the 1990s, focusing on product differentiation in beef cattle and citrus farming. In the beef cattle sector, enhancement of meat quality has accelerated with increased production of Japanese Blacks, a breed in which marbling is easier to achieve. In the citrus fruits sector, enhancement of sweetness of Satsuma mandarins was achieved with development of technology. As for miscellaneous citrus, development of varieties unique to Japan progressed. Japan's strategy can be summarized as "product differentiation" to avoid price competition with imported produce. The background which prompted adoption of this strategy is twofold. First, acknowledgement by Japanese producers that it is impossible to win a global low-price competition. Second, acknowledgement that Japanese consumers question the quality or safety of imported products and are not averse to paying higher prices for domestic products. Recently, economic development of Asian nations suggests a potential expanded interest in Japanese high-quality products, which may afford an opportunity to transform the "domestically focused" mindset into an "export-oriented" mindset among Japan's agricultural sector.

Keywords Globalization · Trade liberalization · Beef and orange · Agricultural management · Product differentiation strategy

1 Introduction

Today, as globalization of economy accelerates, the move to abolish non-tariff barriers is gaining traction around the world, resulting in the expansion of trade in agricultural produce. In Japan, due to the increased industrialization and shift towards service economy after the second world war, agriculture lost much of its economic significance, resulting in increased import of agricultural produce. Japan

A. Kawakubo (✉)
Faculty of Law, Toyo University, Tokyo 112-8606, Japan
e-mail: kawakubo@toyo.jp

A. Taira and R. D. Schlunze (eds.), *Management Geography*, International Perspectives in Geography 19, https://doi.org/10.1007/978-981-19-4403-1_10

has now become a net importer of agricultural produce next to China, and one reason for this is the extremely small export of Japanese agricultural produce. This means that any increase in imported produce could easily compress the demand for domestic produce, and this in turn has been bearing a significant influence on the restructuring of regions that are dependent on agriculture and the continued management of farms. If so, how have Japan's agricultural sector been planning for their survival by adopting what kind of management strategy, as competition with imported produce intensified? The aim of this chapter is to shine a light on such unique characteristics of the management strategy adopted by Japan's agricultural sector, and the challenges the regions face going forward.

Movements concerning the trade in agricultural produce with Japan have been attracting the attention of the world due to the sheer scale of it. Friedmann (1993) pointed out that when Japan invested in Brazil as a new source of imported soybean in the early 1970s, thus diversifying its source of grains, this led to the collapse of the food regime which centered on the USA, whilst Sumner and Lee (1996) pointed out that opening the Japanese rice market pursuant to the GATT Uruguay Round Accord boosted the rice market in California, USA, which produces high-quality Japonica rice, thereby prompting the increase in cultivation acreage. Oro and Pritchard (2010) have shown that the direct investment in Australia made by Japanese corporations from the late 1980s in the period leading up to the beef import liberalization resulted in the rapid development of feedlot sector, and subsequently contributed to the expansion of trade in beef.

On the other hand, in a study which analyzed the response of Japan's agricultural regions to the increase in imported produce, Takayanagi (2006) pointed out that it was important to enhance the quality of agricultural produce and seek increased brand values, so as to avoid competing on price with imported produce. As a means of enhancing the sustainability of farming in rural villages, which have shrunk and have been reorganized, Seki (2014) noted that outlets that sell agricultural produce, as well as factories that process agricultural produce and rural restaurants, which are founded on the farmers' market, are contributing to the revitalization of the rural areas through the so-called sixth industrialization. Tabayashi (2015) considered the status quo of recent farming villages from the viewpoint of "commodification of rural space," and reported that tourism and recreational activities linked to agriculture are leading to the preservation of agriculture and the scenery of farming villages. These researches can be described as important achievements which demonstrate, through case studies, the decline of the rural villages and areas due to globalization and their reaction to it, but in this chapter, the primary focus will be on finding a "management strategy to counter imported agricultural produce" which will be fundamental to the Japanese agriculture as a whole. To this end, the subject of analysis in this chapter will be those sub-sectors of agriculture that involve agricultural produce that are cultivated or reared widely across Japan, and are significantly affected by the increase in imported produce.

As shown in Table 1, Japan's import of agricultural produce increased rapidly over the 1960s and 1970s, but most of this were grains other than rice (primarily wheat) and soybean.[1] Subsequently, in the 1980s and 1990s, all sub-sectors of agriculture, including vegetables, fruits, meat, and dairy products saw an increase in imported produce, resulting in a major decline in self-sufficiency rate, which used to exceed 80%. As a background to this development, there was the widening of the domestic and foreign price difference due to the appreciation of Japanese Yen in the wake of the Plaza Accord of 1985; the resulting increase in cheap imported produce benefited the Japanese consumers. However, because the aforementioned four sub-sectors of agriculture are heavily reliant on full-time farmers, it was feared that the price competition with imported produce could force many farmers out of business, and eventually lead to the economic collapse of the rural regions. If so, how have these sub-sectors been planning for their survival by adopting what kind of management strategy, as competition with imported produce intensified? Analyzing this very point is likely to lead to the elucidation of the "Japanese characteristics" which this chapter seeks.

Accordingly, meat and fruits—two sub-sectors that have seen a dramatic decline in self-sufficiency rate from the 1980s onwards (Table 1)—and specifically, beef cattle farming and citrus farming are chosen as the subject of analysis of this chapter. These two sub-sectors are representative of commercial agriculture that grew rapidly

Table 1 Changes in import quantity and self-sufficiency rate of main agricultural products in Japan

	1960	1970	1980	1990	2000	2010	2019
	Import quantity (1,000 tons)						
Rice	22	2	3	5	88	83	87
Other grains	428	1,579	2,503	2,761	2,676	2,521	2,405
Tubers	0	0	21	40	83	120	118
Beans	118	347	471	468	517	375	365
Vegetables	2	10	50	153	312	278	303
Fruits	12	119	154	264	484	476	447
Meat	4	22	74	151	276	259	326
Dairy products	24	56	141	218	395	353	524
	Self-sufficiency rate (%)						
Rice	101.9	106.2	87.0	100.1	96.9	94.9	98.2
Other grains	52.6	6.9	3.9	4.6	3.4	3.0	5.2
Tubers	100.2	100.1	95.7	92.6	82.7	75.6	73.1
Beans	44.3	13.0	6.6	7.8	6.7	7.9	7.5
Vegetables	100.0	99.4	97.1	91.1	81.4	80.9	79.4
Fruits	100.3	83.9	81.2	63.1	44.3	38.3	38.2
Meat	93.4	89.3	80.4	69.5	52.5	55.7	51.8
Dairy products	89.1	89.4	81.8	77.5	68.4	67.1	59.3

Note Dairy products include milk
Source Ministry of Agriculture, Forestry and Fisheries, "Food Balance Sheet"

from the 1960s onwards; beef ranks second amongst meat whilst citrus ranks 1st amongst fruits in terms of production output. Therefore, during the agricultural trade negotiation held in the 1980s when Japan–US trade friction had intensified, the Japanese government was strongly opposed to the opening up of the markets for beef and oranges. However, because the Japanese government was unable to resist US pressure and proceeded to open its markets for both produce in 1991, the amount of import greatly increased afterwards, and resulted in a dramatic change to the market condition. As such, these two sub-sectors present themselves as excellent cases that merit examination in order to achieve the objective of this chapter.

2 The Rise in Imported Beef and Management Transformation of Beef Cattle Farming

2.1 The Rise in Imported Beef and Its Impact on the Production and Supply of Domestic Beef

Figure 1 depicts the changes in the supply of beef by separating domestic beef from imported beef. Based on this chart, of the 600,000t of beef supplied in 1980, approximately 70% was domestic beef, but from the late 1980s, when the import quota was increased through the Japan–US trade negotiation, the amount of imported beef increased rapidly; in 1991, when the beef market was liberalized, approximately 45% of the 1,050,000t of beef supplied was imported beef. The amount of imported beef continued to increase afterwards, and in the late 1990s, it surpassed domestic beef to reach 900,000t level; one reason for this is the increased demand for rib meat for use in beef bowl which was met by cheap US produce. However, in the 2000s, the amount of imported beef starts to decline. This is primarily due to the cooling of the demand for beef resulting from the discovery of BSE-infected cattle in Japan in 2001, and the import ban resulting from the discovery of BSE-infected cattle in the USA in 2003. After that, imported beef recovers slightly and continues to shift in the region of 700,000t, representing a 40% increase to the level of import seen in the run-up to the liberalization.

On the other hand, unlike imported beef, the supply of domestic beef has not seen any major change, and from the mid-1980s onwards, it remains more or less steady in the region of 500,000t (Fig. 1). This indicates that imported beef served to raise the demand for beef as a whole, but has not directly led to the decline in demand for domestic beef. Nevertheless, the supply of domestic beef, which was on the rise, started to decline from the late 1990s when the amount of imported beef was at its peak, so it could be said that imported beef had the effect of putting a brake on the growth in supply of domestic beef.

Although imported beef had no major impact on the supply of domestic beef, it did have a major influence on the price of domestic beef. As shown in Fig. 2, the price of imported beef—in the ten-year period following the liberalization—has

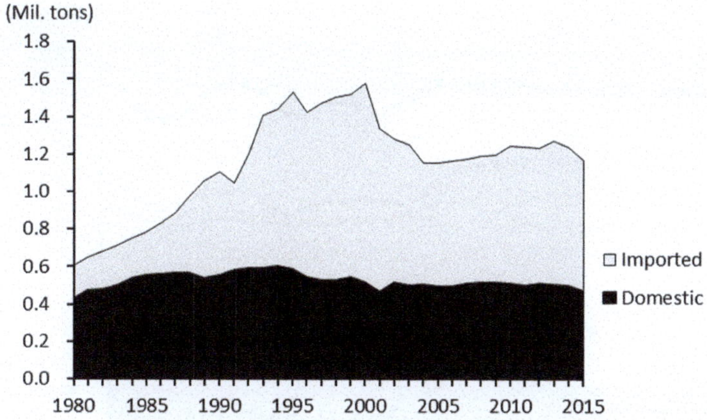

Fig. 1 Changes in domestic and imported beef supply in Japan
(*Source* Various years of "Food balance sheet" compiled by Ministry of Agriculture, Forestry and Fisheries)

seen a major decline from around JPY700/kg to around JPY400/kg, and as if to be dragged by this decline, the price of domestic beef has also fallen. Here, it should be noted that among the domestic beef, the rate of decline of beef breed (*Kuroge Washu* or Japanese Black, a representative breed of Wagyu) is smaller than that of dairy breed (Holstein). This is because Wagyu beef could be clearly distinguished from imported beef by its marbling, and avoided becoming involved in a straightforward price war. Moreover, whilst the price of domestic beef saw a major increase in 2004–2007, when the supply and demand were compressed due to the import ban on US produced beef and the age restriction imposed on beef shipimportedment, the margin of increase was also larger for beef breed.

Thus, it can be said that the liberalization had a more serious impact on dairy breed in the longer term, as reflected in the changes in the number of cattle reared. According to Fig. 2, the number of dairy breed reared kept on increasing from the 1970s, but it begins to stagnate shortly after the liberalization, and by 2015, the number has fallen to 830,000, which equates to 77% of the number at the time of liberalization. On the contrary, the number of beef breed reared saw no major change even after the 2000s, and as of 2015, the number still stood at 1,660,000, which equates to 96% of the number at the time of liberalization.

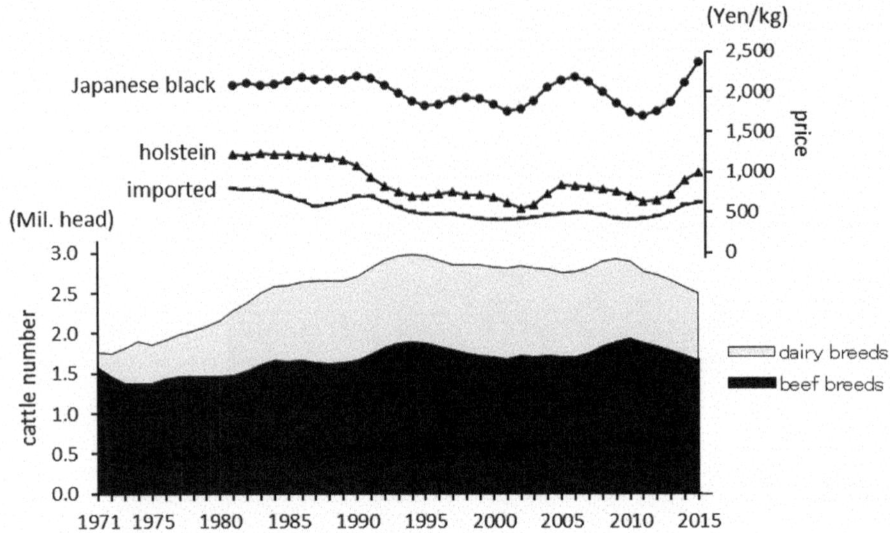

Fig. 2 Changes in cattle numbers and beef prices by category in Japan
(*Note* Price is three-year average price. *Source* Various years of "Statistical survey on livestock" and "Survey on livestock products marketing" compiled by Ministry of Agriculture, Forestry and Fisheries. Various years of "Trade statistics of Japan" compiled by Ministry of Finance)

2.2 Beef Cattle Farming After the Beef Trade Liberalization

2.2.1 The Change in Cattle Farm Management and Regional Characteristics

Figure 3 shows the number of beef cattle reared in 1991 and 2015 for the different breeds and regions, in order to examine the changes in beef cattle farming after the liberalization. According to this chart, the proportion of dairy breed has greatly decreased whilst the proportion of crossbreed (between beef breed and dairy breed, denoted as filial 1 hybrid[2]; in Fig. 2, this crossbreed is counted as dairy breed) has increased, but this shift was aimed at bringing the quality of meat closer to that of the beef breed, with a view to achieving differentiation from imported beef. Additionally, as the number of cattle reared per farm has more than tripled from 13 to 46, one could consider that a certain degree of cost reduction was achieved.

By contrast, if the change in number of cattle reared in the different regions is examined, a significant difference can be noted. This is the significant decline in the number of cattle reared in regions other than Hokkaido and Kyushu, from which one could conclude that beef cattle farming is becoming concentrated in the northern and southern extremes of Japan. However, there is a major difference in the approach to management of cattle farming in these two regions. This is the fact that the scale of cattle farming significantly increased in Hokkaido whilst maintaining a high proportion of dairy breed, but the scale of cattle farming in Kyushu remained below

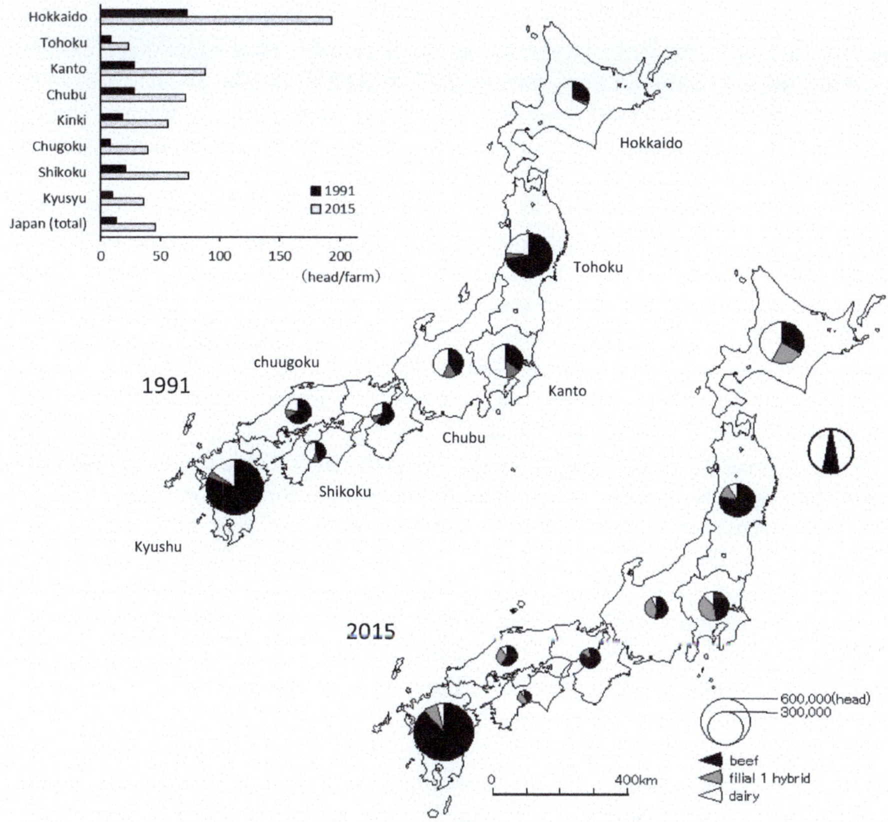

Fig. 3 Regional changes in cattle numbers by breed and farm scale in Japan (*Source* Various years of "Statistical survey on livestock" and "Census of agriculture and forestry" compiled by Ministry of Agriculture, Forestry and Fisheries)

the national average even though the proportion of beef breed increased. Therefore, it is conceivable that Hokkaido and Kyushu adopted different management strategies following the liberalization in order to develop their respective producing regions. Accordingly, this chapter will consider below the post-liberalization management strategies in the case of dairy breed management in Hokkaido, and in the case of beef breed management in Kyushu.

2.2.2 Survival Strategy for Dairy Breed Management: The Case of Hokkaido Region

The reason why Hokkaido alone was able to expand beef cattle farming primarily through the use of dairy breed, which has seen a worsening of market condition after the liberalization, owes much to the presence of a unique environment. Specifically, it is the geography which enables the expansion in the scale of farming, as well as the plentiful supply of bullocks and fodder made possible by the fact that Hokkaido is Japan's largest region for dairy farming and crop farming. The Tokachi area in the south-eastern part of Hokkaido is an archetype of such region, and the town of Shihoro is selected as an example below in discussing the post-liberalization management strategy.

Shihoro is a town situated in the north of Tokachi area, and its core industry is mixed farming. Beef cattle farming started to gain momentum from the 1970s, and the number of cattle reached 20,000 in 1990 immediately before the liberalization, but the number continued to increase, and in 2015 the number reached 60,000 (of which more than 90% is dairy breed). The number of cattle reared per farm also increased significantly from 540 in 1990 to 990 in 2015 (Census of Agriculture and Forestry), and it can be seen that following the liberalization, proactive investment was made to achieve expansion of scale.

Such expansion was realized by support from the Beef Cattle Centres, which was established with capital provided by the Shihoro Agricultural Cooperative. In 2011, there were twenty-nine large-scale farms within Shihoro that kept 500 or more cattle, and eighteen of them were served by the Beef Cattle Centres. Beef Cattle Centres vary in their scale from 500 cattle to 3,000 cattle, and even after 1988, when the liberalization in three years' time was confirmed, five of them were established, and it can be seen that steps were taken to address the price competition with imported beef that would follow the liberalization. The management policy of Beef that would follow the liberalization. The management policy of Beef Cattle Centres was to prioritize cost reduction above all else, and from the 2000s onwards, reduction of the feed cost was prioritized, whilst shipment age was reduced from twenty months to nineteen months. For these reasons, the grading of dairy breed carcasses, which depends on the extent of marbling etc., began to result more frequently in B2 (second from the bottom of five grades), rather than B3 (the middle of five grades), the grade at which the difference from imported beef becomes clear. Additionally, almost 100% of the cattle that are fattened are Holsteins that come from the local dairy farms, and no movement to raise the quality of meat by introducing filial 1 hybrid cattle can be observed.

On the other hand, insofar as marketing is concerned, a strategy which makes use of the strength as a major beef-producing region was taken. This approach involved a meat processing public corporation purchasing more than half of the carcasses produced locally in Shihoro, and marketing them under the brand of "Shihoro Beef." This public corporation was established in 1987 with the lead of the Shihoro Agricultural Cooperative, and once the carcasses are butchered into different cuts by the corporation, all of the cuts are sold to a meat wholesaler in the Chubu region. As stated above, the quality of beef produced in Shihoro is not necessarily high, but ever since BSE-infected cattle was discovered in Japan, consumers increasingly began to demand beef with clear provenance. Consequently, retailers too show a keen interest in continuously sourcing beef from a producing region that can offer a stable and high-volume supply of beef, thereby sustaining the consistent sales at a higher price than imported beef.

Nevertheless, even with a large-scale cost reduction which extends to distribution, finances of cattle farms in Shihoro still operate at deficit most of the years, and without the subsidy provided through the Agriculture and Livestock Industries Corporation, it would be difficult for those farms to sustain their operation. The provision of this subsidy is triggered when the market price of beef cattle calf/carcass undercuts the profitability threshold, and the underlying scheme was established in the wake of the liberalization, with the tariff imposed on imported beef as the source of funding. The profitability threshold is standardized across Japan, and in practice, the scheme operates so as to be advantageous for those producing regions where low-cost operation is feasible. This is a background to the fact that Hokkaido alone was able to continue/expand beef cattle farming through the use of dairy breed.

Yet, it can be seen that cost reduction was not the only step which was taken. The other step which was taken is the production of beef which placed the emphasis on "assurance and safety," and it started in the town of Memuro in the Tokachi area. This business model was mediated by HOKUREN Federation of Agricultural Cooperative where cattle are fed exclusively on expensive antibiotic-free and non-GMO fodder and sold directly as "Mirai Memuro Beef." In addition, the rearing period is also extended to twenty months. As such, rise in cost is unavoidable, but a grocery chain in the Shikoku region which sources this beef has succeeded in selling this beef notwithstanding its higher price, by emphasizing its appeal as a "produce without compromise"—with clear provenance as well as transparent husbandry and distribution route—to the consumers.

Similar business models whereby the producers directly market their produce are adopted by other towns in Hokkaido as well, but in such cases, consumer bodies—such as Consumers' Co-Operative—which place greater emphasis on animal husbandry and food safety over price are quite often present in the background. Additionally, it can be said that such business strategy is made possible only in Hokkaido because of the existence of many large farms that can offer a stable supply of beef at a scale that exceeds 1,000 cattle per annum.

2.2.3 Development Strategy for Beef Breed Management: The Case of Kyushu Region

After the liberalization, the proportion of beef breed reared increased across Japan, but the only region where this increase led to an increase in the number of cattle raised was Kyushu. As a background to this can be cited the fact that mixed farming continued to remain the core industry of this region due to the fact that the region was far removed from major metropolitan areas, thus delaying its industrialization/urbanization. That the region was geographically blessed with sub-montane land suited to grazing, and that breeding management was an important industry for the region's islands were also significant.

Bearing the foregoing in mind, what kind of management strategy was adopted in Kyushu after the liberalization? It is the differentiation of Japanese beef from imported beef through improvement of meat quality, and farmers in Kyushu implemented two management transformations. One way of achieving this is to increase the proportion of Japanese Blacks—a breed which achieves the highest grades in terms of marbling—that are reared. In certain parts of Kyushu, *Akage Washu* or Japanese Brown used to be popular, but its number has declined significantly after the 2000s and as of 2015, the proportion of Japanese Blacks among the beef cattle raised has reached 97%. Another way of achieving differentiation is to build a track record of producing high-quality carcasses, by continuously breeding heifers and bulls whilst placing the emphasis on pedigree selection. Generally speaking, in terms of the ranking of beef breed carcasses, the top two of the five grades (A5/A4) can be treated as high quality beef, and of the beef which are traded in Kyushu's wholesale meat market, the proportion of beef which are graded as A5/A4 has increased from 56% in 1991 to 80% in 2015.

Additionally, the branding tactic employed has also contributed to differentiation from imported beef and sales at higher price. The "All-Japan Wagyu Performance Fair" (*Zenkoku Wagyu Nouryoku Kyoshin Kai*) is a livestock competition for beef breed (Wagyu) which has been held in Japan every five years since 1966, and at start of the 2000s, Miyazaki prefecture and Kagoshima prefecture—both situated in the southern part of Kyushu region—have won the first prize in succession. These two prefectures have historically boasted some of the highest numbers of cattle reared in Japan, but with the award of this prize, the quality of their beef has also been assured, and the value of the brand of beef produced by these two prefectures—"Miyazaki Wagyu" and "Kagoshima Wagyu"—have greatly increased.[3] As a result, Wagyu beef produced by these two prefectures came to command a high price in the market, and at the same time, it is also now sourced by increasing number of butchers and exclusive restaurants. More recently, Wagyu beef is increasingly enjoyed at home or at travel destination as a form of "small indulgence," and its demand as a gift is also rising. Wagyu has also come to be recognized overseas—mainly by those with higher social status—as the ultimate beef, and from 2007 onwards, export is continuing to increase at a price which does not differ much from the domestic price.

Therefore, beef breed management of recent years can be described as enjoying a level of price rise and increased profitability never seen before, which surpasses the level seen before the liberalization. Even so, and notwithstanding such favorable market condition, the number of cattle reared across Japan is showing a downward trend. Kyushu is no exception, and the biggest reason for this is the small-scale farms that go out of business and struggle to find successors. Livestock farming involves working with animals; those in the trade not only struggle to take holidays, but they also have to undertake many physically demanding tasks, such as the disposal of feces and urines. In breeding management, the use of pasture is being considered as well but it is not easy for each breeder to secure the necessary land. Meanwhile, full-time farmers face hurdles in expanding their scale of operation. Typically, the capital required to construct livestock barns is available in the form of loan granted by agricultural cooperatives or as subsidized support provided by the government, but farmers who attempt to build barns near their own property meet the resistance of nearby residents who oppose "livestock pollution," and it's not always possible to meet the ideal conditions for construction. In breeding management, it is critical to secure the supply of rice straw as roughage, but expansion of scale makes this challenging. Moreover, securing the additional labor required in the expansion of scale is not easy in an area where a mature labor market for industries other than agriculture exists (Kawakubo 2011).

Such restrictions are inconceivable in Hokkaido, which fits the image of a traditional farming village surrounded by vast expanse of farmland, and one hopes corporations will enter the market. However, the rearing of beef breed (Wagyu)—and breeding management in particular—requires greater proficiency when compared to dairy breed, especially in relation to feeding and veterinary care for calves, hygiene maintenance of cattle barns, etc. and is therefore not suited to management by large corporations. Moreover, not only is Wagyu traded at three times the price of dairy breed, its shipment age is also long at approximately thirty months. This is a reflection of the significance of the risk associated with cattle dying whilst being reared, and it is one of the reasons why corporations hesitate to participate in the market. Beef breed management is one of the few areas of Japan's mixed farming not depressed by imported produce, but ironically, intensive management to create high quality beef restricts the growth of family farms to corporate management, moreover the sector is suffering from a severe shortage of participants.

3 The Rise in Imported Citrus and Management Transformation of Citrus Farming

3.1 The Rise in Imported Citrus and Its Impact on the Production and Supply of Domestic Citrus

Figure 4 depicts the changes in the supply of citrus (fresh and juice) by separating domestic citrus from imported citrus. According to this chart, in 1980, only 300,000t of citrus were imported, with the bulk of the import comprising grapefruit and lemons; this corresponds to not even 10% of the domestic produce. However, because the import quota for oranges was increased in 1985 and the import of oranges was liberalized in 1991, the amount of imported citrus reached 550,000t by the mid 1990s. Nevertheless, in the 2000s, the import of oranges and grapefruit have both significantly declined, and whilst the import of mandarins have increased in recent years, import of citrus on the whole has fallen to as low as 250,000t.

On the other hand, the supply of domestic produce, which stood at 300,000t in 1980, has more or less steadily declined, and has shrunk to one-third in 2015. This is due to the stagnation of price from the mid 1970s onwards, but the extent of shrinkage is greater in the ten-year period following the late 1980s, when import increased, suggesting that the pressure from imported produce also had a significant impact. Still, from late 1990s onwards, the shrinkage has remained small, and if anything, the share of domestic produce has increased. Therefore, the reduction in

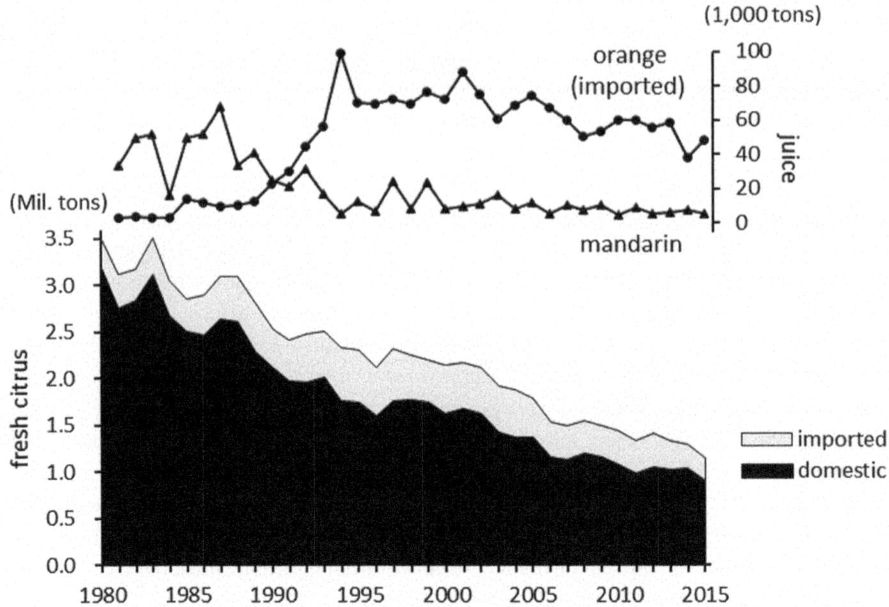

Fig. 4 Changes in fresh citrus fruits and the juice supply of domestic and imported products in Japan
(*Source* Various years of "Survey on vegetables and fruits wholesale markets" compiled by Ministry of Agriculture, Forestry and Fisheries. Various years of "Trade statistics of Japan" compiled by Ministry of Finance. Various years of "Fruits statistics" compiled by Japan Fruits Growers Cooperative Association)

domestic citrus production in recent years can be considered to be largely due to competition with other fruits, or alternatively, the reduced consumption of fruits in general, mainly by the younger generations.

Still, the liberalization of orange juice in 1992 had a devastating impact. This is because mandarin[4] juice lacked competitiveness not just in terms of price, but also in terms of aroma and sweetness. According to Fig. 4, in the 1980s, approximately 50,000t per annum of mandarin juice—mandarin being a key variety of domestic citrus—was produced as concentrate, but in the early 1990s, when the import of orange juice dramatically increased, the production rapidly declined, and it has stagnated at around 10,000t per annum in recent years. Naturally, the price of mandarin juice collapsed as well. This led to the increase in closure of groves in producing regions where much of the mandarins produced were shipped for processing (Kawakubo 1996).

If so, what kind of impact did such pressure from imported produce have on citrus farming in Japan? Fig. 5 shows the cultivation acreage of citrus from the 1970s onwards, by separating mandarins from other varieties of citrus (hereinafter, "miscellaneous citrus"). From this chart, it can be seen that: the planting of mandarins peaked in the mid-1970s; the planting of miscellaneous citrus peaked in the early

1980s; after reaching the peak, planting of both citruses continued to decline; and in recent years, the proportion of miscellaneous citrus has been steadily rising. On the other hand, insofar as price is concerned, a major shift triggered by the liberalization of oranges can be seen (Fig. 5). That is to say, the price of mandarins rose rapidly from the end of the 1980s onwards, whilst the price of imported oranges collapsed. This is due to the improvement in balance of supply and demand, which stemmed from the fact that oranges lost their value as gifts, and the fact that, immediately prior to liberalization, closure of mandarin groves was encouraged by the government with offer of cash incentives. Furthermore, the price of miscellaneous citrus has also been moving favorably, so much so that from the 2000s onwards, it has been surpassing the price of mandarins; one could consider that citrus farming in recent years has, contrary to the trend in production, stabilized at a high standard in terms of management.

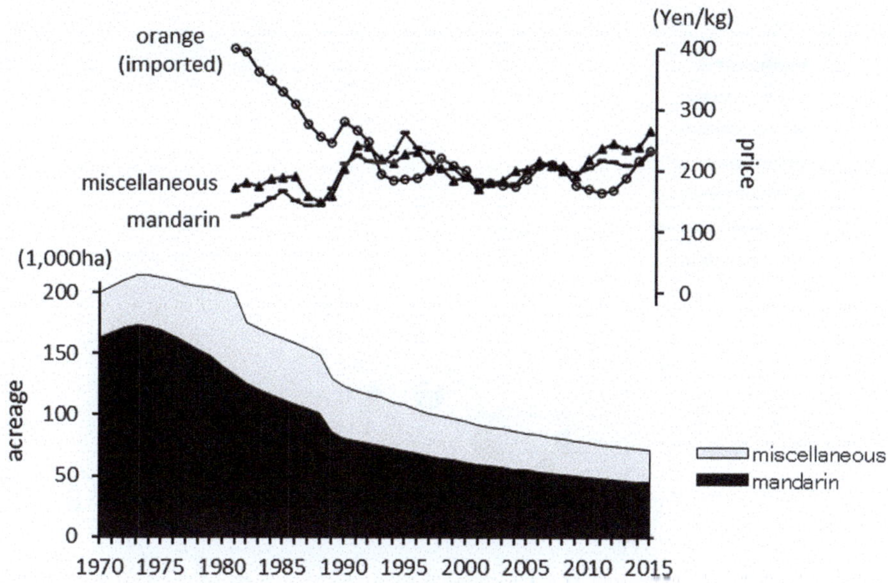

Fig. 5 Changes in citrus fruits cultivation acreage and the price of domestic and imported citrus fruits in Japan
(*Note* Price is three-year average prices. *Source* Various years of "Crop survey" and "Survey on vegetables and fruits wholesale markets" compiled by Ministry of Agriculture, Forestry and Fisheries)

3.2 *Citrus Farming After the Orange Trade Liberalization*

3.2.1 The Change in Citrus Farm Management and Regional Characteristics

Figure 6 shows the citrus cultivation acreage in 1991 and 2015 for the different varieties and regions, in order to examine the changes in citrus farming after the liberalization. According to this chart, there has been a major decline across Japan, but the scale of groves that grow mandarins, which is a key variety, has only increased slightly from 0.46 ha per farm to 0.61 ha per farm, suggesting that the move to consolidate groves and develop them into a large-scale corporate management was weak. As for the composition of varieties, there is a slight increase in the proportion of miscellaneous citrus; in particular, the increase in the proportion of sour citrus is notable, and it can be seen that diversification has progressed.

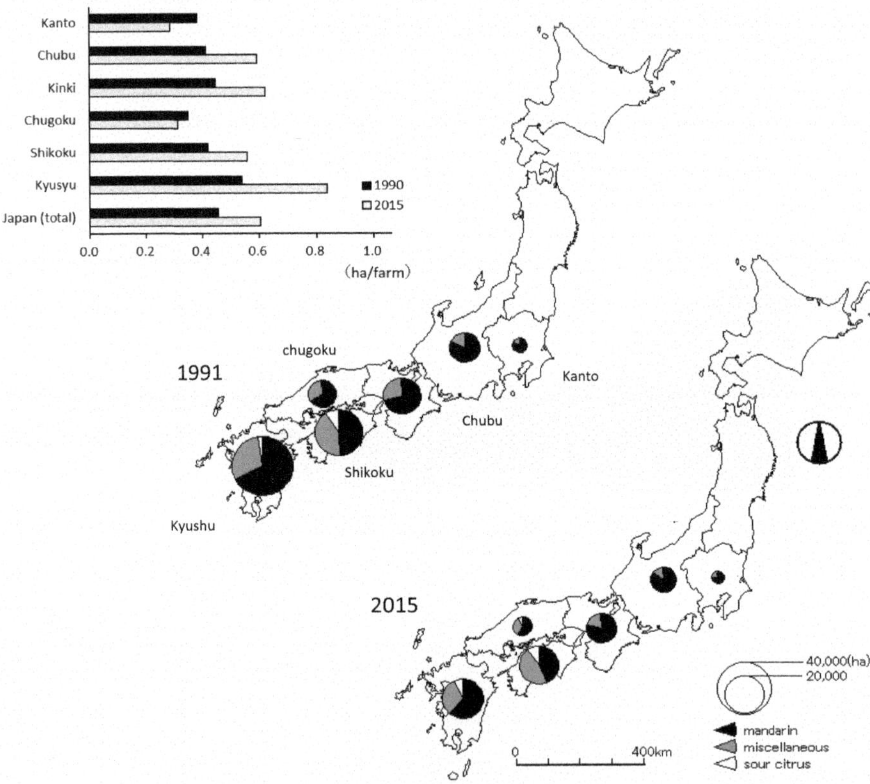

Fig. 6 Regional changes in citrus fruits cultivation acreage and farm scale in Japan (*Source* Various years of "Crop survey" and "Census of agriculture and forestry" compiled by Ministry of Agriculture, Forestry and Fisheries)

Now, by focusing on regional differences, it can be seen that the decline in cultivation acreage is relatively modest in the Chubu, Kinki, and Shikoku regions. However, there is a major difference between Chubu/Kinki regions and Shikoku region in terms of changes to the composition of varieties. That is to say, in the former two regions, the proportion of mandarins has increased, but in the latter region, the proportion of miscellaneous citrus has increased. Furthermore, Chugoku and Kyushu regions, where the decline in cultivation acreage was large, are also showing their own unique trend, such as the increase in proportion of sour citrus. Thus, in the citrus-producing regions after the liberalization, the measures adopted by the regions in order to sustain and develop groves management have diverged, depending on whether the regions have chosen mandarins or miscellaneous citrus as their pillar. Accordingly, the management strategies adopted by both types of regions are considered in detail below.

3.2.2 Quality Enhancement Strategy with Mandarins as the Pillar: The Case of Chubu/Kinki Regions

In citrus-producing regions where mandarin cultivation was chosen as the pillar, a management strategy to maintain domestic demand through enhancement of quality was adopted, but the key to this strategy was to increase the sweetness (increase to 12°Brix or higher being the aim) and to that end, the following three approaches implemented by the corporation of the local agricultural cooperative and farmers proved to be successful.

The first approach was to introduce varieties with high sweetness and utilize branding; this approach quickly took hold in the prefecture of Shizuoka in the Chubu region. Among the citrus-producing regions of Japan, Shizuoka has a relatively cool climate and it was not possible to expect sales at higher price through early shipment. Therefore, much of the mandarins grown there were of the late-maturing variety, and "Aoshima" was an archetype of such variety. Aoshima mandarin is large and has a squashed shape, so it isn't necessarily great in terms of appearance but it is rich in flavor and high in sweetness, so it was rated highly in the market. Thus, in Shizuoka, the shipping of batches that were clearly marked as Aoshima began in earnest in the late 1970s, and by the late 1980s, the move to switch other mandarin varieties to Aoshima had gained momentum. Today, the proportion of Aoshima among mandarins produced in Shizuoka as a whole has risen to as much as 70%. However, Aoshima was a variety which was discovered in Shizuoka, and it was not suitable for cultivation in producing regions with different climate. For this reason, today, the selection and development of varieties with high sweetness is undertaken across Japan,[5] and branding which gives center stage to the name of the variety is being pursued.

The second approach was to develop a way to grow mandarins in hothouse. The prefecture of Aichi in the Chubu region is a producing region which is a pioneer of this approach, and in the late 1980s, it achieved harvest of house-grown mandarins which was one and a half times greater in terms of volume and five times higher in terms of price than field-grown mandarins; its technical prowess and high profitability greatly contributed to the spread of house-grown mandarin cultivation to other producing regions. As a mandarin-producing region, Aichi was small and feeble, and for this reason it was suffering from declining sales in the 1980s under the unforgiving market condition. Thus, it embarked on building facilities with a view to achieving shipment in the early summer—something that is impossible to achieve with open field cultivation—and in the process, it also established the technique to increase sweetness by controlling irrigation prior to harvest. One could say that this is what has enabled sales at the kind of elevated price which would be inconceivable with field-grown mandarins, but depending on the cost of fuel required to heat the hothouse, the profit can become destabilized. Therefore, whilst house-grown mandarins maintain their higher price to this day, their production volume across Japan is trending towards decline.

The third approach was to selectively ship mandarins with higher sweetness as separate batches, and it quickly took hold in the prefecture of Wakayama in the Kinki region. This approach seeks to achieve price premium at the point of sale by guaranteeing high sweetness, and it came to be adopted across Japan in the late 1990s, owing to the development of fruits grading machine which could measure the sweetness of fruits without destroying them. So successful was this approach that it has now become customary for large retailers to include information concerning sweetness in the price labels, and for consumers to treat that as one of the criteria for selecting produce. This resulted in citrus-producing regions showing a keen interest in increasing sweetness, but originally, raising sweetness was not easy in open field cultivation, which is influenced by natural conditions such as sunlight, drainage, etc. However, the situation changed a lot when mulching using white sheet made of Tyvek—which allows moistures to permeate but repels water—became popular. This was because covering the grove ground with Tyvek sheet for a set period prior to harvest made it possible to suppress the amount of rain water entering the soil, and also because the reflection of sunlight from the sheet had the effect of improving the lighting at the base of the trees, which would otherwise remain shaded. Therefore, notwithstanding the increased cost, many producing regions adopted mulching, and mandarin groves covered in white became a common sight in autumn. Moreover, the sweetness data of the fruits accumulated by the citrus packing houses are fed back to each farmer, and proactive farmers began using such data to expend even greater efforts in quality enhancement. One could say that the sorting of shipment by sweetness and the setting of retail price based on such sorting have brought about a major change to cultivation technique as well as the farmers' mindset.

Such approach which puts the emphasis on quality is beginning to manifest in juice production as well. As stated above, the production of mandarin juice declined greatly after the liberalization of orange juice, but this merely means that the manufacture of products for the masses based on concentrate in large scale factories had declined, and the manufacture of non-concentrate juice products that boast high quality have in fact flourished since the start of the 2010s. This resurgence is driven mainly by a group of small and medium-sized local enterprises from the producing region, including entrepreneurs who are former farmers; by adopting a manufacturing method which entails "juicing after peeling" a method which won't appeal to large corporations due to its inefficiency—they have succeeded in maintaining the flavor of mandarins and the freshness of the juice to a great extent. Needless to say, the price has to be set high, but a viable business is made possible by emphasizing the appeal of the juice as a "produce without compromise" to the wealthy, tourists, and health-conscious consumers.

3.2.3 Diversification Strategy with Miscellaneous Citrus as the Pillar: The Case of Shikoku/Chugoku Regions

In citrus-producing regions where miscellaneous citrus was chosen as the pillar, a management strategy to seek differentiation from imported produce by emphasizing the uniqueness of domestic produce through diversification of variety was adopted. One such approach is the attempt to rally domestic demand by developing and releasing citrus varieties that are unique to Japan. As Fig. 5 shows, the cultivation acreage of miscellaneous citrus has been on a downward trend from the 1980s onwards. Notwithstanding this trend, the development of new varieties is being pursued rather vigorously, and of the miscellaneous citrus other than sour citrus, varieties that have cultivation acreage of 100 ha or greater has increased from 16 in 1990 to 23 in 2015 (two varieties have disappeared, and nine varieties have been added). This movement is most prominent in the prefecture of Ehime in the Shikoku region, and more than 50% of the newly added nine varieties are grown in Ehime. In Ehime, when miscellaneous citrus was introduced, tangor varieties which are larger than mandarins, such as Iyokan (*Citrus iyo*) and Kiyomi (*Citrus unshiu x sinensis*), were selected by the local agricultural cooperative's initiative. However, from the 2000s onwards, in response to demand for sweet fruits that were easy to peel and more conveniently sized, varieties which are hybrids of mandarins such as Satsuma Mandarin (*Citrus unshiu*) and Ponkan (*Citrus reticulata var poonensis*) were increasingly released; these varieties were given endearing names which in turn gave the fruits a feminine image, which helped to garner attention. In particular, "Beni Madonna" and "Kanpei" developed at the Ehime Fruit Tree Experiment Station are not permitted to be cultivated outside Ehime due to restrictions relating to plant variety rights, and have achieved success in cementing of the brand, as well as the redistribution of profit to the producing regions.

Yet another approach is the attempt to use sour citrus as a raw ingredient, with a view to vitalize the producing regions through collaboration between farming, commerce, and local industry. In Japan, indigenous varieties of sour citrus such as Yuzu (*Citrus junos*), Sudachi (*Citrus sudachi*), and Kabosu (*Citrus sphaerocarpa*) have been cultivated since ancient times, and they have been used as ingredient of seasoning such as *ponzu* which is used in Japanese cuisine, but in recent years, lemons produced mainly in the prefecture of Hiroshima in the Chugoku region have been attracting attention. Domestic lemons were devastated after the import of lemon was liberalized in 1964 and American lemons swept in, but from the 1980s onwards, domestic lemons came to be appreciated as safe and sound domestic produce which do not receive post-harvest treatment, so much so that in 2015, their cultivation acreage came to exceed 200 ha. This was due to the success of marketing campaign which focused on the fact that lemons are customarily consumed with rind; in order to emphasize the freshness, fruits that haven't fully ripened are also being shipped as "Green Lemon". In recent years, the use of lemons as raw ingredient has also been rising rapidly. Their use include not just drinks and seasoning, but also extend to cakes, snacks, dried provisions and delicacies, and cosmetics; the backdrop to such broad use is the establishment of the "Setouchi Lemon" brand. Setouchi is a reference to the "Seto Inland Sea," the archipelago spreading between the Chugoku region and the Shikoku region, and cultivation of lemons in the Hiroshima prefecture takes place almost entirely on the islands in this area. The islands of Seto Inland Sea are designated as one of the first National Parks, and the beautiful scenery there overlaps with the image of lemons, thereby increasing the appeal of the lemons to the consumers. It is for this reason that processed food and goods which stress the use of Setouchi Lemon are rapidly increasing; this not only leads to differentiation from imported lemons, but also contributes to the development of local processing industry, as well as the development of retail and hospitality businesses that are linked to tourism.

4 Conclusion

This chapter analyzes the unique characteristics of the management strategies adopted by the agricultural sector of Japan—one of the largest importers of agricultural produce in the world—by considering how those regions have been planning for their survival by adopting what kind of management strategy, as competition with imported produce intensified. The sectors chosen as illustrative examples are beef cattle farming and citrus farming, which experienced dramatic changes to the market conditions due to the import liberalization in 1991. As a result, the following matters became evident.

First of all, in beef cattle farming, the use of dairy breed—which suffered a significant drop in price—rapidly declined whilst the introduction of crossbreed progressed. Hokkaido is an exception in that the region pursued large-scale low-cost management, but at the same time, sales of beef which put the emphasis on safety/assurance and traceability was also strengthened. In beef breed management, enhancement of meat quality and use of branding accelerated, and the proportion of Japanese Blacks—breed with which marbling is easier to achieve—among the cattle reared rose even further.

On the other hand, in citrus farming, the liberalization resulted in acceleration of the already existing downward production trend, but insofar as mandarins were concerned—mandarin being a key variety—development of technology to increase sweetness and marketing to stress the same took hold. With respect to miscellaneous citrus, development of new varieties was proactively pursued, and collaboration between farming, commerce, and industry—which utilized sour citrus as raw ingredient—was progressed. However, swept away by imported orange juice, the production volume of mandarin juice declined dramatically.

In addition, from the perspective of the managerial actors, family farms comprise the majority of both cattle and citrus farming and development of the corporate management or agribusiness is rare. Therefore, the strategy planner of management transformation was mainly farmers, agricultural cooperatives, public experiment stations and local processing industries.

If so, what is the unique characteristic of the management strategy adopted by Japan's agricultural sector in order to counter globalization? It can be summarized as "product differentiation (enhancement of added value)" to avoid price competition with imported produce. In beef cattle farming, the rearing of dairy breed—which is closest to imported beef in terms of the characteristics of its meat—declined dramatically and conversion to crossbreed progressed. In respect of citrus farming too, the development of varieties unique to Japan was progressed, and added value was enhanced through the development of processed food and goods which utilized sour citrus. The development of products that extol their safety/assurance can also be said to form part of such differentiation. Additionally, one aspect of quality enhancement is to achieve differentiation from cheap imported produce for the masses. The improved marbling in Wagyu beef, enhancement of the sweetness of mandarins, and the resurgence of non-concentrate juice products are typical examples of this; such products, including those that are sold as gifts, serve to anchor the domestic demand.

But what lies in the background which prompted the adoption of such management strategy? One relevant factor is the long-held stoic realization on the part of the producers that "it's not possible to win in a price competition," and this realization was made definitive by the appreciation of Japanese Yen from 1985 onwards. Another relevant factor is the peculiarity of the Japanese market, namely the existence of consumers who are sensitive to quality or safety of products and are not averse to higher price, or alternatively, have a fondness for products without compromise that offer high added value. These factors are closely related to the fact that Japan is a high-income nation with a mature society, but it can be said that it was this very fact which dictated the behavior of the producers, who are preoccupied with securing their share of the domestic market, and do not venture overseas to develop markets for export.

That being said, if one was to be realistic, it is obvious that under the pressure that came from imported produce from the 1980s onwards, neither the beef cattle farming sector, nor the citrus farming sector was in any position to sustain its productivity. In 2015, the number of cattle reared had fallen to 89% of the number in the inaugural year of the liberalization, whilst the citrus cultivation acreage had fallen to 60%. Furthermore, bearing in mind the reality that the market is on a downward trend due to decreasing birthrate and ageing population, one cannot hope for any major change, but insofar as trade in agricultural produce is concerned, there has been a slight change in the environment surrounding Japan. This is the increase in the affluent class which accompanies the economic development of Asian nations. If in the future the demand in these markets for agricultural produce which offer high added value in terms of quality, safety, etc. was to rise, this is likely to be an opportunity to transform the "domestically focused" mindset which characterized the management strategy of Japan's agricultural sector into "export-oriented" mindset. In fact, from 2004 onwards, owing in part to the government's export drive, export—mainly to Asian nations—has increased considerably.

However, in order to maintain this upward trend going forward, it will be necessary to expand the target consumer groups and usage for the exported produce, whilst developing an understanding of the target country's food culture. Moreover, even if the higher price was accepted, the taste of the consumers will act as a barrier to daily consumption. For example, Wagyu beef with its characteristic marbling, mandarins with high water content and delicate sweetness, and the sticky short grain rice that is Koshihikari are all varieties of foodstuff adored by the Japanese, but they are rarely, if ever, produced overseas and consequently not well known overseas. It would be interesting to learn how the increasing number of tourists who have been visiting Japan from overseas in the recent years evaluate foodstuff produced in Japan, but in the near term, it is inconceivable that the boom in Japanese cuisine in the Asian nations would directly lead to significant export of agricultural produce as food.

That being said, given that the domestic market is continuing to shrink, a stimulus to production that comes from export will help in sustaining agricultural production and revitalizing the regional economy of rural regions. From now on, one should explore a way forward by redirecting the energy of those in the field—which have historically been expended on securing domestic market share—to marketing activities overseas. In that sense, growth of the export-oriented corporation/agribusiness is expected.

Notes

1. As a background to the reason why increased import of wheat and soya did not become a political issue, it is to be note that the domestic production level of these crops had always been low, and it would have been unrealistic to meet the rapidly increasing demand for the raw ingredients for baked goods, noodles, tofus, soy sauce, etc. solely with domestic produce.
2. In Japanese cattle farming, Japanese Black comprises 97% of beef breed and Holstein 99% of dairy breed. Thus, the majority of filial 1 hybrid cattle are crossbreeds between these.
3. The practice of marketing beef using branding is done all over Japan, but because the regional differences in terms of the breed or pedigree of the beef cattle, fodder used, etc. are lessening each year (Takayanagi 2007), winning a seal of approval at livestock competition carries a significant meaning.
4. Author's remark: Except where expressly stated otherwise, reference to "mandarin" in this chapter from this point onwards should be taken as reference to the so-called Satsuma mandarin (Citrus unshiu).
5. According to the Crop Survey, of the new varieties of mandarins released in the period from 2003 through to 2015, there were eight extra early-maturing varieties, eight early-maturing varieties, ten normal varieties, and four late-maturing varieties, indicating that early-maturing varieties, whose sweetness is difficult to raise, have become more popular in recent years.

References

Friedmann H (1993) The political economy of food: a global crisis. New Left Rev 197:29–57

Kawakubo A (1996) Changes in Japanese mandarin-producing areas with liberalization of the orange juice trade. Jimbun Chiri (Jpn J Hum Geogr) 48:28–47 (J)

Kawakubo A (2011) Upgrading a scale of Wagyu cattle breeding and the future issues in further development of the large-scale farming in Nango district, Nichinan city, Miyazaki prefecture. Chiikichirikenkyu (J Syst Reg Geogr) 17(1):1–18 (J)

Oro K, Pritchard W (2010) The evolution of global value chains: displacement of captive upstream investment in the Australia-Japan beef trade. J Econ Geogr 11(4):709–729

Seki N (ed) (2014) Rokuji sangyoka to chusankanchiiki: Nihon no mirai wo sakidoru Kochiken chiiki sangyo no chousen (Sixth industrialization in hilly and mountainous areas: challenges of local advanced industry in Kochi prefecture). Shinhyoron Publishing Inc., Tokyo (J)

Sumner DA, Lee H (1996) Economic prospects for the California rice industry. California Rice Promotion Board, Sacramento

Takayanagi N (2006) Global transformation of spatial structure in agro-food systems. Tsukuba Shobo, Tokyo (J)

Takayanagi N (2007) Fabricating local embeddedness of foods: branded beef and revitalization of the rural economy. Keizaichirigakunenpo (Ann Jpn Assoc Econ Geogr) 53(1):61–77 (J)

Tabayashi A (ed) (2015) The commodification of rural space for regional development. Agriculture and Forestry Statistics Publishing Inc., Tokyo (J)

(J) denotes literature in Japanese

Index

A. Taira and R. D. Schlunze (eds.), *Management Geography*, International Perspectives in Geography 19, https://doi.org/10.1007/978-981-19-4403-1

The manufacturer's authorised representative in the EU is Springer Nature Customer Service Centre GmbH, Europaplatz 3, 69115 Heidelberg, Germany. If you have any concerns regarding our products, please contact ProductSafety@springernature.com

Printed and bound by CPI Group (UK) Ltd, Croydon, CR0 4YY
30/09/2026
02225315-0002